T0311669

EXPECTATIONS AND THE MEANING OF INSTITUTIONS

FOUNDATIONS OF THE MARKET ECONOMY SERIES

Edited by Mario J. Rizzo, *New York University* and Lawrence H. White, *University of Georgia*

A central theme of this series is the importance of understanding and assessing the market economy from a perspective broader than the static economics of perfect competition and Pareto optimality. Such a perspective sees markets as causal processes generated by the preferences, expectations and beliefs of economic agents. The creative acts of entrepreneurship that uncover new information about preferences, prices and technology are central to these processes with respect to their ability to promote the discovery and use of knowledge in society.

The market economy consists of a set of institutions that facilitate voluntary cooperation and exchange among individuals. These institutions include the legal and ethical framework as well as more narrowly 'economic' patterns of social interaction. Thus the law, legal institutions and cultural or ethical norms, as well as ordinary business practices and monetary phenomena, fall within the analytical domain of the economist.

Other titles in the series

THE MEANING OF MARKET PROCESS
Essays in the development of modern Austrian economics
Israel M. Kirzner

PRICES AND KNOWLEDGE
A market-process perspective
Esteban F. Thomsen

KEYNES' GENERAL THEORY OF INTEREST
A reconsideration
Fiona C. Maclachlan

LAISSEZ-FAIRE BANKING
Kevin Dowd

EXPECTATIONS AND THE MEANING OF INSTITUTIONS

Essays in economics by
Ludwig Lachmann

Edited by Don Lavoie

London and New York

First published 1994
by Routledge
2 Park Square, Milton Park, Abingdon, Oxfordshire OX14 4RN
Simultaneously published in the USA and Canada
by Routledge
711 Third Avenue, New York, NY 10017
First issued in paperback 2014

*Routledge is an imprint of the Taylor and Francis Group,
an informa business*

© 1994 Don Lavoie

Typeset in Garamond by Intype, London

British Library Cataloguing in Publication Data
A catalogue record for this book is available from the British Library.

Library of Congress Cataloging in Publication Data
Expectations and the meaning of institutions : essays in economics by
Ludwig Lachmann / edited by Don Lavoie.
p. cm.
Includes bibliographical references and index.
1. Economics 2. Rational expectations (Economic theory)
3. Financial institutions. I. Lachmann, Ludwig M. II. Lavoie, Don, 1951-

ISBN 978-0-415-10712-9 (hbk)
ISBN 978-1-138-00677-5 (pbk)

This book has been sponsored
in part by the Austrian Economics
Program at New York University.

CONTENTS

Editor's note   vii
Acknowledgements   viii
INTRODUCTION: EXPECTATIONS AND THE
MEANING OF INSTITUTIONS   1
Don Lavoie

Part I Uncertainty, investment and economic crises

1 COMMODITY STOCKS AND EQUILIBRIUM [1936]   23

2 UNCERTAINTY AND LIQUIDITY-PREFERENCE
   [1937]   29

3 INVESTMENT AND COSTS OF PRODUCTION
   [1938]   42

4 COMMODITY STOCKS IN THE TRADE CYCLE
   [1938] (with *F. Snapper*)   57

5 ON CRISIS AND ADJUSTMENT [1939]   76

Part II Capital and investment repercussions

6 ON THE MEASUREMENT OF CAPITAL [1941]   91

7 FINANCE CAPITALISM? [1944]   107

8 A NOTE ON THE ELASTICITY OF
   EXPECTATIONS [1945]   124

9 INVESTMENT REPERCUSSIONS [1948]   131

Part III Diagnosing the Austrian School's 'great depression'

10 AUSTRIAN ECONOMICS UNDER FIRE: THE
    HAYEK-SRAFFA DUEL IN RETROSPECT [1986]   147

11 THE SALVAGE OF IDEAS: PROBLEMS OF THE
    REVIVAL OF AUSTRIAN ECONOMIC
    THOUGHT [1982]   164

12 JOHN MAYNARD KEYNES: A VIEW FROM AN
    AUSTRIAN WINDOW [1983]   184

13 REFLECTIONS ON HAYEKIAN CAPITAL
    THEORY [1975]   198

Part IV Subjectivism and the interpretation of institutions

14 CARL MENGER AND THE INCOMPLETE
    REVOLUTION OF SUBJECTIVISM [1978]   213

15 VICISSITUDES OF SUBJECTIVISM AND THE
    DILEMMA OF THE THEORY OF CHOICE [1978]   218

16 FROM MISES TO SHACKLE: AN ESSAY ON
    AUSTRIAN ECONOMICS AND THE KALEIDIC
    SOCIETY [1976]   229

17 G. L. S. SHACKLE'S PLACE IN THE HISTORY OF
    SUBJECTIVIST THOUGHT [1990]   241

18 THE FLOW OF LEGISLATION AND THE
    PERMANENCE OF THE LEGAL ORDER [1979]   249

19 THE MONETARY SYSTEM OF A MARKET
    ECONOMY [1986]   261

20 SPECULATIVE MARKETS AND ECONOMIC
    COMPLEXITY [1988]   270

21 AUSTRIAN ECONOMICS: A HERMENEUTIC
    APPROACH [1991]   276

APPENDIX: BIBLIOGRAPHY OF WORKS BY
LUDWIG M. LACHMANN   291
    Compiled by *William Tulloh*

Notes   297
References   316
Index   323

EDITOR'S NOTE

This selection of essays by Ludwig Lachmann (1906–90) includes the most important of his works in English which were previously published only in scattered places, and not included in his own books. An excellent collection of many of his essays was put together by Walter Grinder in 1977, but there are many significant works that did not fit in that collection, and several others which have only appeared since 1977. In particular, the collection featured heavily what could be called Lachmann's middle period, that is the 1950s and 1960s, but included no essays from the 1930s and only three from the 1940s. This collection then fills in the gaps, including nine essay from the early period, spanning from 1936 to 1948, and twelve from the later period, from 1975 to 1991.

Two of the essays, 'Reflections on Austrian capital theory' and 'Vicissitudes of subjectivism and the dilemma of theory of choice', have not been previously published. The essays have been reproduced with no editorial alterations to the content, except for the insertion of some section headings to improve consistency.

ACKNOWLEDGEMENTS

I would like to thank Bill Tulloh, whose work in gathering together the bibliography, and talking with me at length about the meaning of Lachmann's work, was instrumental in moving this project forward. It was gratifying to see most of our entries verified in the bibliography that was separately collected by C. S. W. Torr, S. Böhm, and K. H. M. Mittermaier for the *South African Journal of Economics*, but there were a few items they found that we had missed, and we thank them for this help. Robert Baldini helped with the proofreading.

Alan Jarvis of Routledge encouraged me in the idea of this book from the beginning, and never lost patience with my plodding efforts.

INTRODUCTION
Expectations and the meaning of institutions
Don Lavoie

> The main social function of the economist is to provide the historian and the student of contemporary events with an arsenal of schemes of interpretation.
>
> *Ludwig M. Lachmann*[1]

Professor Lachmann's contributions to economics, spanning six decades, and addressing issues in microeconomics, macroeconomics, methodology and the history of thought, are a treasure chest. His essays are consistently well written and extraordinarily insightful, yet his message has not yet been adequately appreciated, even by those who know some of his major works. As a dissident member of a dissident school of thought, the Austrian school, his work is not well known in the economics profession at large. Yet as these essays show, Lachmann's challenges to mainstream economics in general, and to mainstream Austrian economics, even those he penned a half century ago, strike at the very heart of what has gone wrong with 'the dismal science'.

Lachmann lived through dramatic changes in the status of the Austrian school during his long career. He began his academic life when the school was at its peak, witnessed its rapid decline throughout the 1930s, survived its dark ages during the next three decades, and then contributed to its resurgence during the 1970s and 1980s.[2] His work is now the inspiration of a growing group of Austrian-oriented critics of mainstream economics who are trying to recover what might be called its interpretive dimension.[3]

Among Austrian economists he is best known as the leading representative of the 'radical subjectivist' wing of the school. His allies understand this to be an honourable position and his critics

1

understand it to be a serious danger: too much subjectivism, say the critics, undermines the ability of economics to describe market processes as systematic in any sense. The critics' concerns that Lachmann's work leads to nihilism have, I think, been misplaced. They have distorted the main thrust of Lachmann's work, by making it seem as though the issue his work is raising is some kind of metaphysical doubt about whether economic reality might be beyond any systematic understanding because it is completely chaotic, or even whether the real world exists at all. This is especially unjust in that Lachmann was in fact far more oriented to the real world of the economy than the vast majority of his professional colleagues. To treat *this* economist – who was as much at home discussing the latest news from the financial press or the intricate details of stock market options as he was discussing economic theory – as if he entertained doubts about whether there is a real world out there, is utterly absurd. The essays collected in this book make clear that on the contrary Lachmann's contributions are precisely aimed at helping us to understand the systematic order and empirical complexity of real world market processes.

Lachmann's message does, to be sure, identify a conflict between neoclassical economics and the real world, but it is not the real world that he is saying needs to go. His work is as uncompromising a challenge to mainstream economics as can be found anywhere. It resembles in this respect, the work of his good friend George Shackle. But in one important respect he differs from Shackle. Lachmann saw his work not only as a criticism of mainstream economics, but as a constructive effort in building an alternative sort of economics, an alternative he thought could be put together primarily from the resources of the Austrian school, although freely borrowing from other sources.

POST-MODERNISM AND THE CRISIS OF ECONOMICS

Contemporary economics appears superficially to be a discipline that is in perfectly good health, spawning numerous journals, graduating thousands of economics majors in universities, and scores of Ph.Ds. But a closer look suggests that it is working itself into a major crisis of relevance. While over the past sixty years it has happily and unselfconsciously proceeded along a 'modernist' philosophical path, the centre of gravity of academic life has meanwhile grown deeply disenchanted with modernism.

2

Modernism can be defined as the rationalist and/or empiricist view that knowledge is the result of the knowing subject achieving a detached objectivity in relation to the objects of study. The 'truth' is thought to follow from the strict application of 'scientific methods' in theorizing (where mathematics and logical deduction is privileged as a superior form of reasoning), and in empirical work (where the verification or falsification of hypotheses through statistical testing is privileged). In effect, if not always in its explicit formulations, it systematically discounts forms of empirical research based on ethnography and archival historiography, and forms of theoretical research based on philosophy and the history of thought. It has been the dominant philosophical orientation of the social and natural sciences since the Enlightenment.

Today modernist views are being routed from all directions. Philosophical ideas from the continent, such as post-structuralism and hermeneutics, are exposing the weaknesses of modernist assumptions about science, knowledge and truth, about the scientific ideal of detachment and objectivity, about the nature of causation and explanation. These challenges are not confined to what can be set apart from substantive economics and labelled the philosophy of science, or methodology, but penetrate right into the core of key concepts used throughout economic analysis, questioning what used to be taken to be self-evident interpretations, for example, of the individual, of language, of choice, and of time.

Modernism distorted economics and other social sciences in their conception of the nature of both theory and empirical research, as well as in their conception of the relationship between them. It misled economists into seeing a need for expressing theory in mathematical language, which it presumed to be, at least potentially, a universal language freed from the ambiguities of natural language. It misled empirical researchers into seeing a need for conducting all their empirical work in the mode of the search for statistical regularities in quantitative variables.

Modernist prejudices concerning the relationship between theory and history make it necessary to privilege one or the other. Approaches in mainstream theoretical economics tend to be a prioristic in a sense that privileges theory over the facts.[4] Theory is thought of as based deductively on 'first principles' in such a way as to essentially insulate it from empirical critique. Approaches in mainstream empirical work, on the other hand, tend to be a posterioristic in a sense that privileges facts over theory. Here theory is thought of as strictly hypothetical, such that the facts are seen as testing the theory. A hermeneutical approach to these issues would, however, refuse to privilege either theory or history, so that theory 'tests' historical facts, in the sense that facts need to be checked for theoretical coherence, *and* the facts test theories, in the sense that theories need to be tried out on real world circumstances to be sure they are relevant.

The consequences of philosophical hermeneutics for both theoretical and empirical work in economics are profound. Without modernist prejudices about language, the natural languages are restored to their rightful place, and formal mathematical expression of theoretical ideas is no longer privileged. For example the kind of conceptual clarification in words of economic principles, in which the Austrian school, and most of economics before the rise of formalism, was engaged, is legitimated. Without modernist prejudices about empirical work, forms of empirical investigation other than statistics, such as historical case studies or in-depth ethnographies, are permitted.[5]

Modernistic notions that used to be powerful weapons economists could use to proclaim their superiority over other social sciences now make the whole field susceptible to easy attack. When modernistic assumptions were dominant throughout academia, the discipline's presuppositions only served to give it pre-eminent status among scholarly disciplines, such that it was widely considered the Queen of the social sciences. Most economists are blissfully unaware of the fact that the modernist ground upon which their profession has been standing has been shifting out from under them. The earthquake has proceeded now to the point where some economists are starting to realize that their whole approach is at risk of being rejected by the academic world at large.[6] If economics is still the 'queen' it may only be in the sense in which, in a post-monarchist age, one may find a remnant of royalty that is subject more to ridicule than respect.

Many critics of mainstream economics have been frustrated by what appears to be an impenetrable wall protecting neoclassicism from any fundamental challenge. Neoclassicism on the one hand is thoroughly imbued with modernistic philosophical assumptions that ensure that any efforts to make substantive contributions which do not play by modernistic rules of discourse are routinely rejected from all the prestigious journals. Empirical work that does not take the form of tests of quantitative statistical hypotheses is rejected out of hand as unscientific, or at least as belonging to some other discipline. Theoretical work that is not a matter of mathematical modelling is not taken seriously as a contribution to contemporary economics, and is consigned to the corner of the profession where the history of economic thought is carried on. And yet neoclassicism, while deeply committed to modernistic methodological notions, thinks of itself as unphilosophical, as committed to no methodological precepts whatsoever, but simply dedicated to doing good substantive work. Any explicitly methodological challenge to modernistic prejudices is itself ruled out of order, as belonging to philosophy. The would-be critic seems caught in a catch–22 situation whereby if one tries to do substantive work it is labelled anthropology or history and kept outside the wall, and if one tries to mount a challenge to the philosophical rules of the game it is labelled philosophy and is still kept out.

On the other hand, this wall may be offering economists little more than a false sense of security. Economics is increasingly isolated from adjacent disciplines in a way that could end up leading to its wholesale rejection.[7] There is a risk that economists are becoming so out of touch with the overall tendencies of scholarship that they will one day find themselves utterly ignored. All of the wisdom economics has accumulated over the past two hundred or so years could be lost only because the field over the last several decades mistakenly came to see itself as founded on modernist grounds that have now turned to quicksand.

LUDWIG LACHMANN AND THE AUSTRIAN ALTERNATIVE

The significance of Lachmann's work, and of the so-called Austrian school of which it is a part, may be seen in terms of this danger. The Austrians were not of course innocent of all of the modernistic tendencies of the last couple of centuries, but they were arguably the one school of thought in the history of economics that resisted more of these tendencies than any other. They may be seen as the school that offers the most promise of rescuing the truths of economics from the sinking ship of modernism. And in the recent revival of the school they are one of the few schools of thought that has explicitly embraced a post-modernist philosophical position, that of philosophical hermeneutics, and has started to re-interpret economics in these terms.[8]

Lachmann's methodological approach can be seen as one which tries to see theory and history as complements of one another. As he puts it in one passage,

> We believe that in promoting a more perfect harmony between theory and history the theorist will be most useful if his approach is made along the following line: He must, first of all, attempt to understand what problems the historians are trying to solve in evolving their various schemes and models. He should then examine the facts which figure prominently in these models as to whether they are facts relevant, or the facts most relevant, to the problems to be solved. If he is not satisfied with the relevance of the facts stressed by the historians, he must send them out for new facts. If he is satisfied with the relevance of the facts gathered by the historians, but finds their model incoherent or otherwise inadequate, he must out of the same facts construct a better model.
>
> (1944: 64)

While contemporary hermeneutical writers would be unsatisfied with the language in which this statement is put, the spirit of the argument, stressing the mutual interdependence of theory and history, exemplifies the ideal of an interpretive social science. By the time Lachmann wrote *The Legacy of Max Weber* (1971) he had become a thorough-going advocate of an interpretive economics.[9] He was proposing that we view economic phenomena, such as prices, capital goods, or institutions, as 'texts' which need to be 'read'. His summary of the interpretive method from that work will sound familiar to contemporary hermeneuticists:

> In interpreting a text, what essentially we are trying to do is to identify a 'meaning,' an idea, to which the text in question is designed to give expression. In other words, interpretation is a method of comparative study by means of which we are attempting to establish a relation between an observable event (a readable text) and an idea which existed in a human mind prior to the writing of the text, and to which the latter is designed to lend expression.[10]

The Austrian school was born together with neoclassicism in

the marginalist revolution of the 1870s, and did not at first consider itself to have a distinctively interpretive methodological stance. On the strength of the contributions to subjective value theory by Carl Menger, the school prospered in the first thirty years of the twentieth century alongside the other two schools of neoclassicism, the Marshallian and Walrasian approaches. The three branches of neoclassicism understood themselves to be variations on a common theme (variously identified as 'marginalism' or 'subjectivism') and to be separated more by the accident of the geographical and linguistic distance among Vienna, Lausanne and Cambridge, than by any significant substantive ideas.

To the extent that the Austrian school thought of itself as distinct, it was only in the sense that it had its own angle on monetary theory and the theory of capital (itself owing a great deal to the work of the Swedish economist Knut Wicksell) which the Austrians felt had not been adequately absorbed in the other branches of neoclassicism. The school's business cycle theory was conceived as a combination of these two themes. In monetary theory the Austrians were unhappy with both the quantity theory approach that held sway in English economics, and with the rather untheoretical empirical work in business cycle research that held sway in Germany. In capital theory, the Austrians were unhappy with the tendency of their neoclassical allies to ignore the 'time structure of capital'. Austrians insisted on the temporal heterogeneity of capital goods, and the importance of understanding the systematic relationship among stages of production that were more or less remote from the final consumer goods from which capital goods ultimately derive their value.

During the 1920s, when Lachmann was a graduate student in Germany, the Austrian school was flourishing in Vienna and beginning to spread its influence around the world. Its leading figures, Ludwig Mises and the young Friedrich Hayek, were actively developing the school's trade cycle theory. They were enjoying the effects of the growing influence of Mises's work in monetary theory, his famous critique of socialism, and his early writings on methodological and epistemological problems of economics.

Lachmann completed his dissertation in 1930 at the University of Berlin under the supervision of Werner Sombart, who was hardly an ally of the Austrians, but Lachmann had already taken an intense interest in the Mengerian branch of neoclassicism. He was attracted by the fundamental idea of subjectivism from

Menger, by the methodological writings of Mises which suggested the relationship between Mengerian subjectivism and the *Verstehen* [understanding] school of German social thought of which Sombart was a part, and by the new work coming out of Vienna on monetary theory, capital theory, and business cycles. The impact of the Great Depression in the early 1930s only intensified Lachmann's interest in trade cycle theory. From his earliest reading of Menger and Mises, Lachmann became an enthusiast, and committed himself to advancing the subjectivist ideas he found in the Austrian school.

Throughout his career Lachmann was always self-conscious of the fact that he was not simply a contributor to a homogeneous 'economics', to an objective account of the economy as it really is in itself, but a proponent of a particular school of thought, a definite perspective, which was differentiated from others by crucial paradigmatic beliefs. Karl Mittermaier quotes an unpublished remark Lachmann once made that

> At LSE in the 30's we were all encouraged to think of our work as 'economic science,' a uniform subject, and of 'schools of thought' as belonging to a not quite reputable past. We were all economists! Coming from Berlin, and having read Mannheim's *Ideology and Utopia*, I felt somewhat skeptical . . . When Keynes began to talk of 'classical economics,' it shocked some people, but not me.[11]

Sometimes, to be sure, the attitude of being dedicated to a self-consciously separate school can contribute to unnecessary divisiveness. In every school of thought can be found some who use the notion of school to wall themselves off from the rest of the discipline. But Lachmann's distinctiveness was not the kind that stems from those who only want to talk to their own clique. Lachmann always insisted on widening the definition of the school of 'subjectivism' to embrace anyone who recognized and resisted the objectivizing tendencies he saw happening to mainstream economics. He sought out alliances with the institutionalists and post-Keynesians, for example, at a time when other Austrian economists were ignoring them. And he always resisted the beliefs he did not share by trying to actively engage them, never by running away from them.

But Lachmann also saw through the objectivistic self-deception of 'schoollessness', of failing to bear in mind the particular perspective from which one sees the world. He challenged the pretence prevalent among economists that in doing one's research one was directly seeing the world as it is in itself, as if one observed reality unmediated by an interpretive framework.

Two themes, one methodological, the other substantive, that integrate all of Lachmann's work could be designated under the headings of Meaning and Expectations. The methodological goal of his contributions has been to construct *an economics of meaning*, that is, an approach to the subject that emphasizes the meaning that economic institutions have to the acting human subjects who participate in them.[12] From the beginning Lachmann saw the principle economists call 'subjectivism' as much more than a technical issue in value theory, but rather as a philosophical theme about the nature of the human sciences. Economics is for Lachmann a subject that needs to deploy the methods of *Verstehen*, of the interpretation of meaning, and not think of itself as a natural science trying to establish causal laws. The distinctive contribution of the Austrians was their aspiration to take this subjectivist principle to its logical conclusion, to rid economics of the many objectivistic elements that it retained from its Ricardian heritage. Lachmann agreed with John Hicks's contention that classical economics was focused on a completely different question, 'plutology', the (macroeconomic) study of the causes of economic wealth, as opposed to the issue that became central with the subjectivist revolution, 'catallactics', the (microeconomic) study of how markets work.

For Lachmann subjectivism relates not only to the direction of human intentions and plans, but also to the discussion of those resultants of human action that are unintended, that is, to the whole realm of economics the Austrians called spontaneous orders. Social institutions such as money and law are understandable in relation to the human purposes that give rise to them, even though they go beyond the intentions of any of the participants.[13]

And yet the shortcomings of the school, Lachmann felt, had to do with the fact that it had not extended its subjectivistic approach consistently enough. In particular, it had not worked out the implications of subjectivism for the issue of expectations. The substantive theme that unifies Lachmann's work is his tireless emphasis on the importance of expectations, and on the significance of the fact that expectations are necessarily diverse. The function of organized stock markets and financial markets, Lachmann contended, was not to eliminate differences among expectations but to co-ordinate those differences, to bring about a balance of the market into bulls and bears.

Both of these themes make Lachmann an uncompromising critic of equilibrium theories of social systems.[14] Walrasian general equilibrium analysis is a style of theorizing that moves in the opposite direction from an economics of meaning, and it necessarily obscures the problem of expectations. Throughout his career the economics profession was increasingly preoccupied with the static and formal analysis of end-states, while Lachmann was trying to draw its attention to the interpretive analysis of dynamic processes of adaptation in time.[15]

Lachmann's work can be divided roughly into three periods, corresponding to his residence in England, South Africa, and the United States. When Lachmann moved to England in the spring of 1933 the Austrian school was beginning to have a significant influence in economics, especially through Hayek's elaborations of trade cycle theory. This theory was looked at by many with the hope that it might help explain how the world had found itself in such a severe economic depression. Lachmann's first essays in the 1930s and 1940s were directly aimed at improving the Austrian school's theory of business cycles. His distinctive contributions were to bring more focus on expectations into the Austrians' theory of the initial causes of the downturn, and to elaborate on the idea of a 'secondary depression', which tried to explain how the economy may have become stuck in the depression once it got there.

His middle period from 1950 to the mid–1970s was spent at the University of the Witwatersrand in Johannesburg in intellectual isolation, but those years were certainly not unproductive. In this period he produced three of his best works, the books *Capital and Its Structure* (1956), *The Legacy of Max Weber* (1971) and the monograph, *Macroeconomic Thinking and the Market Economy* (1973). Several of his most interesting essays in this period (collected in the 1977 book *Capital, Expectations and the Market Process*) began to take a wider focus on the nature of economics as a whole. The Austrian school during these years was enduring its darkest hour. Hayek had turned his interest to political philosophy, and most of the former followers of Mises and Hayek, such as Fritz Machlup, Abba Lerner and Lionel Robbins, had turned away from the Austrian approach. Ludwig Mises, and later his student Israel Kirzner, held a modest foothold at New York University, but there was hardly anywhere in the world where someone could take up the serious study of the Austrian tradition. Lachmann almost single-handedly kept the Austrian tradition alive during those years, working on the margins of a profession that was paying him no heed.

And then, Lachmann attended a conference on Austrian economics at South Royalton Vermont, sponsored by the Institute for Humane Studies, which marked a new phase in his career. Lachmann was energized by the interest he found there among a younger generation in Austrian ideas, and when Kirzner launched the Austrian economics programme at New York University, Lachmann took a position at NYU. After so many years in isolation, Lachmann flourished in the resurgent atmosphere of the NYU programme, and his work continued to widen its focus. He completed his last major work, The Market as an Economic Process in the mid–1980s, which summed up his constructive vision of where subjectivism needed to go next.

Lachmann's presence at NYU in the 1970s and 1980s, and his several visits to the Austrian programme at George Mason University in the 1980s, gave the neo-Austrian movement the benefit of his decades of reflection about what had gone wrong, the opportunities the older Austrian movement had missed, the mistakes it had made. And he gave the young American enthusiasts of the Austrian approach his own enthusiasm and his own vision of what a truly interpretive approach to economics can be like.[16]

EARLY ESSAYS: 1936–48

Lachmann's intent to develop an economics of meaning is evident from his first published article in economics, 'Commodity Stocks and Equilibrium' (1936). Lachmann criticizes an article by Oskar Lange on the 'cobweb theorem' for assuming that 'on each market-day supply is entirely elastic'. That is, Lange is taken to task for completely ignoring the fact that, except for in the special case of perishable goods, producers will prefer to hold commodity stocks in the expectation of better prices in the future, rather than accept any price they can get. This insistence on the distinction between markets that are primarily flows from those which involve the holding of stocks, and the special significance of expectations in the latter case, was to be a recurrent theme in his writings. Another recurrent theme, that what is important in dynamic analysis is the path of adjustment and not just the equilibrium end-state – or as we might say, that history matters – is stressed in the article's closing comment: '[Commodity stocks] are a result of the path towards equilibrium rather than a result of equilibrium itself. Their existence appears to justify the suggestion that for dynamic analysis bygones are not necessarily bygones.'

Lachmann's view of the importance of uncertainty is elaborated in his second essay, 'Uncertainty and Liquidity Preference' (1937). Lachmann criticizes the partial views of uncertainty contained in Paul Rosenstein-Rodan's and J. M. Keynes's analyses of liquidity preference. The other essays appearing in Part I: Uncertainty, Investment and Economic Crises can be seen as contributions to Austrian business cycle theory. Here Lachmann was primarily elaborating themes concerning the time structure of capital which Hayek had developed, with the difference that Lachmann was insisting on the distinctiveness of the secondary depression. In 'Investment and Costs of Production' (1938) he mounts a critique of the Keynesian multiplier, based on the heterogeneity of capital. He points out that increasing demand for consumption goods does not necessarily lead to an increasing demand for investment goods. Keynesian theory misses this because of its overly aggregative approach to investment. Lachmann points to Eric Lundberg's Wicksellian analysis which shows why 'the types of investment most likely to react to changes in interest conditions are least likely to respond to changes in consumption demand and *vice versa.*'

Lachmann's disaggregative approach to investment is further illustrated when he undertakes an empirical analysis (co-authored with F. Snapper) of the changes in commodity stocks during the course of the business cycles in 'Commodity Stocks in the Trade Cycle' (1938). And in the last paper in this section, 'On Crisis and Adjustment' (1939) he points out that Keynesian critics of Hayek's theory have misunderstood it to be about aggregate demand or aggregate employment, when in fact the theory has almost nothing to say on such matters.

In several of the essays in Part II, Capital and Investment Repercussions, Lachmann develops his reasons for insisting on the heterogeneity of capital goods. 'On the Measurement of Capital' (1941), he attempts to outline ways in which capital might be tentatively measured without doing essential violence to its diversity. As he points out,

> As social scientists we are, of course, entitled ... to reject the claims of a spurious 'scientism' which harbours an almost superstitious belief in numbers and identifies measurability with intelligibility. But there is surely no reason why we should not try to measure where measurement helps us to a better understanding of social phenomena. (368)

The essay on 'Finance Capital' (1944) raises the question of who makes investment decisions in modern capitalistic economies. The Marxian theorist Rudolf Hilferding contends that in 'late capitalism' it is the financial sector which takes over the entrepreneurial task of determining the direction of new investment. Lachmann brings empirical evidence from England, Germany, and the United States to bear on the question, and finds no evidence for a special stage of finance capital. But he does note that at any stage of capitalism it will on occasion (in particular when the management of investment is deemed to have been poorly done) be necessary for financial decision-makers to intervene in management. The paper thus not only challenges Hilferding's analysis, but offers a constructive analysis of its own of the relationship between financial capital and industrial capital.

The last chapter in Part II, 'Investment Repercussions' (1948) is an early statement of the set of themes about capital that were to constitute Lachmann's major work, *Capital and Its Structure*. Once one takes the proposition that capital is heterogeneous seriously, it becomes clear that, contrary to the assumption of Keynesian models, an increase in investment does not necessarily reduce the value of existing capital. Investment goods need to be studied in regard to whether they stand in a complementary or a substitutive relationship to the existing capital structure. Lachmann argues that in fact the main function of the entrepreneur involves the invention not of whole new production plans, but of new uses of capital goods that are 'discarded from plans that had to be revised' (1948: 704), which he was to later call 'fossils of old plans'.

> In a dynamic world the successful performance of this function, based on realization of the effective possibilities of capital regrouping which are inherent in a given situation, is the real test of entrepreneurship. (705)

RECENT ESSAYS: 1975–91

The essays in Part III: Diagnosing the Austrian School's 'Great Depression' come from the later period of Lachmann's career, but refer back to those early years. While the economy was undergoing a great depression in the 1930s, it might be said that the Austrian school went through one as well. Lachmann often commented on the fact that the Austrians began the 1930s at the very top of the economics profession, and ended the decade at the bottom. These essays represent Lachmann's reflections on what went wrong in this tragic decade. They are the first that are out of chronological order, but they are arranged in an order intended to refer to the chronology of the events taking place in the period they examine.

Hayek's books *Prices and Production* (1931) and *Monetary Theory and the Trade Cycle* ([1929] 1933) met with an initial enthusiasm from most English-speaking economists for whom the Austrian business cycle theory was a new and promising approach to understanding the severe depression into which the whole Western world was sinking. But Hayek's views sustained a series of blows during the decade, beginning in 1932 with a ferocious attack by the esteemed historian of thought, Piero Sraffa. In 'Austrian Economics Under Fire: The Hayek-Sraffa Duel in Retrospect' (1986) Lachmann examines the episode which began to shake the confidence English economists had initially gained in Hayek's theory of business cycles. Lachmann shows that one factor that led to the strength of Sraffa's critique was that Sraffa never revealed the underlying objective value theory from which his attack was launched. Observers of the intense controversy never realized the extent to which the basis of the challenge to Hayek was a position even more foreign to their own than the Austrian standpoint from which Hayek's analysis proceeded.

In the mid–1930s the Austrians sustained an attack from an unexpected direction. Frank Knight, who was an ardent supporter of the Austrian methodological position of *Verstehen*, and who unlike Sraffa had great sympathies with the Austrians' market-oriented policy perspective, severely criticized the Austrian view of capital (1933; 1934; 1935). In 'The Salvage of Ideas: Problems of the Revival of Austrian Economic Thought' (1982), Lachmann interprets this challenge, and helps us to see why Hayek and Knight were talking past each other. It appears that they were addressing very different questions, and doing so from, respectively, a catallactic and a plutological perspective. At the time of the controversy, however, the very vehemence of the challenge, as with Sraffa's, diminished Hayek's stature in the English-speaking world.

The same essay takes up two philosophical themes the Austrians were never able to convince their fellow economists about during the 1930s, with tragic consequences for the overall trend of economic thought. Hayek met with bafflement when he tried to clarify the importance of knowledge in economic processes in his 1936 presentation to the London Economic Club (1937) and his later essay on 'The Meaning of Competition' (1940). Lachmann suggests that Hayek (and later Shackle) was introducing an idea of practical knowledge or 'know-how' into economic discourse, without making it sufficiently clear that this was a very different thing from the kind of propositional knowledge economists and philosophers were used to discussing.

Another philosophical issue of great importance was articulated by the Austrian economist, Hans Mayer in his 'Der Erkenntniswert der funktionellen Preistheorien' (1932). The fundamental problem with mainstream economics was its preoccupation with 'functionalistic' explanation instead of 'causal-genetic' explanation.[17] Causal-genetic explanation addresses the issue of 'how prices come into being rather than what system of prices will secure equilibrium' (1982: 633). Mayer's main conclusion was that

> '[F]unctional price theories,' i.e., general equilibrium theories, are incapable of explaining how prices are actually formed in real markets, and by implication, that Austrians had no reason to give up their own analytical efforts, and accept the conclusions of the School of Lausanne.
>
> (1982: 632)

Other than Mayer, who never had any significant influence over the world of English-speaking economics, the Austrians never took the offensive on this fundamental level, and so were unable to persuade most economists of the shortcomings of equilibrium theorizing. As Lachmann was to argue, the tragedy of economics is that it failed to follow the subjectivist revolution to its logical conclusion, and instead found itself returning to the Ricardian vice of abstract theorizing, or as he liked to call it 'late classical formalism'.

The biggest blow to the Austrians in the mid–1930s, of course, was the rise of Keynesian economics. In 'John Maynard Keynes: a View From an Austrian Window' (1983), Lachmann examines the uneasy relationship between Keynes and the Austrians, and clarifies the areas of agreement and disagreement. He finds more areas of agreement than most Austrians or Keynesians would have expected, and concludes the essay with an appeal to Austrians to apply their own subjectivistic approach to the way they undertake the interpretation of alternative schools of thought. As he points out, 'those who act and those who formulate generalizations about such action face the same problem.' Those who study real situations in which men have to act have a duty, he says, 'to pay heed to the variety of perspectives from which they may be viewed. *Verstehen* as the method of enquiry specific to the social sciences may be said, like charity, to begin at home' (1983: 324–5). It must be said that particularly with regard to Keynes, the Austrians were often guilty of failing to read the author in a manner in which one tries to make the most sense of what is being said. When Lachmann was at NYU he so often enjoined on his fellow Austrians this hermeneutical principle of charity in interpretation that we came to call it Lachmann's Law.

One of the main ways in which the Keynesians failed, in their turn, to comprehend the Austrian school's message was the fact, illustrated in the Austrians' controversy with Knight, that the school had never made its theory of capital sufficiently clear. Hayek's last major work of technical economics was his *Pure Theory of Capital* (1941), but this too failed to rescue the school from the decline it had suffered during the 1930s. In a previously unpublished essay, 'Reflections on Hayekian Capital Theory' (1975), Lachmann asks why Hayek's effort met with so little success. He concludes that the difficulty arises from Hayek's attempt to use equilibrium analysis as a means towards a causal-genetic explanation of disequilibrium processes. There are two kinds of processes, he argues, which could be called 'mechanical' and 'orientative', and a theory of equilibration, such as that which Hayek deploys, may be appropriate only for the former. What is needed, then, to restore capital theory to its rightful place in economics is to develop an orientative causal-genetic theory of capitalistic production processes.

The essays in Part IV: Subjectivism and the Interpretation of Institutions elaborate on the direction Lachmann felt economics needs to take if it is to recover from the rise of formalism. Lachmann thought that what went wrong with economics was that it never saw the subjectivistic revolution of the 1870s through to its logical conclusion. As his short piece entitled 'Carl Menger and the Incomplete Revolution of Subjectivism' (1978) points out, he is not trying to blame Menger for not having seen all the radical implications of his challenge to classical economics. Nevertheless it is valuable to try to identify what elements of Menger's thought were inconsistent with what might be called the essential message of his subjectivism. Menger's interpretation of the 'marginalist' revolution in value theory turns out in retrospect to have much larger significance than simply the logic of value. The Austrian school began, especially with Mises's work, to realize that the principle of subjectivism was the fundamental methodological idea of all of economics. It has come to be not only one among several principles of economics, but in a sense the meta-principle against which others are judged.[18]

The previously unpublished paper entitled 'Vicissitudes of Subjectivism and the Dilemma of the Theory of Choice' (1978) provides an overview of how the initial move towards subjectivism was subverted in neoclassical economics. In microeconomics, which is ostensibly a theory of individual choice where subjectivism ought to have flourished, mechanistic methodological presuppositions undermined it. In macroeconomics subjectivism was advanced by Keynes's introduction of expectations into economics, but this was a very selective and arbitrary subjectivism. Keynes brought expectations into his argument 'when it suited him, and left them out when it did not'. (1978: 12) And most of Keynes's followers backed off from even the limited subjectivism of their master.

One of the Keynesians who did not abandon Keynes's move into subjectivism, but instead radicalized it, was Lachmann's close friend George Shackle. The two essays on Shackle in this section clarify Lachmann's view of the specific ways in which the Austrian school never went far enough in the subjectivist direction in which Menger pointed. In 'From Mises to Shackle: An Essay on Austrian Economics and the Kaleidic Society' (1976) he compares the work of Shackle to that of Mises, and suggests that Shackle points beyond the traditional value subjectivism of the Austrian school toward the subjectivism of expectations. The essay 'G. L. S. Shackle's Place in the History of Subjectivist Thought' (1990) elaborates on this theme, identifying three stages of the progress of subjectivism. Menger's work marks the first stage, the subjectivism of wants. Mises's work marks the second, the subjectivism of means and ends, but for Mises still the ends are taken as 'given'. Shackle moves subjectivism to a more radical stage, the subjectivism of the 'active mind', thus bringing into the analysis the role of the imagination and expectations.

For Lachmann subjectivism was not merely an abstract methodological principle of how to view the nature of choice. The application of subjective thinking to economics implies that we need to view social institutions in terms of the way they serve as points of orientation for the plans of human actors. The essays 'The Monetary System of a Market Economy' (1986), 'The Flow of Legislation and the Permanence of the Legal Order' (1979), and 'Speculative Markets and Economic Complexity' (1988) illustrate how Lachmann applied his subjectivism to the institutions of money, law, and financial markets.

The last article in this collection, 'Austrian Economics: A Hermeneutic Approach' (1991) was first prepared as the keynote address for a conference held at George Mason University in 1986. Here Lachmann sums up his critique of 'late classical formalism', and points to contemporary work in hermeneutics as a way to renew the interpretive dimension of economics.

When Lachmann, whose exposure to the hermeneutical tradition came at an early stage with the influence of writers such as Weber, Schütz, and Mannheim, endorses 'hermeneutics', there may be some question about whether he would be willing to follow out the more radical implications of contemporary hermeneutics, such as in the work of Heidegger or Gadamer. In some of my last correspondence with Professor Lachmann I had been asking him to consider Gadamer's work as perhaps a better basis for our effort to construct an interpretive economics than can be found in the traditional *verstehen* school. He responded with the following comments:

> So as to be able to look you straight in the face I have read some Gadamer lately. I looked at *Truth and Method* (4th German ed., 1975) where I found the Epilogue (*Nachwort*) of particular interest. By sheer accident I came across an interview with G. in one of the German periodicals in our Library here (*Sprache & Literatur*), a most interesting piece of literary journalism of the higher kind. I must say I quite

liked what I read. Quite an attractive character emerged from the pages I read. His balanced judgment on the 'Positivismus-Streit,' the quarrel Popper and Albert had with the Frank-furters around 1970, struck me as eminently sound.

That no ready recipe is to be found in his work for how to go about reforming Economics is probably all to the good. We have to do the thinking.

CONCLUSION: A LARGE MESSAGE IN SMALL PACKAGES

Although the works Lachmann was most influenced by, such as Max Weber's *Economy and Society* ([1921] 1978), Ludwig Mises's *Human Action* ([1949] 1966), and George Shackle's *Epistemics and Economics* (1972), were large, and astonishingly bold works, each of which can be called a *magnum opus*, Lachmann's own contri-butions were never undertaken on so grand a scale. He seemed to view his role as a humble interpreter of the great masters who inspired him, not as one of them. The mode of writing in which Lachmann excelled and which he made his own was the relatively short and focused essay. Even the three works he published which had bigger ambitions, *Capital and Its Structure*, *The Legacy of Max Weber*, and *The Market As an Economic Process*, are really integrated collections of essays each of which could stand on its own, rather than major books. One does not encounter the kind of breathtaking works aimed at radically transforming our thought, but smaller scale, careful clarifications of issues which the more ambitious works he admired left unclear.[19]

And yet we should be careful not to let his unassuming manner or his preference for the shorter essay mislead us. Taken as a whole the incisive ideas contained in his writings do in fact add up to a radical challenge to our thinking. Lachmann gives us big ideas wrapped in small and misleadingly modest packages. In spite of his own view of himself, I think he was one of the great economists of our time. If we take his challenges seriously we may find ourselves changing our whole vision of what economics is really about.

Part I

UNCERTAINTY, INVESTMENT AND ECONOMIC CRISES

1

COMMODITY STOCKS AND EQUILIBRIUM [1936]

INTRODUCTION

Of all the intricate problems which beset the path of those who endeavour to evolve a dynamic theory of economic equilibrium, none is more formidable than that presented by the existence of different velocities of adjustment of different data. Adopting Mr Kaldor's terminology we may define as 'velocity of adjustment' 'the time required for a full quantitative adjustment to take place (either on the supply-side or on the demand-side) corresponding to a given price-change, i.e. the time elapsing between the establishment of a certain price and the full quantitative adjustment of that price.'[1] Now, it goes without saying that, where the velocity of adjustment of some datum is so small that, while its adjustment is taking place, other data are liable to change, equilibrium becomes hopeless and only 'perfect foresight' seems capable of saving the situation. It has been pointed out in recent discussions,[2] however, that 'perfect foresight' cannot be regarded as a notion suitable for a starting-point of a science which (besides the drawing of so-called 'indifference-curves') is concerned with the explanation of human actions. The question therefore arises whether a satisfactory theory of dynamic equilibrium, i.e. a theory describing the movement from one equilibrium to another as a process in time, can be based upon conditions embracing imperfect foresight.

If we confine ourselves to the study of cases, where data are constant, but velocities of adjustment differ, it becomes clear that even with imperfect foresight a stable equilibrium may be reached, if foresight is inversely proportionate to velocity of adjustment, i.e. where those have the greatest foresight whose adjustment takes the longest time. If, e.g., demand reacts instantaneously to price-changes, but supply requires several months to adjust itself, final equilibrium may be reached without any foresight at all on the part of the consumers, if only the producers are able to foresee for such a period. In the real world, however, we always have to deal with several data and several velocities of adjustment, and since, moreover, the velocity of adjustment of a datum need not always be the same, there is no reason why in reality foresight should necessarily be inversely proportionate to velocity of adjustment. However, as all assumptions involving different degrees of foresight have invariably a somewhat arbitrary touch, it seems most useful to begin the study of dynamic equilibrium with the discussion of a case with no foresight at all and different velocities of adjustment, i.e. a case where all individuals are behaving as if in stationary equilibrium, and base their actions on present circumstances only.

II

The case mentioned has become generally known by the title of 'the cobweb theorem' and was first expounded by Professor Schultz[3] and Professor Ricci.[4] They argued that where supply requires time in order to adjust itself to price-changes, but demand reacts instantaneously, the final attainment of stable equilibrium depends on the condition that demand is more elastic than supply (in this case 'the cobweb will be contracting'). Otherwise, a kind of economic *perpetuum mobile* will be set up, i.e. market-prices will move more and more away from equilibrium ('the cobweb will be expanding') (see Figure 1.1).

The theorem thus appears to raise a serious objection to traditional 'static' equilibrium-theory in that it purports to show that even with constant data (i.e. within the realm of static assumptions) no final equilibrium need be reached.

The cobweb theorem has recently been subjected to searching criticism by Dr Lange.[5] He pointed out (as had, indeed, Mr Kaldor before him)[6] that the possibility of a *perpetuum mobile* depends entirely on the condition that supply-adjustments are not only delayed but also discontinuous, and concluded that if the dangerous gap between an entirely inelastic market-day supply and a relatively elastic long-run supply can be filled by inserting intermediate stages of partly adjusted supply, prices will move less vehemently and final adjustment will be greatly facilitated. From

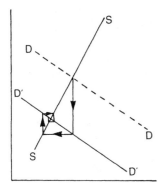 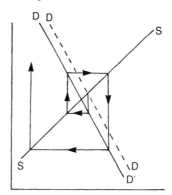

Figure 1.1

this he has inferred that the *perpetuum mobile* has its place in agricultural marketing, where for obvious reasons supply is bound to be discontinuous. On the other hand, on industrial markets, where the adjustment of supply is a continuous function of time, producers are always able to test the desirability of further adjusting operations by current prices and thus to reach stable equilibrium.[7]

Valuable though this criticism undoubtedly is, Dr Lange appears to have overlooked the weakest point in the cobweb theorem. For even he avers that producers are willing to sell their products at *any price*, i.e. that on each market-day supply is entirely inelastic. Now, except for perishable goods this is hardly a realistic assumption, and we need not introduce foresight in order to understand why producers under certain conditions will accumulate stocks of unsold goods rather than sell. Even with no foresight at all, even where nobody is capable of or concerned with forecasting future price-movements, it seems legitimate to expect that producers are not prepared to throw their products upon the market regardless of price. If we simply assume that (let alone expect that) at certain prices producers prefer holding goods to selling them (and the 'motives' of preferences are outside the realm of economic theory) market-day supply will not be entirely inelastic, the dangerous margin between the elasticities of market-day and 'long-run' supply will be narrower, and the velocity of adjustment will lose much of its significance. We thus may expect a stable equilibrium to be reached. Where no producer is willing to sell his products below cost, it will even be reached at once.

Once the hypothesis that everybody is willing to sell at any price has been removed, and allowance made for 'propensity to hold', the existence of (variable) commodity stocks will also exert its influence in the opposite direction. For, as in our previous case of demand falling short of supply, so with demand exceeding supply market-day supply will no longer be entirely inelastic, and producers by diminishing stocks will check the rise in prices. We thus may conclude that the cobweb theorem, i.e. the assertion that where supply is more elastic than demand, no definite equilibrium will be reached, rests on the tacit assumption of the impossibility of keeping unsold goods in stock.

CONSISTENCY WITH EQUILIBRIUM

It may be objected that the introduction of commodity stocks, variable in size, is inconsistent with the postulates of equilibrium analysis and that with any such stocks in existence no equilibrium can be determinate. For, is it not a generally accepted condition of equilibrium that there must be either no carry-over at all or at least a constant carry-over?[8] This objection seems to overlook two points.

First, as regards market equilibrium, it is, of course, true that equilibrium implies that demand equals supply and no carry-over is left, *but at equilibrium price*. Thus stocks do not impair market equilibrium if their holders are not willing to part with them except at a price above equilibrium price.

Second, it is true that full (long-period) equilibrium requires a constant (or no) carry-over, but what we are concerned with at present is not so much this final position as the description of the path leading to it. Final (long-run) equilibrium will be approached by a process of continuous variations in the size of the carry-over; once it is reached the latter will remain constant.

CHANGES IN THE DATA

From this analysis of the economic function of commodity stocks under conditions of constant data with non-instantaneous reactions of supply, we may now proceed to extend our investigation to cases of changes in data. If demand fluctuates to such an extent that the velocity of change in demand is greater than (or equal to) the velocity of adjustment of supply, the situation, as we said at the beginning, becomes hopeless and equilibrium seemingly unattainable. Under such circumstances, in the absence of stocks, producers will find it impossible to adjust production according to market-prices, and since they have to base their actions upon something, will probably have to fall back on 'anticipations', however imperfect and futile. In this case, the dynamic function of commodity stocks is evident in that the rate of change in their size assumes the character of an indicator of the urgency of demand which is, in many respects, superior to the market-price.

For not only, as in our previous case, will the existence and variability of carry-over tend to narrow down the range of price fluctuations and thus serve to facilitate the adjustment of supply, but also besides this mere buffer-function its significance lies in the fact that in what is called 'the statistical situation of the market' it provides producers with a second clue for their operations. Where, as we have seen, market-prices are no longer a reliable guide for the entrepreneur who does not want to fall back upon anticipations, the rate of change in commodity stocks will furnish a useful second criterion. Under such circumstances a price change accompanied by an inconsiderable change in the size of stocks, such as might be caused by a temporary fluctuation in demand, will not induce producers to change their output. But a considerable depletion (or accumulation) of stocks, which would assure them that a change in output is necessitated by the 'statistical situation of the market', will induce them to adjust supply.

CONCLUSION: THE IMPORTANCE OF CARRY-OVER

It follows from the preceding discussion that dynamic equilibrium analysis has to take account of the existence and variability of carry-over. The question therefore arises of how to deal with it and insert it into our system of variables. The situation is different according to whether we concentrate upon the magnitude of the carry-over at each point of time or study the changes in this magnitude due to the passage of time. On each market-day the size of stocks and their supply schedule – the scale of prices at which their owners are willing to part with them – are given as independent variables not determined by current supply and demand. What is determined by the latter is only that change in size which stocks will undergo as a result of market-operations on that day. If, however, we consider the dynamic process as a whole – i.e. the whole period of time that elapses between the point at which the old equilibrium is upset and the point at which the new equilibrium is reached – it becomes evident, supposing no stocks existed at the beginning, that the size of carry-over is simply a function of everything that happens during this period. If some carry-over did exist at the beginning it has to be regarded as a function of the process which formerly led to the old equilibrium.

Hence, for the analysis of the process carry-over is a dependent variable. It, so to say, embodies the history of all the daily disequilibria the aggregate of which forms the path towards final equilibrium. The 'final carry-over' we may say – its magnitude when final equilibrium is reached – is a result of the past but a datum for the future.

Commodity stocks owe their existence to the divergences in the velocities and adjustment of different data, hence their size depends on those changes of data and processes of adjustment which have taken place in the past. They are a result of the path towards equilibrium rather than a result of equilibrium itself. Their existence appears to justify the suggestion that for dynamic analysis bygones are not necessarily bygones.

2

UNCERTAINTY AND LIQUIDITY-PREFERENCE [1937]

INTRODUCTION: WE CANNOT AVOID MOTIVES IN MONETARY THEORY

The prominent place which the concept of liquidity-preference has been occupying in recent literature on economics may be regarded as an indication of the urgent desire for an exhaustive investigation into the forces determining the demand for money. The importance of the problem for both theoretical and practical purposes need not be stressed. In monetary theory no satisfactory progress can be hoped for without the help of marginal utility-analysis, a type of investigation which is inapplicable as long as we remain ignorant of the character of the need which the possession of money satisfies. For monetary policy, on the other hand, it is vital to have a satisfactory criterion for the division of the total quantity of money into the 'effective' (business-funds) and the 'ineffective' (hoards) circulation, if we want to be able to form reliable estimates of the efficacy of monetary measures.

In analysing the forces which determine the demand for cash-balances the economic theorist cannot hope to accomplish his task adequately, if he confines himself to the enumeration and classification of the various 'reasons for holding money'. In this field, as we shall see presently, 'motives' are, indeed, a tricky subject.

For in examining the causes of liquidity-preference we are actu-ally side-stepping from the highroad of economic science, where preferences are identical with motives and must not be further analysed. Whereas, in general, economic theory strives to reduce all economic phenomena to consumers' (and savers') preferences, in the case of money this procedure will not do. Why the connoisseurs of modern painting prefer pictures by Picasso to pictures by Utrillo is a question with which it has been generally agreed that the economist is not concerned. But why sometimes owners of wealth prefer holding their assets in form of cash-balances to other forms of investment is a problem which the monetary theorist cannot afford to shirk. The causes of liquidity-preference have therefore to be sought in a field which lies beyond the realm of preferences: in our case preferences cannot be regarded as ultimate determinants.

But where have these causes to be sought, and by what forces are they determined? In order to overcome this dilemma we have to remember that what as social scientists we are concerned with are not individual acts but mass-phenomena. Mass-phenomena have to be made intelligible by reference to the similarity of the conditions under which different individuals have to act. The conditions the similarity of which makes different individuals, who are subject to them, act in an identical manner, may be either of a subjective (psychological) or an objective (institutional) nature: i.e. they may either exist purely in the imagination of the acting individuals or have a (socially) objective existence. Thus, e.g., the financial panic often accompanying the outbreak of a major crisis may either be explained by taking recourse to alleged phenomena of mass-psychology (the famous 'waves of optimism and pessimism') or by the working of certain institutions like banks.

Men may act identically, either because they are all subject to the same mass-psychological influences or because they all have to operate within the same institutional framework. As our knowledge of mass-psychology is rather scanty compared with our comprehensive cognition of institutions and the way they work, it might be useful to lay down as a preliminary rule that if in the course of the following investigation a mass-psychological and an institutional hypothesis come to compete for the role of a 'cause', preference will be given to the latter.

UNCERTAINTY IN ROSENSTEIN-RODAN'S MONETARY THEORY

In recent literature there seems to exist a fair amount of agreement among writers that uncertainty has to be regarded as the major determinant of movements in the size of cash-balances, i.e. as the main cause of liquidity-preference. At closer inspection, however, this apparent harmony emerges as somewhat problematical, because different writers give this word a different meaning. In the following we shall confine ourselves to the examination of two examples of monetary theories in both of which the leading role is assigned to uncertainty, and we shall find that in each case the word has a different meaning. Afterwards we shall make use of the result of our critical examination of these theories in order to find that meaning of 'uncertainty' which will enable us to regard it as the cause of liquidity-preference.

In a study on 'The Co-ordination of the General Theories of Money and Price'[1] Dr Rosenstein-Rodan uses the word uncertainty 'in its original meaning of doubt, of a vague and dumb feeling of not knowing'.[2] This 'vague and dumb feeling' is, however, according to him, of causal significance for the existence and magnitude of cash-balances. This result is obtained by means of contrasting our world of frictions and unforeseen changes to a frictionless world of perfect foresight. 'In an economy without frictions, where everybody foresaw with perfect certainty his tastes, income, future prices, and therefore the dates as well as the size of his purchases, nobody would keep a cash-balance' (271). Hence, 'Money (as cash-balances) exists only and in so far as general foresight is not certain, it is the function of the individual's feeling of uncertainty, a means of meeting it, a good satisfying the want for certainty' (272).

This statement, however, is later on qualified in a footnote, where we read that 'The function of uncertainty about income and prices will be *naturally* a function of many variables' (p. 272, footnote 3);[3] i.e. translated from the language of functional into that of causal-genetic analysis, uncertainty is but one of many causes of liquidity-preference. Moreover, the statement about the functional relationship between uncertainty and cash-balances has to be read in the context of Dr Rosenstein's discussion, in an earlier part of his article, of the store-of-value-function of money (266–7). Here we are told that money, although being the only good capable of fulfilling the functions of unit of account and medium of exchange, is 'only one of many goods fulfilling what one may call a cash-balance-function'. And, significantly enough, the author adds that, even where money is established as the standard of deferred payment, it will not be the only store of value.

The conclusion which we have to draw from Dr Rosenstein's

argument thus appears to be this: There exists a certain functional relationship between uncertainty and the demand for cash-balances. Yet, neither of the exact form of this relationship nor of the other variables and their relative significance have we the slightest knowledge. We are left much in the position of King Crœsus, who asked the Oracle of Delphi about his chances in the war he was going to wage on his neighbour and received the reply that he would destroy a great empire.

If a causal-genetic investigation like ours is to be conducted on Dr Rosenstein's line of approach, two main questions have to be answered. First: Can increased uncertainty not be accompanied by a diminution in the demand for money, viz. a 'flight from the currency'? Secondly: Are we not familiar with examples of cash-balances held not because of uncertainty but because of the (subjective) certainty of their owners that prices will fall? If in both cases the answer is in the affirmative, this would mean that it is impossible to assign to uncertainty *in this sense* the role of a cause of liquidity-preference.

In both respects the lesson of experience seems to be clear. Uncertainty may result in an increased demand for cash-balances. But if at the same time the future of the currency is deemed to be in danger, we know by manifold experience that people will feel induced to exchange their cash for highly illiquid goods like furs, jewels, and furniture.[4] Uncertainty may generally induce people to restrict the volume of their current liabilities. But if it also affects the future value of money: people may even borrow for buying commodities of the kind mentioned. When will they act in this, when in that manner? We do not know; our functional relationship does not provide us with a satisfactory criterion.

While our conclusion is thus of little, if any, help to the monetary theorist and, of course, entirely useless for purposes of monetary policy, it would be unfair to blame Dr Rosenstein for it. For the task he had set himself was to co-ordinate the general theories of money and of price, and since he endeavours to do it on the Lausanne model, he is entitled to confine himself to inserting a new set of variables into a system of simultaneous equations. As in this system all quantities are interdependent, it is sufficient to show that any variation in uncertainty must have some repercussion on some other magnitudes in order to make the system work and safeguard it, on its own level of abstraction, against theoretical objections. That this type of functional analysis does not solve the problems we have set out to solve is no argument against it; that it 'does not tell us anything about the real World', is a true, but by no means a novel gravamen. Slightly varying Professor Ricci's comment on Pareto one feels tempted to say that, while adding with great architectural skill to the beauty of the famous castle that was erected on the shores of the Lake of Geneva, Dr Rosenstein has still left the housing problem unsolved.

UNCERTAINTY IN KEYNES'S MONETARY THEORY

Perhaps our failure to establish a causal relationship between uncertainty and liquidity-preference is due to our having used the word uncertainty in too wide and too imprecise a meaning. Perhaps it is futile to believe that any definite form of conduct can be the outcome of 'a vague and dumb feeling of not knowing'. On the other hand, our failure to derive a definite demand-function from uncertainty in its most abstract and general sense suggests that a better result may be expected, provided the notion of uncertainty can be given a more concrete meaning. Perhaps, if we can make our notion more concrete by providing it with an 'object' of uncertainty, by making clear what exactly people are uncertain about, our endeavour will be attended by more success.

For Mr Keynes in his 'General Theory of Employment, Interest and Money' uncertainty in such a concrete sense, i.e. a very special kind of uncertainty, is, indeed, the main cause of fluctuations in liquidity-preference. It is uncertainty as to the future rate of interest which, according to him, 'is the sole intelligible explanation of the type of liquidity-preference' which he believes to be of importance (201). Among the motives for liquidity-preference we first come across the *transactions-motive* (which later on is subdivided into the income- and the business-motive, p. 195), described as 'the need of cash for the current transaction of business and personal exchanges', and thereafter 'the precautionary-motive, i.e., the desire for security as to the future cash-equivalent of a certain proportion of total resources' (170). Both these are, however, treated by Mr Keynes as being of no causal significance and as mere functions of total income (Y).

There is, however, a necessary condition failing which the existence of a liquidity-preference for money as a means of holding wealth could not exist. This necessary condition is the existence of *uncertainty* as to the future of the rate of interest, i.e. as to the complex of rates of interest for varying maturities which will rule at future dates. For if the rates of interest ruling at all future times could be foreseen with certainty, all future rates of interest could be inferred from the *present* rates of interest for debts of different maturities, which would be adjusted to the knowledge of the future rates'. (168)

In the absence of such certainty we have thus the third incentive to liquidity-preference in 'the speculative-motive, i.e. the object of securing profit from knowing better than the market what the future will bring forth' (170). In other words: If the price of 4 per cent bonds stands at 100, a person expecting the rate of interest to rise by more than 0.16 per cent in a year will gain by selling his bonds and waiting for the new price-level.

This seems plausible enough, but two sources of doubt remain. In the first place, why is the motive of an activity purporting to secure profit from speculation described as 'uncertainty'? A man who believes that he knows the future rate of interest better than the market, and who is prepared to forego present income in order to secure future profit from his apparently superior foresight, must, it would seem, be pretty certain of his 'hunch'. In what sense can we call him 'uncertain'? To this Mr Keynes's reply would probably be that he is uncertain whether the present valuation of the market is the right one. This leads us to our second doubt arising out of Mr Keynes's peculiar assumptions about the structure of the market for securities.

Mr Keynes attaches great importance to the existence of an organized market. 'For in the absence of an organized market, liquidity-preference due to the precautionary-motive would be greatly increased; whereas the existence of an organized market gives an opportunity for wide fluctuations in liquidity-preference due to the speculative-motive' (170–1). At closer inspection, however, Mr Keynes's organized securities market emerges as a particularly hybrid type. For it appears that, 'perfect' though his market may be in any meaning attributed to this word by traditional 'classical' doctrine, it certainly is *not* organized with a view to facilitate those operations we are most interested in, i.e. intertemporal exchange-transactions actuated by the speculative motive. In other words, it is just because Mr Keynes's market is not an organized forward-market that here 'bearishness' entails liquidity-preference! For on a market which is organized for intertemporal exchange, everybody is able to express his expectations for the future by buying or selling for delivery in the future.[5] On an organized forward-market it would certainly not be true that 'the individual, who believes that future rates of interest will be above the rates assumed by the market has a reason for keeping actual liquid cash, whilst the individual who differs from the market in the other direction will have a motive for borrowing money for short periods in order to purchase debts of longer term' (170). On an organized forward-market both individuals could express their expectations by forward-transactions which do not require any cash. Where the market for securities is fully organized over time, the owner of 4 per cent bonds who fears a rise in the rate of interest has no incentive to exchange them for cash, for he can always 'hedge' by selling them forward.

We do not, of course, mean to deny that, with or without a forward-market, expectations will affect the rate of interest. As there are no carrying-costs involved in keeping securities, spot-price and forward-price must always be equal. Whether securities are sold spot or forward will thus make no difference as far as prices are concerned. What it will make a difference to is liquidity-preference, for whereas spot-transactions involve cash-payments, forward-transactions do not. On an organized forward-market for securities 'bearishness' will therefore not lead to a desire of bond-holders to exchange their assets against cash, but to a desire to 'hedge', which will bring down the forward-price and, via arbitrage, also the spot-price. Negligible effects on liquidity-preference may here occur to the extent to which the spot-market 'lags' behind the forward-market; that is to say, to the extent to which spot-buyers are not quick to lower their demand-prices in accordance with the lower forward-price, and actual spot-transactions are necessary in order to adjust the spot price, which otherwise will almost automatically – and without any actual transactions being necessary – follow the forward-price.[6]

THE PRECAUTIONARY MOTIVE: MONEY DISCHARGES DEBT

Our attempt to establish a causal relationship between uncertainty and liquidity-preference has so far turned out to be a complete failure. When we interpreted uncertainty in the widest possible sense, we learned that it might lead to anything and therefore could prove nothing. When we tried to give it a narrower and more concrete meaning, we had to realize that with organized intertemporal exchanges no appreciable effect on liquidity became visible. Confronted with this dilemma we have to fall back on the other 'motives for liquidity'.

There is, first of all, the precautionary motive. 'To provide for contingencies requiring sudden expenditure and for unforeseen opportunities of advantageous purchases, and also to hold an asset of which the value is fixed in terms of money to meet a subsequent liability fixed in terms of money, are further motives for holding cash' (196).

The first part of this sentence is left comfortably vague, since, as we have seen, for the purpose of meeting unforeseen circumstances, money is just as good or as bad as any other good, and all depends on the nature of the circumstances. Its second part, however, contains the whole truth. If by uncertainty we understand the anxiety of the debtor, whose debt is due on demand, regarding the future actions of his creditor, then, at last, we can say that uncertainty is the cause of liquidity-preference.

This may sound quite plausible. The danger, however, is that economists who are brought up in an atmosphere of genuine contempt for 'institutionalist' argument will admit the possibility, but refuse to see its implications. And while probably prepared to grant that there might be some connection between the existence of money-debts and the demand for money, they may not accept our main contention that it is only because of this connection that such a thing like liquidity-preference does at all exist, and that the sole intelligible reason why people prefer money to commodities is the debt-discharging quality of the former. They may admit that uncertainty of the type described is *one* of the causes of liquidity-preference, but will probably deny that it is the only one.

As it is obviously impossible to demonstrate a contention like ours by a process of logical deduction, we shall have to convince the reader by drawing his attention to the difference between the functions of money and money's exclusive function, between what money *does* and *what only money can do*.

Money is an economic good, and money is legal tender. Is there a necessary connection between the two? At first sight apparently not, for money fulfils several functions. Being an economic good it has utility which is derived from the satisfaction of several wants.

In the first place, as medium of exchange, it yields indirect satisfaction, i.e. its utility is derived from that of the goods it is exchanged against. This has in our case the particularly awkward consequence of making marginal-utility-analysis inapplicable. For where both utilities (that of money and that of the good it is exchanged against) are derived from the satisfaction yielded by the same good (the non-money-good) we cannot attribute changes in the exchange-ratio to changes in either of them.[7] As, however, liquidity-preference and marginal utility of money are two expressions for the same thing, it follows that the relationship sought cannot be established.

In other respects money yields direct satisfaction,[8] e.g., in its function of a store of value. But we have already seen that in this respect it has almost as many substitutes as there are (non-perishable) goods, and that it is impossible to predict when it will be used as store of value and when something else. Sometimes the satisfaction derived from its possession will be even more 'direct'. Molière's Harpagon, e.g., derives as much 'direct satisfaction' from the contemplation of his hoarded treasures as does the spectator from seeing him on the stage. Yet, Harpagon – although a type rather than a character – is not a type appearing frequently enough in reality to account for the mass-phenomena we observe. Those fluctuations in the demand for cash which we observe in reality and have to explain in theory cannot be reduced to the preference-scale of an Harpagon.

At this juncture let us remember what at the beginning we said about mass-phenomena and their alternative explanation in terms of mass-psychology or institutions. There are, no doubt, some economic phenomena – mostly connected with the 'psychology of markets' – which justify and require an explanation in terms of mass-psychology. But with most of the manifestations of liquidity-preference this is far less obvious, and even if it were, our present knowledge of this kind of psychology is, at any rate, too inadequate to cope with them. Therefore, in order to account for those recurring oscillations in the demand for cash which manifest themselves as identical actions of a multitude of individuals, we have to fall back on the institutional setting within which these individuals operate. Their identical actions have to be explained as the outcome of identical objective conditions in which they find themselves.

Of all the institutions within the framework of which the human actions described by economic science are performed, the existence of money-debts is doubtless one of the most important. Now, money is the legal means of payment, i.e. its owner can use it for discharging debts.[9] This is the only use in which it has no substitutes, for its very institutional character excludes that. On the worst days, when all instruments of exchange fail us, when all markets and banks are closed, when the most liquid assets have become entirely illiquid, money – and only money! – will still serve to discharge a debt. But it must be added that this may easily be the only service it would render under such circumstances; whether it would buy even the smallest quantity of food is rather doubtful.

It therefore seems legitimate to infer that (apart from the reasons implied by intertemporal imperfection of markets) it is principally because of its debt-discharging quality that money is demanded. The fluctuations in the demand for cash which we observe in reality have thus to be explained as manifestations of debtors' uncertainty. As the security of a loan depends on the financial strength of the debtor, i.e. the relative value of his assets and liabilities, it follows that every time the money-value of assets has declined, creditors will demand repayment of loans, and debtors will have to take precautions. What this entails on trade cycle theory we shall see presently.

THE TRANSACTIONS MOTIVE

Before proceeding to the application of the results of our study we still have to examine the 'transactions-motive'. Two questions arise: to what extent does this motive determine the demand for cash? And: how far is uncertainty here of causal significance?

While Mr Keynes on the whole rather tends to minimize the importance of the transactions-motive for the demand for money, the point has recently been stressed by Mr D. H. Robertson.[10] He accuses Mr Keynes of having neglected the difference between money in the hands of entrepreneurs and money in the hands of the public ('those who desire to hold more money and those who desire to use it')[11] and emphasizes the close connection between the profitability of investment and the magnitude of the business-funds. As the profitability of investment depends on the degree of confidence which enters the 'business outlook', the inverse proportionality between uncertainty and liquidity-preference seems thus rather firmly established.

It is, however, difficult to see why an increase in business activity should necessitate a greater demand for cash for the business-funds. Most commercial transactions in the strict sense (that is, excluding wage-payments and retail-sales) are not carried out against cash. An entrepreneur who wishes to extend his scale of operations can almost invariably obtain credit from the producer of the intermediate products he needs, who thus substitutes claims on his customers for commodity-stocks. Moreover, during periods of industrial buoyancy it is quite usual that bills and similar quasi-liquid assets come to be regarded as being 'almost liquid' and are used like money. 'Trade creates its own means of payment'; there is therefore no such thing as a necessary relationship between total output and the size of business-funds.

If, nevertheless, in reality we observe that enhanced business activity is usually accompanied by increased demand for money, the explanation has to be sought in uncertainty of the type mentioned. Businessmen generally hold cash in proportion to the liabilities falling due in the nearest future. What therefore affects their liquidity-preference is not the absolute level of output, but the rate of increase in their short-term-liabilities. Hence every (even expected) deterioration of the conditions under which credit may be obtained (or extended) will be reflected in the state of liquidity-preference.

CONCLUSION

From what we so far have been setting forth there seems to emerge the general conclusion that uncertainty may be regarded as the cause of liquidity-preference, if the former is referred to the relationship between creditor and debtor. We shall now apply it to trade cycle theory and will attempt to tackle, by its help, a problem which has, of late, attracted the attention of students in this field.

All those who continue to be sceptical regarding the explanatory value of such formidable devices as the 'relation' and the 'multiplier' – or, more precisely, regarding their alleged interrelationship – will have to look out for possible explanations of the fact that economic crises do not ordinarily lead to the readjustment we should expect in theory, but almost invariably degenerate into 'cumulative downward-processes'. Once the 'secondary depression' has been recognized as a distinct phase of the cycle and a separate problem of trade cycle theory,[12] the problem of its causation and necessity poses itself, and it is towards the solution of this problem, that, on the strength of our conclusions, we believe we are able to make a contribution.

In the modern world banks are the most important debtors of loans which are due on demand. On the other hand, the banks are likely to suffer losses already during the 'Primary Crisis', because the processes which have to be liquidated at its end have, directly or indirectly, been financed by bank-credit. In this situation the obvious way out seems to be the immediate writing off of all losses and a subsequent reconstruction of the capital of the banks concerned. There is, however, an alternative solution: As the security of bank deposits is now impaired by the losses the bank has sustained, the latter may now choose to compensate its depositors for diminished safety by increased liquidity. As the banks' uncertainty in the above-mentioned sense must naturally increase, they may try to appease the fears of their creditors by showing them that they are prepared for all possibilities. But this will, of course, only be necessary if the capital of the banks is not immediately reconstructed; for, in the latter case, the security of the deposits will at once be restored.

Now, there is one good reason why we should expect the banks to go in for increased liquidity rather than for immediate reconstruction. For reasons into which we need not go here the rate of interest is likely to be very high during the period under consideration. The new capital which has to be borrowed for the purpose of reconstruction will therefore be relatively expensive, and it is quite natural that the owners of the banks should try to postpone this operation to a point of time when new capital will be cheaper. But as, for the reasons mentioned, depositors must be compensated somehow, the banks will in the meantime have to raise the cash-proportion of their assets. Contrary to Mr Keynes's theory we find that it is the expectation of a future *lower* rate of interest which, because of the increased uncertainty of the banks, leads to enhanced liquidity-preference.

Secondary depression would thus have to be explained on lines exactly similar to the theory of the boom. By raising the rate of interest above the marginal efficiency of capital the banks appear to cause secondary depression and to impose on the economic system a cumulative deflationary process the further stages of which need a more detailed investigation on the lines just sketched out.

As regards practical policy the conclusions of our investigation seem to go far to vindicate the maxims of 'orthodox' banking. For in the light of our results the idea of a cheap money policy as a panacea for crises and depressions loses most of its attractions. And a rigorous banking policy which compels the banks to undertake their immediate reconstruction after the outbreak of the crisis (and which, incidentally, would enforce the early closing of all those banks where this is no more possible) would appear to be the most appropriate method of averting the horrors of the cumulative process of depression.

3

INVESTMENT AND COSTS
OF PRODUCTION [1938]

Most modern business-cycle theories are couched in terms of 'cumulative processes'. Investment creates incomes which are spent on consumption goods, and consumption stimulates investment. The turning points of the cycle, crisis and recovery, have then to be explained by exogenous forces.

It can, however, be shown that the theory of cumulative processes is not beyond doubt. It is generally agreed that for various reasons a process of expansion will be accompanied by rising costs. In a world of immobile labour and specialized equipment, unemployment and idle resources may coexist with scarcity of factors and inelastic supply of output, and the concept of 'full employment' loses much of its meaning. If this is so, increasing demand for consumption goods must, by its effects on costs, adversely affect durable investment. During the upswing, the rise in costs and prices will be accentuated by commodity speculation. The faster the rise the sooner the boom will break, because durable investment becomes unprofitable. The dilemma of a monetary policy which aims at stabilizing the rate of expansion is recognized.

CONTROVERSY IN TRADE CYCLE THEORY CONCERNS EXPLAINING THE PEAK

One of the more gratifying aspects of recent investigations into the trade cycle is the remarkable rapprochement on the nature and conditions of the cumulative processes of expansion and contraction. However much economists may quarrel about the forces determining the 'turning points' of the cycle, i.e. crisis and recovery, there exists today fairly wide agreement that the intermediate periods of the cycle, i.e. prosperity and depression, are characterized by self-reinforcing processes of expansion and contraction of employment and output.

This rapprochement became possible only when it was generally realized that we are living in a world in which the supply of many factors of production, notably labour, is sometimes highly elastic, and where, with the general use of bank deposits as means of payment, fairly large changes in the demand for money can take place without affecting the rates of interest. These two circumstances – the existence of unemployment and the elasticity of the monetary system – are the necessary condition of the cumulative processes. Even about the mechanism of the latter there is today little disagreement.

The fact that ours is a dynamic world, in which inventors are day and night racking their brains to find some slight improvement in productive technique, has so far prevented serious controversies about the causes of recovery by allowing economists to fall back on the convenient expedient of exogenous forces for the explanation of the lower turning point of the cycle. In such a dynamic world, sooner or later, investment opportunities are bound to arise which will tend to raise the marginal productivity of some types of capital above the current rate of interest. With fixed MV this tendency would immediately be checked by the forces of the money market, but where, as in our world, the readjustment of the rates of interest depends on the attitude of the banks, this is, for reasons we need not go into here, unlikely to happen. The inducement to invest thus being untrammelled by monetary forces, investment in the newly opened lines will have its well known repercussions on output and consumption. As soon as consumption increases, whether we accept the acceleration principle or not and with whatever qualifications we do so, there is a high degree of probability that investment will be further stimulated.[1] Thus the wheels have turned the full circle and, with further increased inducement to invest the cumulative forces of expansion, are given free play.

Here agreement ends. It is held by one powerful school of thought that, theoretically at least, the cumulative process of expansion could go on until 'the point of full employment' is reached. But, as we shall see later on, it is by no means easy to give this concept any precise meaning. Moreover, whatever meaning we may attach to it, in reality many booms have broken down long before it was reached. For this reason even the adherents of the above-mentioned school have found it necessary to devise some other theory in order to explain the collapse of expansion.

Mr Keynes has taken a non-committal attitude. According to him every boom causes sooner or later certain expectations to be disappointed. These disappointed expectations manifest themselves in periodically recurrent collapses of the marginal efficiency of capital 'determined, as it is, by the uncontrollable and disobedient psychology of the business world'.[2] A boom is dangerous, because it 'is a situation in which over-optimism triumphs over a rate of interest which, in cooler light, would be seen to be excessive'.[3] Nothing is said about the causes of this undue optimism, nothing about their relationship to the current rate of interest. His followers, however, have tried to give the periodical collapses of the marginal efficiency of capital a more realistic appearance and, as was to be expected, have evolved both over-investment and under-consumption theories.

Mr Kalecki has put forward a theory according to which the high level of investment activity which characterizes the boom reduces the marginal efficiency of capital. The latter, however, is prevented from adapting itself gradually by the existence of technically conditioned time-lags between the moment of investment-decision and the moment at which the new investment goods are ready for use.[4] Hence, the marginal efficiency of capital will fall suddenly and heavily as soon as the new output of investment goods is forthcoming.

Now, Professor Hayek has disposed of the argument that investment must necessarily reduce the marginal productivity of all capital by showing that this proposition involves an undue generalization of conclusions which apply only to the results of investment in a particular field.[5] Moreover, Mr Kalecki seems to have exaggerated the economic significance of his technical time-lags. The mere fact that the production of a good takes time is not in itself sufficient to show why this technical fact can have its economic repercussions only after the good has been 'delivered'. If the entrepreneur who has ordered it is unable to forecast the results of his actions, there are others who will do it for him. There are, in a fully developed free-exchange economy, speculative markets for assets and claims; and on these markets speculators are in the habit of forecasting the results of everything they hear about by raising or lowering share prices. Since in Mr Keynes's theory, share prices express the marginal efficiency of capital,[6] Mr Kalecki's argument is not very convincing.

The under-consumptionist wing is represented by Mr Harrod.[7] According to him, investment is a function of the rate of increase of consumption. As soon as the latter declines (which is, of course, quite possible even where consumption increases absolutely) investment will fall off and the process of expansion will come to an end. This decline is caused by a number of factors which make themselves felt more strongly the longer expansion lasts, and which bring about a 'shift to profits', i.e. an increase in the percentage of profit per unit of output. One of these factors is the 'diminishing elasticity of demand', an alleged tendency of markets to become more monopolistic as people grow richer.[8] But surely, of all phases of the cycle it is during prosperity that we should expect new firms to enter the field. And of the other causes of the shift to profits, Professor Neisser has said that 'the constellation supposed in Mr Harrod's pattern is much more likely to prevent any upswing at all than to explain the end of prosperity and the trade cycle.'[9]

It is, indeed, to the changes which profits undergo during the cycle that we have to look for its causal-genetic explanation; and Mr Harrod is no doubt justified in stressing the importance of 'the observed fact that fluctuations of aggregate profit in the cycle exceed fluctuations of output' (p. 77). But we have only to remember the other well known fact that fluctuations in the output of investment goods exceed those in the output of consumption goods in order to be able to infer that the most violent fluctuations will occur between profits in these groups of industries.

Fluctuations in relative profitability therefore appear to be the most convenient starting point for a causal-genetic analysis of the trade cycle.

ANOTHER LOOK AT CUMULATIVE PROCESSES

In spite of the rapprochement mentioned, there remain grounds for regarding the cumulative process with some suspicion. In this theory an essential point is left in the dark: investment is stimulated twice, first by the divergence between marginal productivity of capital and rate of interest, and afterwards by the increase in consumption. How soon will the two tendencies come into conflict? It is true that builders build cinemas as well as hydro-electric plants, and it is comforting to hear that as long as the supply of factors of production is highly elastic – with 'less than full employment' – one activity need not interfere with the other. Yet, it is generally acknowledged that every process of expansion leads to a rise in marginal costs, and the question is how far this will affect the relative profitability of the two types of investment activity.

It is useless to say that all costs being incomes and (with due modifications for hoarding) all incomes being spent on something, for entrepreneurs as a whole receipts will always equal outlay, precisely because this applies only to entrepreneurs as a whole. It is futile to argue that a general rise in costs (which leaves the ratio of marginal to average costs unchanged) will not affect the profitability of investment, because the income from the latter will rise as much as the cost of it; for this does not tell us anything about the effect on the relative profitability of different types of investment. There is, indeed, every reason to believe that the forces which raise the marginal productivity of one type of capital will lower that of another.

In our case the stimulus to investment originated from the margin between the marginal productivity of some type of capital and the current rate of interest. Our problem therefore is whether, during the subsequent spell of prosperity, increased consumption and the rise in costs accompanying it will affect either of the two magnitudes. Changes in the rate of interest being excluded by our assumption about elastic money supply, it all reduces to the question how far and in what direction our *causa causans*, the marginal productivity which gave the initial stimulus, will be modified.

At the present time, these seem rather pertinent questions to ask. On the one hand, Mr Lundberg has recently shown that precisely those types of investment which are most sensitive to changes in the rate of interest will probably not react at all to changes in consumers' demand and *vice versa*. This clearly is relevant to our problem.[10] On the other hand, recent events in the United States seem to indicate that even where there could be no question of full employment and where the supply of money was as plentiful as one could wish, increasing costs did not fail to have adverse effects on certain important types of investment.

UNDERSTANDING RISING COSTS DURING THE UPSWING

In order to cope with the problems outlined, we now have to examine more closely the causes and effects of the cost movements which accompany the cumulative processes.

It is generally agreed that, even with widespread unemployment and idle equipment, a process of expansion is bound to be accompanied by a rise in marginal costs. It is sometimes thought that this is due partly to the heterogeneity of labour and equipment, and partly to the probability of encountering all sorts of 'bottle-necks' as soon as surplus stocks are exhausted. But, as we shall attempt to show, this is but one aspect of a more fundamental phenomenon governed by forces which deprive the concept of full employment of much of its meaning.

The rise in marginal costs is sometimes ascribed to the fact that the unemployed are necessarily inferior workers; but this is not a convincing argument. It is true that on the whole entrepreneurs will try to keep their best workers even in the depression, but for obvious reasons they may not be able to do so. Moreover, a major depression is usually accompanied by bankruptcies and the closing down of whole factories involving the dismissal of the entire staff. What is probably more important is the observation generally made when the world was emerging from the last slump, i.e. that skilled workers who had been out of work for a long time had lost part of their skill. As regards the equipment with which the newly employed co-operate, there is more reason to believe that equipment which is left idle during the depression is inferior, and during periods of financial strain it has probably not been properly maintained. As to the scarcity of working capital, it would seem that cost movements resulting from this scarcity could be only of a temporary character.

The main causes lie deeper, and the real problems involved are more fundamental than that. Immobility of labour and specialization of equipment are outstanding features of the world in which we are living; and they present serious impediments to any expansion of output. With given technique, the coefficients of production are fixed in the short run, and the elasticities of substitution are extremely low. Hence, a smoothly running general process of expansion would require factors available in exactly those proportions in which they have to be combined. This, of course, is a mere wish-dream. In a world in which children are not born to fit the production function of particular industries, and where many equipment goods are of such highly specialized nature that they cannot be shifted from one line of production to another without total or partial loss of the capital invested in them, scarcity of labour and widespread unemployment may exist at the same time; redundant plant and equipment being used to full capacity may be found side by side.[11] For every combination of factors the elasticity of output depends on the elasticity of supply of the scarcest factor. If a product is created jointly by several factors, full employment of one of them will cause supply to become inelastic, and all further 'effective demand' directed toward that product will only increase the income of the scarce factor; and, by widening the gap between marginal and average costs, it will swell profits without any effect on employment. It is true that, as far as this applies to equipment, the high profits accruing to its owners will probably stimulate further production of that product – in a wider sense these 'bottle-necks', too, may be temporary. This depends, however, on whether these profits are believed to be more than transitory; and, furthermore, the technical time-lags cannot here be neglected.

For our purpose immobility of labour and specialization of equipment are sufficient to establish the necessity of rising costs. As expansion is going on, more and more categories of factors will come to be 'fully employed.'[12] To the extent to which this applies to (non-substitutable) 'key-workers' and 'key-equipment' the rise in costs will become more violent while the decline of unemployment is checked. These 'bottle-necks' cannot be overcome by any dose of credit expansion whatever.

If the supply of different factors becomes inelastic at different points of the cycle, the 'point of full employment' becomes meaningless, and with it goes the criterion of distinction between a beneficial expansionist credit policy and one that is fraught with the dangers of inflation. The 'policy of maintaining full employment' so widely advocated today thus assumes a striking similarity to the policy of 'solving the social question' which in 1848 the French Chamber so warmly recommended to the government. An important corollary is that, once it has been realized that unemployment may coexist with scarcity of factors of production, it will no longer be possible to dismiss theories stressing relative cost movements as causal determinants of crisis and recovery on the grounds that they are 'starting from an assumption of full employment'.

THE LUNDBERG THEOREM

We have now reached a stage of our investigation at which we have only to introduce the Lundberg theorem in order to gather up the main threads of our argument.

Mr Lundberg has recently pointed out that those types of investment which are most sensitive to changes in the rate of interest are least likely to be affected by changes in demand for consumption goods and vice versa that 'the influence of the direct demand for consumption goods on the volume of investments tends to diminish with the rise in value of . . . a magnitude . . . which may be given by increasing durability of the investment goods.'[13] He adds that 'this tendency will be strengthened by the fact that the longer the time-dimension of an investment the less the influences of changes in profits and receipts during relatively short periods upon the volume of investments.'

As the income stream from a durable type of investment (e.g., a house) will extend over a great number of years, the level of demand for its services in every single year will become a matter of relative indifference. The investor will have to make a rough estimate of the average yield to be expected, and if this average refers to, say, 40 or 50 years, the present level of demand will hardly affect his decision at all. But the most durable types of investment are most sensitive to changes in the rate of interest. It follows that the types of investment most likely to react to changes in interest conditions are least likely to respond to changes in consumption demand and vice versa. This already suggests that the cumulative process of expansion may not be such a well-lubricated merry-go-round after all!

It is possible to extend this theorem so as to cover costs other than interest. The rate of interest relates a future income stream to a present capital outlay. With a given rate of interest, the investor's decision depends on the cost of this present outlay and the size of the expected future income stream, i.e. he has to compare a present outlay exclusively determined by the present level of costs and prices with an expected income stream which, as we have seen, is unlikely to be affected by this at all. It follows that, in the case of durable investment, the average yield of which is independent of present conditions, a rise in costs will check the inducement to invest and vice versa.

Mr Keynes's version of this story, i.e. that 'if current costs of production are thought to be higher than they will be later on, that will be a further reason for a fall in the marginal efficiency of capital',[14] contains only half the truth. If the higher level of costs is thought to be permanent, the marginal efficiency of capital will fall just the same. For, when does an increase in current costs give rise to the belief in its permanency? Evidently this will be the case, if – in the opinion of the market and in the sense in which unsophisticated people use this expression – current costs are now, after the increase, 'at their equilibrium level', i.e. at a level at which they are compatible with existing economic conditions.

As opinion on such matters does not change overnight, it follows that, before the increase, current costs were at what according to general opinion was a subnormal level. Hence, there must have been at that time a good deal of 'bargain-hunting', i.e. investment activity induced by the low cost level which now will be discontinued.[15] It follows that, even if the new (higher) level is believed to be permanent, investment activity will tend to fall off.

We are therefore entitled to conclude that a rise in costs such as is bound to occur in every process of expansion will sooner or later lead to a fall in the most durable types of investment activity and may easily bring about a crisis. But the latter will be the case only if the fall in 'primary investment' is not counterbalanced by an increase in investment in the consumption-goods industries. If at the moment under investigation consumption is still expanding, this may be the case, and the increased spending-power of the cost-income receivers may, via the acceleration principle, bring about just the degree of investment required to keep the process of expansion going.

For a number of reasons, however, this could happen only under quite extraordinary circumstances. First, the counterbalancing investment must take place immediately, otherwise the setback in primary investment will have its repercussions on employment, incomes, and consumption. Second, the scope of the acceleration principle itself appears to be limited by the same considerations as have formed part of our argument. According to this principle the effect of a given increase in consumption demand on investment depends on the durability of the latter,[16] but, as we have seen, the more durable the type of investment the smaller the influence of a temporary rise in demand. In our case, the greater the quantity of counter-balancing investment which (technically) a given increase in consumers' demands might induce, the more doubtful it is that entrepreneurs will actually decide on it. But the longer they wait the more certain is the impact effect of the setback we have described.

A rise in costs by checking the inducement to invest is therefore likely to bring about a crisis.[17] This is what seems to have happened in the United States between midsummer and early autumn, 1937.[18]

On the other hand, there must be certain types of durable investment which a fall in current costs (as soon as it is thought to have reached its limits)[19] will stimulate, whatever the present level of consumption demands. This goes far to explain the remarkable role of housebuilding as the type of investment activity which has so often in depressions of the past led the first steps towards recovery.

EVEN IF POLICY-MAKERS LOWER INTEREST RATES...

We have so far rigidly adhered to our initial assumption about a perfectly elastic supply of money. As it was one of our main purposes to show that, even with the most accommodating of monetary policies, the process of expansion will come sooner or later to an abrupt end, this was, indeed, an indispensable hypothesis. It is, however, unlikely that it will meet with the approval of the advocates of an expansionist credit policy. 'If for some reason or other,' they will argue, 'the marginal efficiency of capital falls, the correct policy to pursue in order to prevent investment from falling is to reduce the rate of interest.' If because of the rise in costs durable investment becomes less profitable, is it not possible to restore profitability by reducing the rate of interest? And will this not be all the more adequate as the most durable investments and those most responsive to changes in the rate of interest will be the most adversely affected? Our next task therefore will be to show that this is not so and that, on the contrary, such a 'cheap money' policy by its effects on prices and costs will further add to the difficulties of investment and finally defeat its own ends.

For this purpose we need a set of additional assumptions. We shall assume that in our system there are only two rates of interest, a 'long-term rate' represented by the price level of industrial bonds (capital market) and a 'short-term rate', i.e. the discount at which 90 days' bills of exchange are exchanged against money (money market). Bonds can, by assumption, be used only for financing investment in fixed capital. Capital and money market during the first part of this section are completely isolated so that the monetary authority can operate in either of them without affecting the other.

Hitherto we have been arguing as though prices rose *pari passu* with marginal costs as the process of expansion is going on. In reality, of course, this will not be so; and we find that during prosperity, under the pressure of speculation, prices will tend to 'run ahead of costs'. As soon as expansion is well under way and the aim of monetary policy is generally known to be expansionist, speculators will naturally accumulate stocks of commodities. As few things are more certain in the world in which we are living than that expansion will sooner or later lead to increases in wages and other costs, the accumulation of commodity stocks – the intertemporal transfer of goods from points of lower to points of higher marginal costs – will not be a very risky business. This speculative activity, implying as it does additional investment in stocks, will of course tend to speed up the whole process and thereby to shorten it. Prices will rise faster, and the high prices will make employment, output, and marginal costs rise earlier than they would have done otherwise. Hence, the larger the stocks accumulated the sooner will durable investment become unprofitable and fall off. Moreover, as the activity of the speculators may easily, under changed circumstances, be reversed, and the resulting disinvestment cannot but have serious repercussions on employment, output, and incomes, such a situation must be regarded as very dangerous.

The stocks accumulated have to be financed, and on our assumptions this can be done only in the money market. We now have to make our assumptions about monetary policy a little more precise.

With constant MV, the long-term rate of interest tends to adjust itself to the marginal productivity of (free) capital, and the short-term rate reflects expected changes in the price level of commodities. As the bill of exchange, the object of transactions in the money market, is the principal source of finance for working capital, it seems a legitimate inference that, in Mr Keynes's terminology, the short-term rate will tend to adjust itself to the 'commodity rates of interest'.[20] This appears to be the most plausible explanation of the observed fact that during the cycle the short-term rate oscillates so much more violently than the long-term rate. During the upswing far larger profits are to be derived (for short periods!) from intertemporal transactions in commodities than from investment in fixed capital; but during the depression, where the shorter the horizon the darker the outlook, losses are made on commodities, and short-term rates therefore tend to approach zero. We may surmise that, were capital and money markets completely isolated in the actual world, these oscillations would be even stronger.

We now examine the repercussions of monetary measures on the relative profitability of durable investment and the holding of commodity stocks. We shall first ask ourselves what an elastic supply of money means with regard to capital and money market.

It is, of course, possible, that our monetary authority will pursue its expansionist aim by keeping both long- and short-term rates fixed. It follows, however, from our previous argument that in this case it would defeat its own ends. For by preventing the short-term rate from rising it would remove the only check to commodity speculation that, under such circumstances, could be effective. Keeping the short-term rate fixed would mean to provide the speculators with all the funds they require in order to drive up prices and costs and thus to hasten the collapse of prosperity. It is therefore more likely that our monetary authority will confine its attention to the long-term rate while allowing short-term rates to fluctuate with changes in the size of commodity stocks.

But even so, as we saw in the section on Understanding Rising Costs (pp. 47–9), a moment will arrive when the rise in costs will impair the profitability of durable investment. To reduce the long-term rate under such circumstances in order to maintain the level of investment would mean merely to encourage commodity specu-lators by indicating that the authority will do nothing to prevent costs from rising wherever they might, i.e. that it will 'always satisfy the needs of trade'. Prices and costs will therefore rise all the more violently. Moreover, we have to bear in mind that in the real world capital and money markets are not completely isolated. Not only are there fairly large funds like the liquid resources of insurance companies and similar institutions capable of being invested in either market, but the commodity speculators themselves will possess securities which they can use as collateral and the prices of which would rise if long-term rates were reduced.

Our monetary authority thus finds itself confronted with the following dilemma: a rise in the long-term rate of interest will check the inducement to invest. A reduction will, by its effect on prices and costs, have the same result unless the short-term rate is raised at the same time; but this would be possible only under conditions of complete isolation. If the long-term rate is simply maintained, a restrictionist money market policy can only postpone but not avoid the moment at which rising costs impair the profitability of durable investment. 'Expansionist policy', whatever meaning we may attach to it, emerges therefore as a somewhat doubtful panacea.

DIFFICULTIES OF EXPANSIONIST POLICY

It is beyond the scope of this investigation to formulate general principles of monetary policy in a dynamic world; and it certainly is not our task to say what monetary administrators ought to do when after a prolonged period during which matters have been allowed to drift they are suddenly awakening to a spell of renewed activity. It is easy to see that the problem bristles with difficulties.

As we have pointed out, the 'maintenance of full employment' as a principle of economic policy is highly ambiguous. A 'point of full employment' at which according to the doctrine of fashion a hitherto beneficial expansionist credit policy suddenly becomes inflationary and dangerous simply does not exist. But, as during expansion at almost any point some factors are becoming scarce, the conditions of inflation are *pro tanto* constantly satisfied. If real wages decline with expansion, the decision whether, if we allow a further measure of expansion, its benefits will outweigh the sacrifice in real wages, already involves interpersonal comparisons of utility of the kind to which economic theory has no answer. But this is not all.

In the case discussed in the last section the monetary authority might, by bringing about a sharp rise in the short-term rate accompanied by a smaller increase in the long-term rate, cause such a collapse of commodity prices that its beneficial effects on the cost of investment would outweigh the adverse effect of the (small) increase in the long-term rate. Still, it does not follow that in this way it will succeed in maintaining the level of investment.

First, while a restrictionist credit policy will affect market prices, it will not (under modern conditions) affect wages; and if, as in the case of building, these are an important element of cost, the beneficial effect of the fall in commodity prices will *pro tanto* be weakened. Furthermore, where, as in the case of many important raw materials, output is monopolistically controlled, the fall in prices will lead to a restriction of output, and thus prices may afterwards rise again. This will adversely affect the marginal productivity of capital in the consumption-goods industries, which, while having to suffer from the effects of diminished employment in the monopolized industries, will not be able to benefit from lower raw material prices and probably will restrict investment. All this is merely one aspect of the perplexities besetting economic policy in a world of 'price maintenance' in which wages find it easier to rise than to fall.

There emerges, however, the more fundamental question whether in such a world it would be worth while trying to maintain the level of durable investment. If a monetary authority by restrictionist measures causes market prices to fall to a lower level than can be maintained with given rigidity of costs, this means that it will raise in the investors hopes which are bound to be disappointed. This is just another way of saying that a credit policy stimulating investment at stages where, with a given degree of cost rigidity, it cannot be maintained, is bound to be a dismal failure.

CONCLUSION

We have so far studiously refrained from using the terminology of the Austrian theory of the trade cycle. We have avoided all references to the time structure of production; we have – in the face of the current controversy – steered clear of the problems of saving; and we have constantly been arguing as though the rates of interest were purely monetary magnitudes.

As we are now coming to summarize the conclusions of our investigation, so much forbearance may be dispensed with. As a matter of fact, the Austrian theory comes out fairly completely vindicated. It is often said that its validity depends on full employment; but we have endeavoured to shake this belief. We have pointed out that in a world of immobile labour and specialized equipment, unemployment and idle resources may coexist with scarcity of factors and inelastic supply of output. We have further shown that, if this is so, increasing demand for consumption goods by its effects on marginal costs must adversely affect durable investment (the earlier stages of production); and we have tried to show that this result is quite independent of the monetary policy pursued.

There is, however, scope for doubts as to the effects of the crisis. It is by no means certain that even with the most flexible cost structure it will be possible to complete processes of production which, owing to some shock, have once been interrupted. It is here that the analytical tools of static equilibrium analysis prove of little value. And it is here that the large shadow of secondary depression falls on the field of knowledge we have tilled.

4

COMMODITY STOCKS IN THE TRADE CYCLE [1938]

(with F. Snapper)

INTRODUCTION

In this paper we endeavour to make use of the statistics of commodity stocks in order to throw some light upon the trade cycle and the issues arising from it.

Our main problem is: Do commodity stocks move in positive or inverse correlation with the cycle? Important issues as to the momentum of the 'cumulative process' hinge upon the answer to this question. For, in the case of positive correlation, investment in commodity stocks would be an important accelerating force in the mechanism of booms and depressions, tending to make any increase in investment activity somewhere in the economic system the impelling force of a cumulative process. By analogy, in the case of inverse correlation changes in the size of stocks would be a retarding force.

It would, of course, be most desirable to be able to make use of statistics of the stocks of finished as well as of unfinished goods. For then it might be possible to say something about the relative size of stocks at different stages of production in different phases of the cycle, a very important problem to all those who, unyielding to the attractions of 'macrodynamics', refuse to see in crises simply fluctuations in total investment. Unfortunately, we have at our disposal statistics of unfinished commodities only.[1] There is, however, reason to believe that the stocks of finished products move in positive correlation with the cycle, because they are kept by producers and merchants as a constant percentage of turnover.

We thus shall have to confine ourselves to the study of raw material stocks and try to find out what light they throw upon the trade cycle. So far, Mr Keynes has been the only one to formulate a precise and logical theory of the cyclical fluctuations in commodity stocks.[2]. According to him, 'surplus stocks' must be cleared before recovery is possible, and therefore the depletion of stocks during the depression is a subsidiary force of disinvestment. We shall have to examine this thesis in the light of the statistical facts. On the other hand, if it can be shown that stocks as a rule reach their lowest level immediately before the outbreak of the crisis, this may conceivably give some indication of the causes of the latter. It would purport to show that the point at which 'surplus stocks' are exhausted is not the lower, but the upper turning point of the cycle.

THE NUMBERS

We present below two tables of statistics of movements in stocks of certain raw materials and foodstuffs, the first (Table 4.1) referring to the pre-First World War period and the second (Table 4.2) to the years 1919–37.

INTERPRETATION OF THE NUMBERS

Economists before the First World War assumed that Sauerbeck's index numbers were a fairly good barometer of the general trade cycle. Now there is reason to believe that for the period before the war this contention holds true, although we prefer a production index which is derived from the English unemployment figures. We do not need to explain why certainly after the war the American production index is greatly preferable.

The movements of agricultural raw materials require, however, a separate explanation. We observe that during the period 1873–1913, whereas the general trade cycle reaches its peak in 1881, 1891, 1900, 1907 and 1913, the index numbers of prices of foodstuffs behave somewhat differently. The peaks of this cycle are in the years 1877, 1891, 1900 and 1912. At first sight it may seem that agricultural production as a whole has a cycle of its own, which consists of two components: the general industrial cycle and changes in natural conditions. By natural conditions we mean all those atmospheric and climatic factors which influence the size of crops.[3] The absence of a production function in the strict sense, i.e. the fact that in agriculture output quantities are not uniquely correlated with input quantities, makes the supply of agricultural

Table 4.1

End of Year	Pig Iron North of England 000 tons[2]	End of Year	Pig Iron North of England 000 tons[2]	Copper in Europe 000 tons[1]	Copper in USA	Tin 000 tons[3,4]	Wheat 000,000 bushels[6]	Cotton 0000 bales 1 Aug.[5]
1869	116	1885	517	–		16	–	134
1870	118	1886	652	47		14	–	144
1871	68	1887	637	56		19	–	147
1872	42	1888	473	35		19	–	129
1873	80	1889	262	96		17	–	132
1874	90	1890	256	95		14	126	108
1875	74	1891	263	62		16	175	174
1876	182	1892	164	53		19	194	282
1877	271	1893	163	52		20	206	226
1878	337	1894	216	43		30	200	213
1879	283	1895	306	51		36	186	320
1880	331	1896	163	43		40	151	193
1881	378	1897	97	31		35	126	192
1882	266	1898	138	27		24	113	324
1883	253	1899	71	22		21	160	400
1884	302	1900	44	28		21	163	246
		1901	139	22		26	169	267
		1902	121	16		17	142	267
		1903	97	13		17	133	292
		1904	199	16		17	146	277
		1905	707	13		16	140	504
		1906	537	17		16	151	418
		1907	89	20		15	127	569
		1908	132	57	57	23	132	458
		1909	385	109	66	23	96	568
		1910	519	84	55	20	132	473
		1911	526	57	41	19	185	484
		1912	241	40	48	14	–	681
		1913	230	21	41	16	–	636

Notes: See Table 4.2

produce a relatively independent variable at least in the short period, when acreage and methods of cultivation are given. Hence, if there are cyclical fluctuations in the size of output per acre this would be a sufficient condition for a separate agricultural cycle. So much for the supply side.

On the demand side, of course, the agricultural cycle is linked up with the general trade cycle. Industrial demand for agricultural raw materials depends, of course, on the state of trade. The demand

Table 4.2

End of Year	Copper in Europe 000 tons[2]	Copper in USA 000 tons[2]	Tin 000 tons[3,4]	Zinc 000 tons[3,7]	Sugar 000 tons 1 Oct[3]	Wheat 000,000 bushels[6]	Cotton 0000 bales 1 Aug[5]	Rubber 000 tons[3,8,9]
1919	18	546	20	61	–	347	675	–
1920	20	587	18	81	1338	317	634	281
1921	23	427	24	72	2039	238	968	296
1922	33	344	26	20	868	285	561	358
1923	37	409	21	34	791	339	338	306
1924	51	374	25	42	542	363	276	233
1925	65	322	18	9	2500	323	327	234
1926	48	358	16	20	1919	378	550	311
1927	14	330	16	38	1780	400	784	334
1928	10	315	25	42	1850	565	521	301
1929	12	439	28	75	4047	583	452	382
1930	12	585	42	144	5522	583	619	505
1931	34	722	51	130	7022	608	897	644
1932	48	747	45	125	7099	598	1326	641
1933	39	673	23	106	6264	539	1181	668
1934	69	567	13	120	5396	516	1070	724
1935	104	496	12	84	4128	487	909	637
1936	63	377	20	45	2983	318	696	473
1937	42	505	20	79	3102	346	624	496

Notes:
1 *Year Books of the American Bureau of Metal Statistics.*
2 Monthly Trade Supplement of the *Economist.*
3 *Special Memoranda* of the London and Cambridge Economic Service, nos. 32 and 45.
4 *World Tin Statistics, 1938.*
5 *Cotton Year Book of the New York Cotton Exchange, 1937.*
6 *Broomball's Corn Trade Year Books.*
7 *Statistische Zusammenstellungen der Metallgesellschaft.*
8 London and Cambridge Economic Service, May *Bulletin*, 1938.
9 *Special Memorandum* no. 32, table on p. 19.

for agricultural produce for consumption is governed by the level of income and employment unless the income elasticity of demand is very low. It is clear, for example, that fluctuations in wheat (demand for which is very inelastic) will be entirely governed by the acreage and the output per acre, whereas demand for cotton will depend on factors partly germane to the industrial situation.

We may therefore conclude that the whole conception of an agricultural trade cycle is somewhat doubtful. However, there are very good reasons, as we have seen, to expect production and prices to deviate from the general trade cycle each in its own

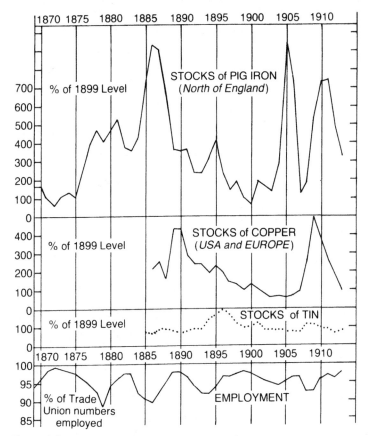

Figure 4.1

way. It would be useless, therefore, to correlate stocks of such commodities to the general trade cycle. We correlated the movements of cotton stocks with the price of cotton in the period 1885–1913, and we found an inverse correlation, after eliminating trend, of – 82. Some economists will find this result very satisfactory, but we beg to differ. We prefer the simple method of graphical illustration to the dubious niceties of correlation analysis.

For the period 1928–36 a recent inquiry has shown how the prices of different commodities like wheat, cotton, coffee, tea, rubber, silk and tin move inversely with their respective stocks.[4] Besides, Figure 4.2 is presented in which the total stocks of the commodities mentioned move inversely with their average price level. To this we added the American index of industrial pro-

61

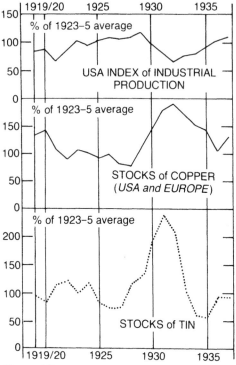

Figure 4.2

duction (Figure 4.3). It is, of course, well known that after the war the trade cycle was more intimately connected with investment in the production of raw materials, particularly in overseas countries.

Sugar shows a peak in 1925 (Table 4.2, col. 6). The explanation is given in a Special Memorandum of the London and Cambridge Economic Service.[5] The cause must be sought in the decision to increase the acreage of plantations in Cuba in 1923. We cannot deal here with all the very interesting questions with which that Memorandum deals. But in our opinion the inverted movement of sugar prices with the stocks in those years is perfectly clear.

The steady rise of stocks of cotton (Table 4.2, col. 8) from 1924–7 is accompanied by a steady decline in price.[6] The fall in stocks in 1928 was due to a rise in price. The same holds true for the years 1921–3, whereas the fall in price from 1920–1 is again accompanied by a rise in stocks.

Stocks of wheat, as Mr Keynes has told us,[7] show maxima in

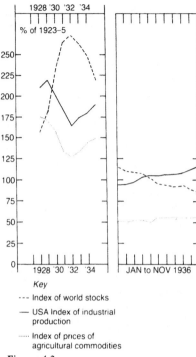

Figure 4.3

1896, 1899, 1907, 1923 and, we can add, 1933. But when we look at the prices we shall find them in these years at their minimum level, with the difference that with regard to the years 1907 and 1933 the price reaches its minimum one year earlier. When we examine those years which according to the *Stanford University Wheat Studies* (the statistics to which Mr Keynes refers) are minimum years for stocks, they appear to be maximum years for prices; we have to add that since then Stanford University has compiled world stocks for the period 1922–34.[8] Moreover, Professor Tinbergen gives also stocks for wheat for the period 1890–1911 which do not differ much from the Stanford statistics.[9]

Finally it should be noticed that the stocks of wheat increase during the year 1937 (Table 4.2, last line); the stocks of rubber and sugar do the same, and when we compare the year end stocks of cotton, we also see a rise[10]: from 6 million bales at the end of 1936 to 8.4 million bales at the end of 1937.

The stocks of pig iron, copper and tin before the war show the inverse correlation with the cycle rather well as is seen from Figure 4.1.

Pig iron stocks after 1896 exclude makers' stocks[11] (Table 4.1, col 4). The sudden fall in 1878–9 (col. 2) – otherwise a time of intense depression – was due to a coal strike in Durham, but it was slight owing to the attempts of ironmasters to raise prices.[12] The enormous increase in 1905 was due to heavy speculation in 'Middlesboro' N. 3'.[13] As will become clearer later on, it was a typical instance of the case where opinions differ widely and dealers were more 'bullish' than either ironmasters or iron consumers.

Copper had a special over-production crisis (Table 4.1, col. 5) in 1889.[14] Afterwards stocks have a falling trend for about seventeen years owing to the steady expansion of the electrical industries.

After the war (Table 4.2) the stocks of copper, tin and zinc show great irregularities, but by 1929 we find them all having resumed the inverse movement to the cycle. Copper and zinc stocks increased in 1937, tin (where production was most rigidly controlled) had already increased in 1936.

It remains for us to discuss the influence of monopolistic restrictions on the size of stocks, taking the case of copper, stocks of which after the war show a very close inverse correlation with business activity, with a lead of one year. The period 1923–9 appears to be very suitable for this purpose. After 1929 the phenomenon is disturbed by the Great Depression.

A combine of copper producers was formed in 1926. Until March 1929, although stocks remained very small throughout this period, this does not seem to have had much influence on the size of stocks. But then a speculative boom broke out. The combine, more interested in high prices than in the stabilization of production, at first allowed stocks to reach a minimum level. After a month the boom collapsed, but the high prices had by then induced producers to increase output, and because of the American anti-trust laws the combine was unable to prevent this. They tried in vain to keep the price high by accumulating stocks. After 1930, however, the accumulation of stocks was no longer deliberate.

Between 1923 and 1929 there was a cartel which tried to restrict the output of spelter. Its efforts, however, were not very successful. Production rose from 960,000 tons in 1923 to 1,440,000 tons in

1929. Moreover, as far as we know, it took no measures to influence the size of stocks.

WHO HOLDS THE STOCKS?

We shall now have to examine the distribution of raw material stocks between different classes of holders. For this purpose we shall divide them into: Producers (of raw materials); Dealers (in raw materials); Manufacturers (of finished commodities in so far as they are buyers of raw materials).

We would expect that because of the costs involved in the storing of commodities, everybody wants to keep his stocks as low as possible. Moreover, we know that entrepreneurs as a rule keep their stocks in a certain relation to their turn-over. We therefore have to find an explanation why the stocks of raw materials do not obey that rule. The obvious reason is that in the case of sudden and unforeseen changes in demand, agricultural and mineral production can only be readjusted with a certain time-lag.

Sometimes another reason is mentioned: speculation – about this point we shall have to say more in a later section of this chapter.

If our explanation of the inverted movement of the stocks of raw materials is correct, we shall expect producers to bear the burden of these surplus stocks, for the dealers and manufacturers, who wish to maintain their proportion between output and stocks, are not responsible for the production of raw materials.

In some cases, however, not the producers but the dealers and manufacturers hold these surplus stocks. Here the explanation has to be sought in the relative ease with which in different industries different classes of entrepreneurs can obtain credit. In some fields of production the producers have a relatively large reserve of capital available, or they may have an easy access to the credit market. In other fields of production producers do not enjoy these facilities and have always to sell to dealers. It is also conceivable that the dealers may be unable to provide enough capital and that they may have to sell a part of those stocks to the manufacturers. We thus can imagine the enormous extra fall in price when at a certain moment during the slump the capital reserves of a certain field of production are becoming insufficient to finance the growing surplus stocks.

Thus the stocks of sugar in Java were negligible before 1929. 'For the crop was always sold forward in its entirety before the grinding season began', as we read in *Special Memorandum* no. 45 of the London and Cambridge Economic Service.[15] After 1929 the stocks in Java (and in Cuba) and in the hands of dealers move very strongly in an inverse relation to the trade cycle.

In the same *Memorandum* is an interesting table concerning the division of rubber stocks during that period.[16] We combined the stocks of UK public warehouses with the stocks of US dealers and manufacturers. Then we subtracted these combined figures from the total amount (See Table 4.3).

Table 4.3 Stocks of rubber at the end of the year (000 Tons)

Year	US and UK	Total	Difference	On estates in Malaya
1928	88	301	213	35
1929	192	382	190	28
1930	320	505	185	26
1931	449	644	195	20
1932	472	641	169	22
1933	457	668	214	21
1934	496	724	228	12
1935	476	634	158	23
1936	301	473	172	26

The conclusion is that in the depression, the manufacturers and dealers in these commodities bear the brunt of the burden. It is interesting to observe how the stocks in the hands of producers (on estates in Malaya) move in opposite direction to the total of stocks. It should further be noticed how during the period total stocks of rubber moved inversely towards the trade cycle.

The division of the stocks of copper, on the other hand, presents entirely different features. Although there are no statistics of copper in the hands of manufacturers we know the stocks in the hands of producers (American smelters and refiners) and (European) dealers.

The stocks of copper are mostly in the hands of producers, but there is a tendency for dealers' stocks to move in the same direction. The reason obviously is that producers have to carry the bulk of these stocks in order to maintain prices. They are able to do it because of the credit facilities they enjoy; they are supported by the Morgan group.[17] The dealers, as a rule, have some financial reserves and their stocks exercise a buffer function as regards changes in demand. At any rate, we are entitled to conclude that the stocks will be held in the strongest hands.

IMPLICATIONS OF THE STATISTICS FOR TRADE CYCLE THEORIES

The main conclusion emerging from the statistics we have presented appears to be that our stocks are inversely correlated with the cycle. As a rule, they reach their lowest level very shortly before the outbreak of the crisis, while their peak level is to be found towards the end of the depression. If this reading of the facts is correct, it is difficult to accept Mr Keynes's theory according to which surplus stocks must be exhausted before recovery can start. On the contrary, the conclusion that seems to suggest itself is that raw material stocks must have reached a certain size if they are to support a lasting recovery. This shows the highly artificial character of the division of stocks into 'working capital' and 'liquid capital' according to 'the normal requirements' of production and illustrates the ambiguity of the concept of 'surplus stocks'; for stocks that may have been surplus with regard to the level of activity at the trough of the depression may be insufficient to sustain a major recovery. It is here that the buffer function of stocks[18] – at least of those goods the supply of which can only be adjusted with a time-lag – comes out most clearly: without ample reserves of raw materials, recovery may soon be checked by all sorts of 'bottlenecks'.

On the other hand, our statistics seem to show that it is at least not impossible that prosperity should come to an end owing to the scarcity of certain factors of production. It is no doubt difficult to generalize from the material presented, because different commodities show different 'leads' against the trade cycle, and it is, of course, by no means necessary that all the crises brought about by scarcity should be brought about by scarcity of the same factor. The coefficients of production being fixed in the short run, scarcity of *one* factor may suffice to stop *all* investment activity. Moreover, as the Austrian Theory has shown, scarcity at one stage of production is quite consistent with unsaleable stocks at another stage. For these and similar reasons, until we have more accurate knowledge about the distribution of stocks between capital goods – and consumption goods industries in general, and of raw material stocks between producers, dealers, and manufacturers of finished commodities in particular, extreme caution in the cyclical interpretation of the low level of stocks seems advisable.

If the statistics presented are representative of the behaviour of stocks of unfinished goods in general, what conclusions have we to draw with regard to the theory of the trade cycle? If these stocks diminish during the upswing they evidently offer no scope for investment. It follows that for the source of that investment activity which characterizes the upswing we have to look elsewhere, i.e. we probably have to seek it in investment in fixed capital. The obverse applies to the downswing, and we are therefore entitled to conclude that investment and disinvestment in staple commodities' stocks, so far from being secondary forces in the mechanism of the cumulative process, actually are retarding forces, offsetting to a certain extent the effects of investment in equipment.

This statement has to be qualified in several respects. In the first place, we have to remember that our statistics refer to unfinished goods only and that, as we said, there is reason to believe that stocks of finished commodities move in positive correlation with the cycle,[19] i.e. that producers and merchants of consumption goods tend to keep their stocks in a certain proportion to their turnover. In so far as changes in raw material stocks merely offset opposite movements in the stocks and production of finished goods – owing to the lag with which raw material production is adjusted to changes in demand – raw material stocks serve as a kind of excess reserve for the industries producing finished commodities (buffer function).

Secondly, the size of stocks has a direct causal influence on the production of raw materials. Not only will output be restricted as long as stocks are accumulating – very much against the wishes of the producers who have to carry them – but even while they are falling it is unlikely to recover before, indeed, stocks have again reached a normal size. Thus, as long as stocks are large, an increase in demand will not immediately lead to an increase in supply; in this case the buffer function of stocks will check the cumulative process.

Another point to be considered in this connection is the relationship between the size of stocks and investment in the production of raw materials. To the extent to which the investment activity characteristic of periods of prosperity is due to investment in raw material production our inverse correlation may not hold. Unless demand grows more rapidly than supply is forthcoming stocks will increase and prices tend to fall. This need not cause a general collapse as long as investment in other parts of the economic system remains satisfactory; it may even stimulate expansion in raw material consuming industries. Still, it is true that investment in the production of raw materials undertaken in the expectation of a rise in demand which does not immediately occur will lead to a, perhaps temporary, increase in stocks. There is every reason to believe that the steady rise in raw material stocks between 1923 and 1929 – in positive correlation with the trade cycle! – has to be ascribed to similar causes.

If it is true that in the past recovery has usually been preceded by an accumulation of stocks of industrial raw materials, it follows that all schemes aiming at a restriction of output by means of monopolistic control have to be regarded as potentially dangerous. One has, of course, to beware of the *post hoc ergo propter hoc* fallacy, and it follows by no means that accumulation of stocks of a definite size is a necessary condition of recovery. It may well be that in the past recovery would have occurred even with much smaller stocks. But we beg to submit that then it may have been much shorter. At any rate, the danger of 'bottlenecks' being encountered would be greater.

For these reasons we are unable to follow Mr Keynes in his advocacy of restriction schemes. It seems to us that such schemes are justifiable only where it is possible for a price fall to lead to readjustment, i.e. where the following three conditions are fulfilled:

1 demand is very inelastic;
2 prime costs are either constant or falling;
3 all producers work under identical conditions so that there are no high cost and low cost producers.

Mr Keynes argues that the present economic system offers no mechanism for the carrying of surplus stocks, hence the necessity of restriction schemes. The material we have presented seems to indicate that in spite of his contention that the holding of large stocks is too costly to be feasible such holding did and does in fact take place, and that stocks do exercise a buffer function.[20]

WHAT ABOUT COMMODITY SPECULATION?

Out of the foregoing there arises the interesting problem of the scope and significance of commodity speculation during the trade cycle. From all we know from the reports and descriptions of contemporary observers of past booms, commodity speculation has always been a strong, and in some instances a decisive factor. But, if stocks of unfinished commodities actually diminish during the upswing, how is commodity speculation possible? The possibility of speculation in finished goods may be dismissed as it is obvious that because of their low 'plasticity'[21] large speculative transactions in them are not feasible. Moreover, we know from experience that speculation is usually most intense on the big markets for staple commodities which offer speculators the greatest facilities. How, then, is the riddle to be solved?

A given change in price is not necessarily correlated with a given volume of transactions. From the financial press we all know instances where 'the movement of prices was out of all proportion to the volume of dealing'. The volume of transactions necessary to bring about a certain price movement is an indication of the division of opinions in the market. If everybody expects prices to rise, they will rise without any transactions taking place. Hence, the more 'bullish' the market during the boom the less transactions are necessary in order to bring about a given price rise. In other words, commodity speculation during the boom will not lead to an accumulation of stocks, if sellers, buyers and consumers are all equally 'bullish'. It follows that stocks can increase only to the extent to which producers and speculators are more 'bullish' than consumers.[22]

Let us restate the same thing in the terminology of the forward market most appropriate where we have to deal with intertemporal price- and quantity-relations. Stocks can accumulate only if the forward price exceeds the spot price by more than the carrying costs, for only then it will be profitable to carry them. Hence, changes in stocks are determined by changes in the forward price relatively to the spot price. It follows that an increase in stocks during the boom can occur only in so far as the spot market tends to lag behind the forward market, i.e. to the extent to which operators in the spot market are less 'bullish' than those in the forward market. Where there is no division of opinions between the two markets, and the spot price immediately follows every movement of the forward price, there can be no change in the size of stocks. Such changes are proportionate to the dispersion of opinions.

We have now seen why commodity speculation during the boom need not lead to an increase in stocks, if optimism is sufficiently widespread. But the inverse correlation between commodity stocks and the price level conceals even more interesting problems. We have found that in the upswing stocks of raw materials actually decrease, i.e. forward prices tend to fall relatively to spot prices. As we pointed out, this may be due to actual shortage of supply. Where production can only be adjusted with a time-lag, a situation may be reached in which present supply is short but future supply plentiful, and where therefore nobody will carry stocks. But the explanation of our inverse correlation in terms of increasing physical scarcity during the upswing is not the only possible one. It may be due to the superior skill of operators in the forward market who in this phase of the cycle already anticipate the next. If a decrease in stocks indicates a tendency of the forward price to fall relatively to the spot price, this shows an increasing divergence of opinions. If this occurs during a boom, it means that forward market operators are less 'bullish' than their colleagues in the spot market. In which case we shall reach the astonishing conclusion that the commodity speculation characteristic of the boom is just speculative activity of people who ordinarily do not 'speculate', i.e. operators in the spot market, which drives up the spot price relatively to the forward price.

If this were true, it would be, in fact, a tribute to the superior foresight of the professional speculators operating in the forward markets, and it would, moreover, show why a free exchange economy with a well-developed system of intertemporal markets operated by specialists can weather many storms. We must not forget, however, that the relationship between the size of stocks and the difference between forward and spot price applies to covered stocks only.

This makes it extremely difficult to use our theorem for the depression. The large stocks characteristic of the downswing are, as we saw, mostly carried by producers very much against their own wishes and for the purpose of preventing a complete collapse of prices. They are probably 'unhedged', since if they were sold forward they would affect prices. Therefore the accumulation of stocks in the depression cannot very well be ascribed to the superior foresight of speculators.

This is, of course, not to say that the existence of large uncovered stocks outside the market will not affect the latter. We know from experience that the existence of huge stocks kept outside the market will by forcing down the forward price cause the liquidation of 'hedged' stocks.

In applying this theory to the tin market during the last thirteen years we find that it is, on the whole, borne out by the facts.[23] Broadly speaking, boom periods are accompanied by a backwardation and falling stocks, depressions by a contango and stock accumulation.[24] In 1926, 1927 and 1928 visible supplies of tin were extremely scarce and did not reach 20,000 tons until October 1928. Throughout this period there was a backwardation which in 1926 and 1927 averaged £6.16 and occasionally reached £10.

From February, 1929, till the end of 1932 total visible supplies rose form 26,000 tons to 46,000 tons while the contango was never less than £1.

By February 1934, stocks had fallen to 21,000 tons while spot and forward prices hardly deviated. This fall in stocks was due to the liquidation of the International Tin Pool.

In 1934, with an average backwardation of 19s. 2d., stocks fell to 12,600 tons. This must have been a minimum level, for whilst throughout 1935 and 1936 the backwardation was never less than £2, stocks remained at a little above 13,000 tons. In November-December 1936, the backwardation disappeared and in January-February 1937, gave way to a contango which by March had brought up stocks to about 20,000 tons.

Monopolistic interference with the tin market started in 1928: 'During the year a syndicate which came to be known as "The Group" was formed to hold tin off the market and the rise in price which began in August may mark the beginning of their operations.'[25] Their activity would explain why stocks rose suddenly between August 1928, and February 1929, in spite of a large backwardation.

The International Tin Pool was formed in September 1931, and by the end of January 1932, had acquired 21,000 tons. Liquidation began in July 1933, and lasted until the early months of 1934. There can be little doubt that but for its sales of spot tin the backwardation which did not exceed £1 before March, 1934, would have appeared earlier.

CONCLUSION

At last we have to discuss what light, if any, is thrown by our investigations upon some modern trade cycle theories. Of course, how one expects commodity stocks in general and raw materials stocks in particular to behave during the trade cycle depends on the type of theory one happens to hold. We have found that the cyclical behaviour of (industrial) raw material stocks conforms to a definite pattern which, it would seem at first sight, must rule out at least some theories.

In fact, however, practically all those theories which stress the importance of fluctuations in investment in fixed capital as the outstanding feature of the trade cycle are borne out by our material. The reason is that an increase in investment activity of this kind involves an increase in the demand for mineral products such as iron, copper, tin, the supply of which can only be adjusted with a time-lag. Hence, in the meantime stocks are bound to decrease as they are likely to augment in the case of a setback in investment activity. It follows that all over-investment theories are consistent with the results of our investigation. On the other hand, recovery cannot possibly start in the raw material producing industries, hampered as they are by large and increasing stocks which have to be cleared before their production can recover.

Unfortunately we are not in a position to judge the relative merits of various over-investment theories. In particular, our statistics neither corroborate nor disprove the so-called 'monetary over-investment theories' of the Austrian School, as we do not know enough about the distribution of stocks among the different stages of production. As we mentioned above, only two of our series include manufacturers' (rubber and cotton) stocks. Mr Blodgett, however, has pointed out that stocks of raw materials in the hands of manufacturers tend, on the whole, to move in inverse correlation to the trade cycle.[26] What would be required in order to verify 'monetary over-investment theories' is exact knowledge about the relative movements in the stocks of the manufacturers of capital and consumption goods respectively, but it is here that we are almost completely ignorant. Where the 'over-investment' of the boom is due to investment in the production of raw materials, stocks may, of course, increase with production, and then their inverse correlation with the trade cycle will be broken.

As we pointed out above, this actually was the case between 1923 and 1929 when all were increasing rapidly.

With regard to Mr Keynes's views on these and similar subjects we have to distinguish between his general trade cycle theory[27] and his thesis about the cyclical fluctuations in commodity stocks.[28] Whereas the former may be described as an over-investment theory the latter does not form a necessary part of it, i.e. the investment activity of the boom is mostly due to investment of fixed capital. The depletion of 'liquid stocks' which in his opinion is a pre-requisite of recovery as well as the increase in 'working capital' accompanying the phase of expansion are, on the whole, secondary forces in the mechanism of the cumulative process which originates from and centres in the investment in equipment. Thus, even if our statistics show that fluctuations in stocks so far from being secondary factors are actually retarding forces, this does not affect Mr Keynes's argument. Moreover, we must not forget that our theory refers to strictly industrial raw materials only.

What are our conclusions to be with regard to under-consumption theories? It is well known that this doctrine cannot be disproved or proved by a mere comparison of total quantities like, for example, investment and consumption. What is required in order to decide whether or not under-consumption was the cause of a crisis is a knowledge of events in their chronological order. In other words, what we would have to know is what increased first, stocks of finished consumption goods, or finished capital goods, or raw material stocks (the problem of 'leads' and 'lags').[29] Raw material stocks alone are an insufficient criterion.

There is, however, a version of under-consumption theory which has a direct bearing on the demand for industrial raw materials. In the 'under-consumption cum acceleration' theory of Professor J. M. Clark and Mr Harrod investment is linked up with the rate of increase of consumption. Hence, every slowing down in this rate of increase entails a setback in investment activity which explains the increase in the stock of mineral products. This version of under-consumption theory is therefore entirely consistent with the statistics we have presented.

The only trade cycle theory which, at first sight, it seems difficult to reconcile with the results of our investigation is that of Mr Hawtrey, who emphasizes investment in stocks as the impelling force of the trade cycle. But, since his theory refers to stocks of manufactured commodities only and not to agricultural and mineral products[30] it does not affect our argument. Moreover, it is highly probable that stocks of finished commodities in the hands of wholesalers and retailers do move positively with the cycle. Still, if our statistical conclusions are correct, the forces released by Mr Hawtrey's movements in finished commodity stocks are largely offset by the economic forces which we have endeavoured to describe.

5

ON CRISIS AND
ADJUSTMENT [1939]

The character of the relationship between economic science and economic policy has always been problematical.[1] Nor were there any reasons to expect that our own epoch would improve upon an age in which free trade was the teaching of science and protection the order of the day. Nevertheless, it is difficult to believe that future historians of economic thought will feel inclined to describe the attitude of economics to the pressing problems of our days as anything but a disheartening spectacle. And nowhere is this more true than in the field of the business cycle.

'When governments perplexed by cyclical mass unemployment and recurrent depressions turned for advice to those whose special subject was the study of this problem,' they will have to report, 'economists seized the welcome opportunity for quarrelling with each other. An intellectual mass-duel between two rival groups, the expansionists and the classicists, shook the seats of higher learning. But the strangest of all was that the struggle was not so much about the measures to be undertaken, as about the time one had to wait before undertaking them.'

That such a situation detracts from the authority of economic science is a commonplace. That its only practical effect will be to encourage politicians to come forward with schemes of their own, which none of the duelling scientists would ever dream of approving, is altogether clear. In this situation it seems pertinent to inquire what, after all, the quarrel is about.

Now, it is relatively easy to describe the position of the expansionists. Their intellectual weapons have been forged precisely in order to meet a situation of chronical underemployment. Whatever the merits of their case, at least they leave nobody in doubt as to what is their diagnosis. Once this is accepted, the therapy follows

logically. In their view an economic crisis is the necessary consequence of a setback in investment activity. They demonstrate that
every change in total investment will have a multiple effect on
total incomes, output, employment, and consumption (the
'multiplier'). On the other hand, changes in consumption are likely
to have repercussions on investment activity (the 'relation' or the
acceleration principle). Thus changes in investment will set up
'cumulative processes' of expansion or contraction. Hence, in order
to maintain a given level of employment and incomes, we have to
maintain a given level of investment activity. And since every
addition to the equipment of society – whether profitable or not
– will serve this purpose, a deficiency in private investment, due,
for example, to a fall in profit prospects, has to be offset by an
increase in public works (or any other policy which will bring
about an expansion in total money incomes).

There can be little doubt that in recent years the expansionists
have made considerable headway. The multiplier gun, the main
piece of their scientific artillery (which seems to lend mathematical
precision to a common-sense argument), has proved a very effective weapon in twentieth century scientific warfare. Confronted
with a formidable array of weapons, the defenders of traditional
'classical' views are having a difficult time. Their artillery has left
impartial observers with the impression that it is slightly out of
date. Moreover, they lack unified command and a comprehensive
treatise to guide them.[2]

Their main argument is the need for 'adjustment'. The exact
meaning of this notion we shall examine presently. They admit the
central importance of investment for employment and incomes,
but argue that, if only adjustments took place, private investment
would recover speedily. It is the delay in adjustment which causes
the delayed recovery in investment. In this way their main line of
advance is covered against the multiplier gun. It is furthermore
now admitted by most of them that a situation as conceived by
the expansionists, a cumulative process of contraction which
nothing but public action will stop, may actually occur. Such a
situation is described as 'secondary depression'.[3] It is, however,
not quite clear whether its occurrence is due to a failure of adjustment[4] or whether it may not occur in spite of adjustment having
taken place.[5] At any rate, all neoclassicists agree that the forces of
adjustment must be given a chance. Only if they fail us shall we
be entitled to follow an expansionist policy.

Here, however, the time factor becomes of importance. For the expansionists are prone to argue that unless investment recovers immediately (during the 'breathing spell',[6] when orders given just before the outbreak of the crisis are keeping up investment activity) it is bound to have its unfavourable repercussions on employment and output. The neoclassicists are thus forced to admit that unless adjustments can be made within a very short time they will not prevent a cumulative process of contraction. It is their task to show what factors will prevent the stage of secondary depression from being reached once a setback in investment has set the ball rolling. We shall therefore have to study the nature of these adjustments in more detail.

THE NEOCLASSICAL THEORY OF CRISIS AND ADJUSTMENT

According to the neoclassical view, crisis is essentially a phenomenon of maladjustment, of price and output dislocation. A crisis occurs because an industry, or a group of industries, is out of tune with the rest of the economic system, because relative prices do not correspond to relative consumers' preferences. In a *free-exchange* economy, consumers direct all productive activity. All entrepreneurial decisions are provisional actions pending the ultimate sanction of the market. In the end, the market decides what quantities of goods are produced and at what prices. But in a dynamic world, entrepreneurs have to guess the verdict of the market and many make mistakes. They may produce too much of one good (i.e. more than can be sold at a price covering marginal cost), too little of another. If such forecasting errors become general in an industry, a crisis is due. The obvious remedy is to shift factors of production from the overexpanded to neglected lines. A fall in factor prices will make the latter attractive to enterprise. Capital invested in the overexpanded line will have to be written off, thus presenting a warning signal to investors. Free capital will now flow into the hitherto neglected branches of production where investment has been made more attractive by the fall in factor cost. It is this change in the direction of the flow of free capital which sets factors on the move.

It is readily seen that, faithful to the traditional teaching of the older classical school, the neoclassicists mean by crisis a partial depression. Only a sector of the industrial system is affected;

the rest remains intact. This complete intactness of the rest of the system in which – at possibly a lower rate of interest – investment goes on just as before is really the *conditio sine qua non* of successful adjustment. The smaller the sector which is affected by the crisis, the larger the absorptive capacity of the system as a whole. If the number of unemployed is small relative to the total working population, the demand for labour will be very elastic. And if investment prospects in the rest of the system are unaffected, the elasticity of demand for capital with respect to the rate of interest and other factor costs will be extremely high.

Where these conditions are not fulfilled, adjustment becomes a very irksome process. What the neoclassical school terms 'frictions' (essentially a long-run concept) may in the short-run be very real obstacles: fixed coefficients of production, rigid wage-rates, and rates of interest which are in part contractually fixed and in part influenced by monetary forces rather than by investment prospects. With given equipment the number of workers who can be employed is limited. Where relative wage-rates cannot change, the unemployed will still wish to move to another industry, but their employment will not be attractive to capital. And the variability of idle balances is by now too familiar a subject to need comment.

The neoclassicists are thus confronted with the dilemma that adjustment in order to prevent a setback in investment and to lead to an immediate recovery has to be so rapid as to be practically impossible. And if it cannot be brought about within the 'breathing spell', the cumulative process will already have started and the poison spread throughout the whole system. Most of the types of investment which adjustment tends to promote will be undertaken only as long as the major part of the system remains intact – or not at all.

THE CYCLICAL FUNCTION OF DURABLE INVESTMENT

There is, however, an important exception. Professor Hansen has recently emphasized the highly significant distinction between those types of investment which are 'closely geared to consumption' and those which are not.[7] To the latter category belong all those which are mainly undertaken with a view to the more distant future. Similarly, Dr Lundberg has pointed out that those types of investment which are most sensitive to the rate of interest, i.e. the most durable ones, are least likely to be affected by changes in demand for consumers' goods and vice versa. 'The influence of the direct demand for consumption goods on the volume of investments tends to diminish with the rise in value of . . . a magnitude . . . which may be given by increasing durability of the investment goods.'[8] He adds that 'this tendency will be strengthened by the fact that the longer the time-dimension of an investment the less the influences of changes in profits and receipts during relatively short periods upon the volume of investments.' The present author has attempted to extend this theorem so as to cover costs other than interest.[9]

> The rate of interest relates a future income stream to a present capital outlay. With a given rate of interest, the investor's decision depends on the cost of this present outlay and the size of the expected future income stream, *i.e.*, he has to compare a present outlay exclusively determined by the present level of costs and prices with an expected income stream which . . . is unlikely to be affected by this at all. It follows that, in the case of durable investment, the average yield of which is independent of present conditions, a rise in costs will check the inducement to invest and *vice versa*.[10]

Types of investment which are not closely geared to the current level of incomes and consumption, but which are highly elastic with regard to costs, are therefore the chief stronghold of the neoclassical position. It is mainly the existence of such investment opportunities which lends plausibility to the thesis that adjustment will ultimately lead to recovery. If it were not for them, the neoclassicists would have to admit defeat and to concede that, since adjustment and the elimination of frictions take time, a setback in investment activity, once it has occurred, is likely to start a cumulative process of contraction.

That, at least in the past, such investment opportunities have existed and led the way out of many a depression cannot very well be denied. The classical instance is residential building (England in 1932); but it seems that during a great part of the nineteenth century, railroad construction served the same function both in America and in Europe.

Theoretically, what happens is that the economic system is dragged out of the depression by that sector which belongs to the future and is therefore relatively immune against present-day disturbances. Or, we may say that a point is reached where, with a low rate of interest and lower costs generally, intertemporal exchange becomes more profitable, i.e. the exchange of present capital outlay against future income. The case is exactly parallel to that of the foreign balance, i.e. where a deflation in a country improves its competitive position in international trade and gives a stimulus to export industries. In both cases, recovery is due to forces outside the system, here in a spatial, there in a temporal, sense.

OVERINVESTMENT AND THE NEOCLASSICAL DOCTRINE

Thus far we have seen that the neoclassical theory of crisis involves the dislocation of a part of the economic system, a distortion of relative prices, and that adjustment is essentially the readjustment of that area which has been hit to the rest of the system that has remained intact. The applicability of neoclassical analysis is therefore confined to cases in which the initial depression is a partial one.

Now, this does not seem to be too unrealistic a picture of what has actually happened in many historical instances. It is, of course, well known that many of the great crises of economic history were connected with overexpansion in particular industries. We are wont to describe the crises of the 1840s and 1850s as railroad crises, to link the crisis of 1901 directly, and that of 1907 indirectly,[11] to the rapid growth of the electrical industries. And as to 1929, among those ascribing the crisis to overexpansion in particular industries, the main quarrel is as to whether it was entirely due to the rise of the automobile industry and to building in the United States or whether the rapid expansion in raw-material production in the twenties (rubber, tin) was an important factor.[12]

There now arises the question of how neoclassical economics proposes to deal with overinvestment crises. Analytically, no particular difficulty seems to be involved. Overinvestment crises are the result of a dislocation of the industrial system; prices of investment goods were too high, too many of them were produced, too many resources were used in their production. The necessary adjustment consists simply in a shifting of factors of production from the capital-goods to the consumers'-goods industries. Here we encounter several practical difficulties. First, in a modern economy the investment-goods producing sector is not a small part of the economic system; an overinvestment crisis due to, say, lack of entrepreneurial foresight regarding demand for capital goods is not just a partial depression. It is difficult to conceive of an overinvestment crisis which would leave the major part of the system intact. Second, since the maladjustment is due to an overexpansion of investment activity, adjustment must necessarily take the form of a reduction of it. But we know that this means a fall in aggregate output, employment, and consumption, and is bound to have further repercussions. No 'compensatory investment' of the kind described in the previous section could help us; on the contrary, every attempt to maintain investment would defeat its own ends by perpetuating the maladjustment. It would serve to keep investment-goods prices permanently above their equilibrium level. How then is adjustment possible?

The answer is briefly that in the case of an overinvestment crisis the basic dislocation consists in a maladjustment between investment and consumption. What is needed is a diminution of investment *accompanied by an increase in consumption*. In the language currently in fashion: If the marginal propensity to consume increases, we may have the same aggregate output and employment with less investment. What we need for a frictionless adjustment is not compensatory investment, but compensatory consumption. Are we likely to get it in the normal course of events?

A rapidly growing number of students of business fluctuations has come to agree on the essentially discontinuous character of economic progress. In a dynamic world, investment is governed by profit prospects which turn up at irregular intervals. When they appear, they give a fillip to investment and employment; the economic system 'expands'. When they have been exhausted, when all the resources necessary to exploit them have been installed, the system will have a relapse.

> A transcontinental railway is completed – a mercantile marine is converted from a coal to an oil basis – a steel industry has shifted its location and modernised its plant – arrears of housing or armament are made up – every American citizen has become possessed of a motor-car, wireless set and refrigerator – China or Peru after a period of chaos has resumed its place upon the economic map. Good – all to the

good – man must progress. But what is the next thing, please?[13]

In a world of this kind, stability could only be obtained by a propensity to consume inversely correlated to the level of investment and fluctuating as widely as the latter. What is required is such an intelligent behaviour on the part of consumers that they will reduce their consumption whenever new investment opportunities appear on the horizon and expand it immediately after these have been exhausted. To formulate these conditions is, for all practical purposes, to question the possibility of their ever being realized. If industrial progress is discontinuous, income-receivers would have to save discontinuously, but such is not their inclination. Nor is there any mechanism which would make them do it. If consumption ever did increase simultaneously with a fall in investment, it would be nothing but a happy accident. Even those for whom the rate of interest is not a preponderantly monetary phenomenon will have to admit that, while it may have some influence on saving, it is unlikely to bring about those wide fluctuations we require.

MONETARY OVERINVESTMENT THEORY AND ADJUSTMENT

We have thus far attempted to describe the neoclassical notion of adjustment, and to examine the conditions contingent upon its attainment. We came to the conclusion that this type of analysis fits best the case of partial depressions, where the system as a whole has remained unaffected, but encounters considerable difficulties in the case of overinvestment crises. We now shall have to study the views of an important group of neoclassical economists, the outstanding representative of whom is Professor Hayek.[14] This separate treatment of the 'monetary overinvestment theory' of the 'Austrian School'[15] seems to be justified by the peculiar conclusions at which this group, starting out from the common body of neoclassical doctrine, has arrived as regards both the causes of crises and the conditions of successful adjustment.

The Austrian analysis of crisis runs in neoclassical terms. An economic crisis is due to a dislocation of the structure of production, expressed by distortion of relative prices of producers' and consumers' goods. The cause of the maladjustment has to be sought in a rate of interest which was 'too low', i.e., at a level lower than can be maintained, if a constant increase in the quantity of money and, ultimately, an explosion of the price system is to be prevented. Under the stimulus of the low rate of interest, entrepreneurs begin to embark upon investment projects; but since, as we saw, the rate of interest cannot permanently be kept at a level which entails progressive inflation, they find it impossible to complete these projects (or to maintain those that were completed).

As long as the rate of interest is kept below its 'equilibrium level' and the increase in the quantity of money continues, these investments can go on, financed as they are by the 'forced savings' of the fixed-income receivers. But once the rate of interest has been raised and the process of inflation been stopped, these investments will no longer be profitable, and it will not even pay to complete them. In other words: Once the supply of money has been 'neutralized', the price ratio between producers' and consumers' goods will again be determined by consumers' relative preference for saving and consumption. High demand for consumers' goods accompanied by lower demand for producers' goods is the symptom of the crisis.

It would appear, therefore, that what in the preceding section we described as a 'happy accident' – an increase in demand for consumers' goods at the moment at which investment contracts – is, from the Austrian point of view, the real cause of the crisis. Considering that the Austrian theory is 'overinvestment theory' just as much as the one described previously, this certainly is a rather startling conclusion. How then is the paradox to be solved?

At this juncture, we may remember that the expansionists are in the habit of charging Professor Hayek and his followers with making the assumption of full employment throughout and thus assuming away the whole problem. In another place, the present author has attempted to refute this charge,[16] which is due to a misunderstanding on the part of the expansionists who like to think of factors of production as homogeneous masses of labour, land, and capital, and who fail to understand that, with the degree of specialization which we find in the modern world, these concepts are meaningless. The Austrian theory can very well include amongst its premises the existence of unemployed labour and idle resources provided only some factors in the system are scarce. The question is whether it can deal adequately with changes in aggregate output and employment.

Economists generally agree that total output is the best measure of prosperity and depression. In Professor Hayek's theory, however, crisis is described as a situation in which investment output falls while that of consumable goods rises. *Thus nothing is said about total output.* There will now certainly be unemployment among labourers who are specialists in capital-goods industries (miners, engineers, shipbuilders), but there will also be more employment for chauffeurs, waiters, and cinema attendants. *Thus nothing is said about total employment.* It follows that the crisis considered by the Austrian school must be something different from what is generally understood by this term. It appears that Professor Hayek's object of study is qualitatively distinct from that of his opponents.

It is now possible to indicate where the difference between the Austrian point of view and that of the majority of the neoclassical writers lies. For the bulk of the neoclassicists, as we saw, crisis means a fall in output in one sector of the industrial system; hence, *ceteris paribus*, a fall in total output. Whether this sectional recession will then be offset by recovery in another sector is just the crucial problem. The neoclassical case against an expansionist policy stands and falls with the possibility of adjustment, the possibility of a compensatory increase in investment – or, in the case of an overinvestment crisis, in consumption – in other sectors. The acid test of their thesis is the demonstration that in our world – in spite of its technical peculiarities, its debt structure, its rigid costs – such adjustment is practically possible. The Austrian writers, however, need not set forth any such demonstration. For them, by definition, the shifting of factors of production from investment to consumption *is* the crisis. Crisis and adjustment are not only simultaneous, so that the time-lag problem which we showed above to be fundamental for the neoclassical position does not arise; it is the same process. What to the Austrian writers are symptoms of crisis are nothing but the hardships of adjustment.

Before concluding this part of our analysis, we may briefly examine the Austrian view on adjustment. This, shortly, is that only an increase in voluntary savings, by curtailing excessive consumption-demand and providing the capital supply necessary for completing investment projects under way, would effectively remedy the situation. It is interesting to observe the difference between this point of view and the theory of adjustment held by the bulk of the neoclassical school. For the latter, adjustment is essentially an equilibrating process, i.e. a process by which the economic system moves from a position of disequilibrium, where it has been brought by the misguided expectations of entrepreneurs, to a position of equilibrium, where once more relative prices will correspond to consumers' preferences. *The neoclassical theory of adjustment is essentially a theory of the path towards equilibrium.* For Professor Hayek, on the other hand, the disequilibrium having been of a monetary kind, no such process is possible. Once the supply of money has been neutralized and the relative prices of producers' and consumers' goods moved to levels corresponding to consumers' preferences, equilibrium has effectively been restored. Society, it is true, has squandered a part of its resources on futile ventures, but this will be expressed by the price mechanism. No further adjustments are called for. What the Austrian remedy – increase in voluntary savings – amounts to is nothing but *a change of data* which will turn data that originally were purely imaginary – entrepreneurs' profit-expectations induced by the low rate of interest – into real data.

CONCLUSIONS

If the preceding analysis is correct, we are now able to draw a number of interesting conclusions. In the first place, on the strength of their own argument, the Austrian writers are not entitled to object to measures destined to raise consumers' purchasing power. For the difference between the situation to which they are referring when speaking of crisis and the one in which such measures are to be adopted lies exactly in the fact that in the former case there is no lack of effective demand while in the latter case there is such a lack.

On the other hand, all this is not to say that a crisis of the Austrian type may not be a very serious matter. We have unemployment of specialized labour, capital losses, disappointed expectations, a stock-exchange collapse and, probably, a number of important bankruptcies. In short, what the Austrian theory depicts in the first place is a financial rather than an industrial crisis. It is clear that some of these events at least are bound to have further repercussions. Owing to the peculiar psychological climate of the stock market, the slump is unlikely to be confined to 'heavy stocks' but will soon spread to all categories of shares including those of the consumption-goods industries which are doing well. Demand for luxury goods will also be affected. Most important of all, the net effect of the financial crisis on the banking system is bound to be deflationary.

Finally, all this will now enable us to understand the significant role which the concept of *secondary depression* plays in the teaching of the Austrian school. Their object of study – the 'primary crisis' – is not identical with a recession in total output and employment. Since, however, all social scientists like to think of their theories as being somehow relevant to the world in which they are living, they have to find some link between the two. They have to evolve a mechanism by which depression spreads from the investment sector throughout the whole system. Such model-mechanism will most suitably run in terms of (bank) deflation and show how the 'primary crisis' starts a chain of events which will ultimately lead to a fall in aggregate incomes. It is then readily seen that the more rigid are prices and costs, the more will a given volume of deflation reduce aggregate output and employment.

We therefore have to conclude that the economists of the Austrian school are only apparently taking part in the battle which is fought between neoclassicists and expansionists. Those who reported to have seen Professor Hayek as a protagonist on the neoclassical side must have been suffering from an optical illusion. In reality his followers are not to be found on the battleground at all. They are sitting on the fence all the time.

Part II

CAPITAL AND INVESTMENT REPERCUSSIONS

6

ON THE MEASUREMENT OF CAPITAL [1941]

INTRODUCTION

Few economists will deny that in recent years the rapid *rapprochement* between theoretical and empirical economics has been one of the most encouraging features of the evolution of their science. The remarkable progress which the investigation of problems connected with the analysis and measurement of national income has achieved gave convincing proof, if such was needed, that co-operation between theorists and statisticians is capable of giving rise to a clarification of concepts as well as to fuller understanding and more exhaustive utilization of available statistical data. Nevertheless, as has often been pointed out, it is a necessary condition of this co-operation not only that theorists present their theses in a verifiable form, but also that econometricians be aware of the economic nature of the processes underlying the phenomena which they are measuring.

To the present day most economic theory has evolved along static lines. The adaptation of its theorems to a dynamic world, as witness the problem of expectations, has proved a more than formidable task. But in no field of economics is the need for a break with the static tradition and for a new and dynamic approach more imperative than in the theory of capital. As Professor Hayek has shown, a world without, or with only generally foreseen, change is not at all a 'capitalistic' world, as in it none of the problems, the solution of which is the typical function of the capital-owner, would present themselves. It was therefore only to be expected that contributions to the econometrics of capital which do not keep abreast of the present level of knowledge of dynamic

91

phenomena as contained in the modern theory of capital would go badly astray.

In this paper we do not propose to make a contribution to this dynamic theory of capital. We have nothing to add to the analysis with which Professor Hayek has presented us, but shall set ourselves to the more modest task of utilizing the light it sheds for the exploration of some problems in the econometrics of capital. In the first part of this chapter we shall examine certain results of a recent attempt at a statistical evaluation of the quantity of capital and its productivity. In this we shall learn that the theoretical study of problems connected with the dynamics of the capital structure, so far from being an intellectual parlour-game for the fastidious, is an entirely indispensable condition for the proper understanding of economic phenomena in a world of change, and that his neglect of it has led a distinguished statistician into serious misinterpretation of his statistical data. In the second part we shall adumbrate a method for the measurement of the productive contribution of capital which, we hope, will at least be unexceptionable on this score, whatever its other defects may be.

MEASURING CAPITAL WITHOUT CONSIDERING MISINVESTMENT

In his recent book[1] Mr Colin Clark devotes a chapter to 'The Role of Capital in Economic Progress' (pp. 374–422). In it he is 'concerned with the relation between long-period economic progress and the accumulation of capital' (374). The measure of this relation he finds in 'the long-period marginal productivity of capital, that is to say, the increase in annual real income in any community consequential upon an increase in its stock of real capital, other factors remaining unchanged' (374). Needless to say, this definition raises at once, in its most general form, an issue pivotal to modern capital theory, which, of course, is based on the proposition that no important change in capital is conceivable which would leave the 'other factors unchanged'. Nevertheless, we shall here refrain from criticism on a priori grounds and adopt the method of immanent criticism instead. In this and the following section we shall confine ourselves to pointing out that even if 'the stock of real capital' were a meaningful concept, Mr Clark would none the less be prevented from measuring it by the inadequacy of his material for his purpose and, in particular, by the fact that the influence of 'other factors', so far from being eliminated, is actually one of the salient features of his time series. We shall therefore not be surprised to learn that our author on occasion arrives at strange results.

Mr Clark shows himself not unaware of the nature of the difficulties confronting him.

> The first difficulties of measurement are theoretical. There are three entirely separate concepts of the basis on which capital can be measured, namely market value, replacement value and cost price. In the case of consumption goods such difficulties do not arise ... But in the case of durable commodities wide differences can and do occur. (375)

However, he comforts himself with the reflection that 'in the long run' forces are operative which tend to tie the three value sources together. 'All that can be said is that with the lapse of time there are forces tending gradually to bring the three values together. If replacement value is high relative to market value, there will be no incentive to erect new buildings, as has indeed actually been the case in many countries in the last twenty years'. But does the example of the building values not suggest that even twenty years may not be long enough to qualify for the 'long period'? Besides, in a period which is long enough to allow such equalizing forces to become operative, new disturbing influences are likely to supervene which may actually make the three values diverge even more. It would seem that this comforting thought of our author is based on a simple confusion between 'long periods' in the ordinary sense, in which any number and variety of factors may come to influence events, and the 'long periods' of economic theory in which by definition nothing ever occurs but the process by which the dependent variables adjust themselves to the change in data which took place at the beginning of the period.

The author believes that, whichever of the three values we adopt as our standard, we shall not go wrong as long as we use consistently the one we select. Price fluctuations are to be eliminated by the use of index numbers. The question is, of course, whether those who made the records on which our data are based used the same consistency of method, but this question is nowhere discussed.

In applying his method of measurement, based on original cost and deflation by price index (376), to fixed capital in manufacturing industries in the United States, Mr Clark finds that the quantity of capital rose from 100 in 1919 to 112.5 in 1929 and afterwards fell to a low level of 94 in 1935.

> Figures of Capital Assets taken from Corporation Income Tax Returns tend to confirm our index ... These returns give $25.46 milliards as value of capital assets (land, buildings and machinery) for 1925 and $25.62 milliards for 1932 ... After 1925, we may therefore safely say, there was no net addition to the quantity of manufacturing capital up to 1932 – a very remarkable conclusion. (382)

But the most remarkable conclusion these figures permit us to draw is certainly as to the inadequacy of a theory of capital in which misinvestment has no place. For what they indicate clearly enough is that more or less all the capital which in the years prior to 1929 had been invested in American manufactures turned out to be misinvested and had subsequently to be written off.[2] What, however, they do not indicate is that in 1935 the American economy was less well equipped with fixed capital in manufacturing industries than in 1919, for it is of the essence of misinvestment that while, like all investment, it adds to the resources of society, it nevertheless adds less than it might have added, and certainly far less than its investors expected it to add. It is this disappointment of investors' initial expectations which the process of writing down asset values reflects.

The dilemma with which misinvestment confronts an investigation of capital changes, the conceptual apparatus of which is exclusively framed in quantitative terms, consists precisely in this: We have to count misinvested capital either at zero value, in which case we underrate the addition to resources, or at cost value, in which case we exaggerate it. Valuation at market value would conflict with the consistent use of our standard unless we assessed all other capital in the same way. Moreover, both timing and extent of the correction of book values are perfectly arbitrary, as is clearly seen in the case of American manufactures from the 'decline in capital' from 104 in 1932 to 94 in 1935, i.e. during a period when the worst of the depression was over. Mr Clark, quite consistently, chooses the first method and identifies misinvestment with no investment, but is thus led to the startling conclusion that then there must have been increasing returns! 'So violent was the tendency to increasing returns in the USA that a greatly increased output was produced from a stationary volume of factors of production' (385).

In the case of Great Britain, Mr Clark finds that the money value of capital increased from £9.435 milliards in 1928 to £11.725 milliards in 1935 (393). As 'Figures for Great Britain, however, have been measured throughout at market values' (376), these figures have first to be converted into 'real terms', and for this purpose our author conceives the necessity to allow for the effect of changes in interest rates on asset values. Choosing the yield on consols as representative interest rate he multiplies both figures by their respective consol yields and thus obtains a 'decline in real terms' from £44 milliards in 1928 to £35.2 milliards in 1935. At this result of his own ingenuity our author shows surprise. 'It is probably the case that by 1935 values of capital goods had not yet adjusted themselves to the strong changes in interest rates and replacement costs which had occurred during the years immediately preceding' (393). But on his own showing this should disqualify the 1935 results from serving as indicators of the long-period growth or decline of capital – if indeed there were any others to take their place.

DIFFICULTIES WITH THIS APPROACH TO MEASUREMENT

For Mr Clark the determination of the quantity of capital is preliminary to the measurement of its long-period productivity. His measure is the quotient of total capital and total output, C/P, in other words the quantity of capital used per unit of output. Its growth or decline, the relative increase of numerator and denominator, are to indicate the existence of increasing or decreasing capital costs. From the table on p. 381 (Clark 1940) we find that in American manufacturing industries C/P fell from 165 in 1919 to 132 in 1929, then rose to 228 in 1932, to fall again to 126 in 1937. But do these figures indicate the quantity of capital *used* per unit of output?[3] It is obvious that the spectacular rise from 1929 to 1932 must be largely due to the inclusion of unutilized equipment in the numerator at a time when the denominator was on the down grade, and vice versa for the heavy fall after 1932. This goes to show that in a society which is making less than full use of its resources the numerical aggregate of these resources, even if it were measurable, is irrelevant to the determination of their productivity unless qualified by an index expressing the degree of their utilization. The main defect of Mr Clark's method is thus seen to lie in the lack of identity between the object of his statistical measurement and the productive agent the contribution of which he wishes to measure. In the case of under-utilization of resources the former concept is wider than the latter, fluctuations in which will therefore appear under the guise of 'variable returns'. But as we saw in the previous section, the reverse may also happen: a change in book values, the basis of our statistical data, would affect our numerator without, of course, having any real effect on productivity. The influence of both factors combined is recognizable in the United States between 1932 and 1935, when total manufacturing output (1919 = 100) rose from 75 to 107, while fixed manufacturing capital, for the reasons previously discussed, declined from 104 to 94. The divergent movement of numerator and denominator, for quite different reasons, thus explains the fantastic fall in C/P from 228 in 1932 to 144 in 1935.

Mr Clark takes a different view. To him these figures mean that

Since 1922, therefore, the USA had witnessed a rapid expansion in the volume of manufacturing output with a decline not only in the labour force but also in the quantity of fixed capital used. This is indeed confirmatory of the idea previously suggested that about the year 1920 some radical change came over the whole productive system of the USA.(382)

Perhaps it will be argued that Mr Clark's failure to establish a satisfactory criterion of measurement for the growth and productivity of real capital has to be ascribed less to any inherent defects of his method than to sheer bad luck in the choice of his time period. It is, of course, true that in no branch of human activity does the inter-War epoch lend itself easily to inductive generalizations. Certainly no period in modern economic history was less well suited to the elimination of 'other factors'. Nevertheless, we venture to doubt whether a series of capital figures taken in the same way from another period in the economic history of a world of change would have yielded very different results. The fundamental dilemma remains, viz., that our period is either so short that changes in the degree of utilization of the equipment overshadow growth, or so long that for a considerable proportion of equipment its original, and even replacement cost, no longer forms a possible basis of valuation. In neither case can the 'other factors' be eliminated.

Nor is this impression incapable of verification. Closer inspection of Table 13 in Professor Douglas' *Theory of Wages*, the cherished prototype of Mr Clark's exertions in the econometrics of productivity, reveals for a different period the same problems and the same bewilderment. Professor Douglas finds that, in American manufacturing industries between 1890 and 1922, C/P, the quantity of capital per unit of output, increased from 100 to 180 while over the same period L/P, the quantity of labour per unit of output, fell from 100 to 67. But had he chosen 1921 instead of 1922 as his terminal year, the figures would have been 233 for C/P and 82 for L/P! Besides, it is difficult to reconcile a rise in L/P from 81 in 1916 to 90 in 1918, evidently indicating a heavy strain on the existing equipment and its utilization beyond its optimum point, with a large rise in C/P from 132 in 1916 to 164 in 1918. It is more than probable that 'write-ups' on the grand scale had something to do with this astonishing figure.

We therefore conclude that Mr Clark's attempt to establish a method for the measurement of the quantity and productivity of capital cannot be described as an unqualified success.[4]

MEASURING THE STREAM OF CAPITAL SERVICES

Thus far this has been an essay in destructive criticism. We have tried to expose the fallacies of a quasi-static theory of capital by showing that, if available statistical records were interpreted in accordance with it, we should obtain an absurd picture of the world. We have seen an attempt to measure the growth of capital in real terms fail, mainly because of the impossibility of eliminating the effects of other factors from the time series. We have found the determination of the productivity of capital incapable of accomplishment because of the lack of identity between the object of statistical measurement and the productive agent the contribution of which is to be determined. The latter fact suggests that 'the total quantity of capital in real terms' may not be a meaningful, and in the present context is not a relevant, concept. The former experience points to the conclusion that even if it were a meaningful and relevant concept, it would none the less be incapable of quantitative evaluation.

Nevertheless, the reader will not, it is hoped, infer from our strictures that where the productive services of non-permanent resources are concerned no meaningful measurement is possible at all. On the contrary, as we shall try to explain, our objections are strictly confined to the measurement of the *source* of these services, but do not extend to the measurement of the services themselves.

As social scientists we are, of course, entitled (and in the circumstances of our time almost obliged) to reject the claims of a spurious 'scientism' which harbours an almost superstitious belief in numbers and identifies measurability with intelligibility.[5] But there is surely no reason why we should not try to measure where measurement helps us to a better understanding of social phenomena.

Where, as is the case with marginal productivity, the main propositions of a theory are stated in quantifiable, if not in quantitative, terms, to renounce all measurement would be to rule out all possibility of empirical verification. Also, in economic policy no rational discussion of the distribution of incomes would be possible inasmuch as all such discussion has to run in terms of a necessarily quantitative comparison between shares in the national income and the productive contributions of income-receivers. Furthermore, it is clear that a concept like 'the rate of profit', pivotal to the dynamics of capital, in itself involves the quantifiability of some aggregate of resources to which it is related as a 'rate'. The conclusion we have to draw is that, whilst 'the total quantity of capital in real terms' may be a meaningless magnitude, and not measurable either, some proportion of it, as also the flow of services emerging from it, is germane to essential propositions of economic theory. But how is this proportion to be determined?

First of all, the productivity of capital involves relationships between three magnitudes, the stock of non-permanent resources, the service stream flowing from it, and the output stream produced by capital services jointly with the services of other factors of production. The main difficulty confronting us lies in that, since the stock of capital resources is capable of giving rise to service streams of various size and shape, there seems to be no determinate relationship between it and the output stream. Hence the relationship determining the productivity of capital has in the first instance to be established between service stream and output stream.

But it is readily seen that in measuring the stream of services flowing from the stock of capital resources[6] we are *ipso facto* measuring the depletion of the stock owing to its productive contribution. Evidently both are two different aspects of the same phenomenon. Here then we have a uniquely determinate relationship between service stream and a *proportion* of the capital stock, and – since with constant co-efficients of production the relation between service stream and output stream is also determinate – between output stream and that proportion of the capital stock of which, owing to its depletion in the process of production, we may say that it 'enters' output. Needless to say, the size of this proportion depends on the length of the period over which we measure the output stream, hence it is a function of time. We also obtain a valuable criterion of distinction between capital changes which are due to the using up of resources in the production of output and capital changes due to causes which are 'external' to the production of output. If only we can contrive to find a satisfactory measure of the stream of capital services, we shall, by the same token, have determined the proportion of capital resources which enters output.

Since this approach involves the time factor, the selection of a suitable period of measurement becomes a matter of some significance to us. The main defect of a theory which operates with the total quantity of capital lies precisely in this: that a period long enough for our proportion to become identical with the total capital stock, long enough, that is, for the stock of non-permanent resources to yield all the services of which it is capable (in other words, a period in which all fixed capital has become circulating, has been used up and written off), is in a world of change apt to bring some unforseen change which will upset all prior arrangements. The period we have to choose for the measurement of the productive contribution of capital thus depends on the time dimension of the productive plans involving the use of it. Here we encounter the familiar difficulty of all period analysis, the lack of synchronization between the production plans of different producers. However, fortunately for us, diverse though the time shape of individual production plans may be, the method of checking results is highly standardized. In business accounting the period for which records are examined, results assessed and a balance sheet drawn up is the year. It seems to us therefore that in a world of change the best measure of the amount of capital used up in production is to be found in the annual depreciation quotas on fixed capital.

In propounding this suggestion we shall, in the first place, try to elucidate a little the economic function of capital accounting in a dynamic world. Thereafter we shall indicate in what way and by what methods data obtained from actual business records have to be modified in order to make them a suitable instrument of measurement for our purposes. Finally, we shall have to show why the method we advocate is not open to the objections which in the first part of this paper we raised to Mr Clark's method.

ACCOUNTING FOR CAPITAL REVALUATIONS

The method which we here advocate for the measurement of the proportion of capital resources which annually enter the social product is a method which Dr Fabricant of the National Bureau of Economic Research employs for the determination of capital consumption in the United States from 1919 to 1935.[7] Though ostensibly his aim is the measurement of the difference between gross and net national income, it is evident that this difference equals the total capital change other than gross capital formation. More important is that for Dr Fabricant, being thus interested in one type of capital change, the determination of capital consumption is only part of his task. For only capital consumption, the amount of capital used up in production, and capital adjustment, the capital changes due to causes external to the production of output, together make up total capital change other than gross capital formation, i.e., the capital change he seeks to determine. The measure of capital consumption he finds in annual charges to income account (depreciation on fixed capital, depletion of wasting assets, plus some minor items like provisions for accidental loss and maintenance and repair expenditure), the measure of capital adjustment in (intermittent) charges to capital account (retirements and abandonments and revaluations of capital assets[8]). In so far therefore as the object of his investigation coincides with ours, i.e. fixed capital used up in production, he virtually employs the method we advocate.

But it may be doubted whether in actual accounting practice the distinction between charges to income account and charges to capital account can be regarded as symmetrical to Dr Fabricant's distinction between 'internal' and 'external' capital change. If there is a parallelism, it is at least not a very close one. On the other hand, obsolescence, certainly the result of 'external' factors, is usually provided for in depreciation in so far as it can be foreseen.[9]

On the other hand, there is the case, well known from the history of all inflations, where depreciation allowances, because based on original rather than reproduction cost, habitually understate the amount of capital used up in production, with the result that sooner or later a charge to capital account has to be made. It seems to us, therefore, that the accounting distinction between charges to income and to capital account is better regarded as reflecting the economic contrast between foreseen and unforeseen changes.[10] Nevertheless, it still remains true that we have to exclude charges on capital account from our computation of capital used up in production. Our next task consists in explaining why this is so.

In a world of perfect foresight depreciation allowances, in so far as they cover 'normal' obsolescence as well as ordinary wear-and-tear, will, as a rule, suffice to ensure capital replacement on a scale commensurate with the permanent flowing of a constant income stream. But in a world of imperfect foresight this need not be so, and the aggregate of depreciation allowances over a number of years may, for familiar reasons, either exceed or fall short of this standard; hence the recurrent necessity of revaluation of capital assets. The frequency of such revaluation offers strong evidence that in a world of change the 'maintenance of capital' is not a practical possibility. Adopting Swedish terminology we might say that depreciation allowances are *ex ante* estimates of the amount of capital used up, whereas the subsequent correction of these estimates by a charge to capital account determines this amount *ex post*.

For the purpose of the measurement of capital changes during a sequence of years there are three alternative methods of dealing with these intermittent revaluations. Each of them has its merits according to the purpose in hand and the aspect of the problem we wish to stress. There is first Dr Fabricant's own method which consists in simply adding up charges on income and on capital account. Since he is interested in total capital change other than gross capital formation over the period 1919 to 1935, this is no doubt an entirely legitimate procedure. A second method, more, we believe, in accordance with the essential meaning of period analysis, would be to include or exclude capital adjustment from our computation according to the length of the period chosen. For instance, when computing the quantity of capital entering annual output we might well confine ourselves to depreciation and disregard revaluation, while we could not afford to disregard it where,

CAPITAL AND INVESTMENT REPERCUSSIONS

like Dr Fabricant, we had to deal with a period of more than fifteen years. In adopting this method we would do more than merely draw a conventional distinction between 'long' and 'short' periods and the forces operating in them; we would, that is, implicitly admit that there are forces making for capital change which are quite unrelated to the productive contribution of capital. It is on a recognition of this fact and its implications that the third method, the omission of capital adjustment from the computation of capital, is based.

We learned above that the difference between foreseen and unforeseen changes provides the economic rationale for the accounting distinction between charges to income account and to capital account. As in general the effect of unforeseen changes on capital value cannot be apportioned to individual income periods, it is only logical to charge it to capital account. Yet this does not equally apply to all types of unforeseen change, and in fact there is a further important distinction which is germane to our argument. There are, on the one hand, changes which, although unforeseen at the moment at which the production plan was made, do not, when they occur, altogether upset the plan, do not necessitate any important modification of the pattern of resource use as chalked out in the plan (there may and always will be minor technical adjustments), and which might very well find their financial expression in charges to income account if accounting methods were more elastic than they actually are. A good instance of this, as was mentioned above, is provided by the history of inflations, in particular their earlier stages: Where in such a situation depreciation methods are based, as they traditionally are, on original rather than reproduction cost, sooner or later a charge to capital account will have to be made, the necessity for which, however, arises not from the nature of the case but from the nature of bad accounting. Where this happens we are, of course, unable to accept depreciation allowances as compiled from actual business records at their face value, and in a moment we shall have to discuss methods of their rational reinterpretation. But there is another type of unforeseen change, arising, for instance, from technical progress or changes in the social environment in general, which upsets the whole production plan and makes it impossible to adhere to the pattern of resource use as originally chalked out in it. In the former case it was still possible, after the change had occurred, to allocate its effects to single income periods. In the case of inflation all we have to do is to allow for the higher cost of replacement goods in the depreciation allowances for subsequent years. But in the latter case no such allocation is feasible, for here the very occurrence of the change marks at the same time the failure, and consequently the end, of the production plan. Now an entirely new plan has to be drawn up, and the failure of the first finds its appropriate expression in a charge to capital account.

We contend that in the computation of the amount of capital which gives rise to a certain stream of services, and hence indirectly to a given output stream, charges to capital account in so far as they reflect the latter type of unforeseen change must be disregarded. In not doing so we would obviate the very reasons for which we adopted period analysis, for our chief reason was our recognition of the fact that in a world of change the measurement of capital over periods so long as to involve alterations in the mode of its use is logically impossible and, if nevertheless persisted in, bound to lead to absurd results. Hence, in applying period analysis we have to select our period so as to make it co-extend with the carrying out of a coherent production plan. But revaluation, as we saw, usually marks the failure of a production plan. It follows that our period has to be selected in such a way as to have it ending before such necessity arises.

However, as we pointed out, in reality asset revaluation often marks not the failure of a production plan but the failure of accountants to understand the nature of the processes the effects of which they are about to assess. Frequently charges to capital account are made where charges to income account would be quite as feasible. It follows that if in our computation of capital resources we disregarded these charges to capital account like all others, we should be disregarding something which really ought to be included in depreciation. Hence, if we wish to omit all charges to capital account from our computation, we must somehow modify depreciation data as compiled from business records in order to make them cover these cases.

Here we are extremely fortunate in being able simply to follow Dr Fabricant, who has worked out most ingenious methods in order to deal with this problem.[11] By making judicious use of an inquiry by the New York Stock Exchange of companies applying for the listing of their securities, he first establishes the principles to which actually the majority of American companies adhere in their depreciation practice.[12] As was to be expected, it is found that the principles underlying their practice are very different from what they would have to be if the data compiled from balance sheets were to be of immediate use for our purposes. Still, the result of the inquiry reveals that, however illogical these methods may be from the economist's point of view, there are certain broad underlying principles to which the large majority of company accountants adhere and which are not incapable of rational reinterpretation.[13] The two main defects of depreciation data are found to be that they ignore variations in the degree of utilization, and that they are largely based on original rather than reproduction cost. But Dr Fabricant shows convincingly that these are by no means insurmountable obstacles. If depreciation allowances are to reflect the amount of capital resources responsible for the output of a period, they will have to be on a 'service-output' basis,[14] i.e. they must vary with variations in output and the degree of utilization. But in practice (this is one of the principles established by Dr Fabricant) depreciation is usually on a 'straight line' basis, i.e. annual depreciation is computed by dividing the original cost of capital equipment through the prospective number of years of its economic life, and irrespective of the variations in output.[15] We therefore have to construct an index of output by means of which we can convert our data from a 'straight line' to a 'service-output' basis.[16] The same applies to replacement cost. Here we have to find the age-distribution of industrial equipment,[17] and then to construct a price index for equipment goods.[18] This done we are able to convert our data from an original cost to a reproduction cost basis.

Finally we have to show why the method here proposed is not open to the objections which in the first part of this chapter we raised to Mr Clark's. After all, it might be said, our data as well as his are finally derived from book values of capital assets, as depreciation allowances computed on a 'straight line' basis are, of course, merely a function of book values. We made our statistical raw material pass through a processing stage, but why could not Mr Clark's data be subjected to similar treatment?

The answer is that by disregarding capital adjustment we contrived to eliminate those capital changes which are due to unforeseen events entailing discontinuity in the mode of use of capital resources, and hence irrelevant to the computation of the amount of capital used up in production. Our main charge against Mr Clark was that the object of his statistical measurement was not identical with the aim of his investigation, viz., the non-permanent sources of productive services. On the one hand, his data were seen to be affected by changes in book values of capital assets which did not reflect concomitant changes in the productive contributions of these resources. On the other hand, his data did not reflect changes, like variations in the degree of utilization, without taking account of which it is impossible to determine the productivity of any factor. The former problem we endeavoured to overcome by ignoring charges to capital account and by the choice of an appropriate time period, the latter by correcting our original data for changes in prices and output. Instead of measuring a stock of resources capable of giving rise to service streams of various length and shape we prefer to measure the depletion of the stock consequent upon the flowing of each service stream.

One objection we hope will not be raised against us, viz., that by basing our computation of capital on subjective estimates we are infringing upon the objectivity of measurement. Such argument would incidentally raise a fundamental issue in the methodology of social science, and it would be possible to meet it on a broader plane by discussing the meaning of objectivity in social life. In the present context we may forestall it by pointing out that in the field of capital, where the physical attributes of the components of this heterogeneous mass cannot serve as criteria of classification, all measurement must necessarily proceed in terms of value relationships, and all economic values are ultimately derived from subjective estimates. We readily agree that where a market is sufficiently large, generally accessible, and continuous over time, it serves to co-ordinate a large number of subjective estimates and thus may impart a moment of (social) objectivity to value relations based on prices formed on it. But it can hardly be said that the second-hand market for industrial equipment, which would be the proper place for the determination of the value of capital goods which have been in use, satisfies these requirements, and that its valuations are superior to intra-enterprise valuation. On the other hand, as Dr Fabricant has found, business accountants in their depreciation practice as a rule follow a general but very distinct pattern of behaviour. If there is such a thing as institutional objectivation of subjective attitudes, it applies to modern business accounting certainly no less than to market values.

We must here confine ourselves to this brief and very sketchy outline of an approach to a problem the intricacy of which has hitherto perhaps not always been fully recognized. We are painfully conscious of its many shortcomings, like the snares implicit in the construction of a price index of capital goods under conditions of technical progress or in disregarding intersectional output variations, but none the less we venture to put it forward as a contribution to the discussion.

7

FINANCE CAPITALISM? [1944]

INTRODUCTION

It is easy to see that the extension of economic research into the realm of dynamics will necessitate much closer co-operation between economic theorists and historians than has existed so far. Not only have historians to provide the empirical material with which to test our dynamic models. But, as it is impossible to conceive of dynamic processes as taking place against the quasi-stationary background of neoclassical economics, we have to provide, first of all, a proper setting for our models, a world in motion of which each dynamic process forms an element and from which it derives its impulse, its direction, and, hence, its significance. This world in motion provides the substance of, if it is not identical with, the historical process itself.

There are, however, obstacles to this closer co-operation which cannot be removed merely by repeated expressions of goodwill. Theorists, for instance, might profitably abstain from flaunting 'general' theories which are readily seen to rest on assumptions which are – and often enough are meant to be – mere transcriptions of the conditions of economic activity during some particular period of time, usually the theorist's own lifetime. Economic historians, on the other hand, are often confronted with a peculiar dilemma. In order to interpret the facts they have collected they need a theory, but the kind of theory best suited to their needs, viz. a theory with a time-dimension, theorists have thus far been unable to provide for them. Are we to blame them if then they evolve theories of their own, schemes of economic development 'by stages', models at the crudity and inadequacy of which the sophisticated may smile, but for which they have no substitute to offer? Or are we entitled to scoff if in their distress they address themselves to the art-historians, their seniors, to borrow their central concept, the Styles of Art, which they then adapt as 'economic systems'?

We believe that in promoting a more perfect harmony between theory and history the theorist will be most useful if his approach is made along the following line: He must, first of all, attempt to understand what problems the historians are trying to solve in evolving their various schemes and models. He should then examine the facts which figure prominently in these models as to whether they are facts relevant, or the facts most relevant, to the problems to be solved. If he is not satisfied with the relevance of the facts stressed by the historians, he must send them out for new facts. If he is satisfied with the relevance of the facts gathered by the historians, but finds their model incoherent or otherwise inadequate, he must out of the same facts construct a better model.

In the present paper we shall follow this procedure in examining certain views on the economic character of our time. In a terminology which seems to have found fairly wide acceptance this is described as an epoch of 'monopoly capitalism' and 'finance capitalism'. The latter epithet appears to merit closer attention than it has hitherto received. A whole literature has grown up in recent years around the problem of monopoly, its theoretical depth has recently been probed by Professor Schumpeter, and the impressive number of volumes embodying the result of the labours of the TNEC investigation testifies to the interest it has found in political circles. But finance capitalism has, on the whole, been neglected since Dr Hilferding first described the phenomenon in 1910,[1] and although a good deal of economic literature on current events implicitly reflects a theory of it, this theoretical position is hardly ever precisely stated or even recognized as such.

What is finance capitalism? Dr Hilferding defines 'finance capital' as 'capital controlled by banks and employed by industrialists' and describes it thus:

A steadily increasing proportion of capital in industry does not belong to the industrialists who employ it. They obtain the use of it only through the medium of the banks, which in relation to them represent the owners of the capital. On the other hand, the bank is forced to keep an increasing share of its funds engaged in industry. Thus the bank is increasingly being transformed into an industrial capitalist. This bank capital, i.e. capital in money form which is thus really transformed into industrial capital, I call 'finance capital'.[2]

Lenin, writing in 1916, thus enlarged on the subject:

> When carrying the current accounts of a few capitalists, the banks, as it were, transact a purely technical and exclusively auxiliary operation. When however, these operations grow to enormous dimensions we find that a handful of monopolists control all the operations, both commercial and industrial, of the whole capitalist society. They can, by means of their banking connections, by running current accounts and transacting other financial operations, first *ascertain exactly* the position of the various capitalists, then *control* them, influence them by restricting or enlarging, facilitating or hindering their credits, and finally they can *entirely determine* their fate, determine their income, deprive them of capital, or, on the other hand, permit them to increase their capital rapidly and to enormous dimensions.[3]

If it were true that finance capitalism, so defined, is one of the outstanding characteristics of our time, this proposition would be significant in at least three respects. It would, first of all, be a genuine contribution to the understanding of our time and its problems. Secondly, it would probably throw light on some problems which have resulted from the theoretical study of contemporary phenomena, like the investment problem or that of the various forms of monopoly, and thus be of help to the theorist. Thirdly, it might possibly establish a test case for the feasibility of 'short-cuts', for the possibility of gaining knowledge directly from the inspection of historical material without the lengthy and awkward roundabout journey of theoretical analysis. For these reasons, if for no others, the problem of finance capitalism would seem to merit a more detailed study.

CLARIFICATION

If we are to follow the procedure just outlined, our first task is to clarify the meaning of 'finance capitalism' by finding out what problem the introduction of this concept was meant to solve. The only way in which we can attribute meaning to a notion purporting to describe an economic phenomenon is by translating this notion into the vocabulary of economic theory. For economic theory provides us with a coherent frame of reference which permits us to see economic phenomena as the – intentional or unintentional – outcome of the pursuit of plans, and it is by reducing 'action' to 'plan' – and by this activity of the mind alone – that we 'understand' human action and can attribute meaning to it. Throughout this paper we shall assume that by finance capitalism is meant a type of economic development which is characterized by the shifting of the entrepreneurial function into the hands of 'financiers', investment bankers, i.e. intermediaries of the capital market, specialists in directing capital flows. We now have to show, first, that this is what our authors – 'really meant', that this is the sense in which their utterances have to be construed; and, secondly, that the thesis that finance capitalism in this sense is an outstanding feature of our age is a meaningful proposition, that whether true or not, and whatever the range of phenomena covered, it 'makes sense'.

Now, as to the first, it is easily seen that if Dr Hilferding says that 'the bank is being transformed into an industrial capitalist', what he means is a shifting of the function of industrial enterprise to the bankers, for the mere legal creditor-debtor relationship is economically irrelevant. If he defines finance capital as 'capital controlled by banks', the word 'control', we submit, must denote the exercise of the active, planning and decision-making function which characterizes the entrepreneur, and which in a dynamic economy determines the direction in which it moves; otherwise the location of this control would economically be a matter of indifference. Similarly, if Lenin says that the financiers 'first *ascertain exactly* the position of the various capitalists, then *control* them, influence them ... and finally they can *entirely determine* their fate'[4] the process he is describing is, we suggest, economically a shifting of the entrepreneurial function.

In order to accomplish the second part of the task of this section, viz. to show that the contention that finance capitalism is an outstanding feature of our age is a meaningful proposition, we must give a brief outline of the position which 'the entrepreneur' occupies in modern economics. As long as the family firm and the private partnership were the preponderant forms of business organization the location of the entrepreneurial function was no problem. There were occasionally 'sleeping' partners, it is true, but as a rule it was not difficult to identify those who were wide awake. But with the growth of joint-stock enterprise the question 'Who is the entrepreneur?' became a pertinent one. It is true that the official legal theory which underlies company law continues to ascribe this role to the shareholders,[5] but a whole literature from Walther Rathenau to Mr Burnham has shown this to be a fiction, even to those naïve minds who had not yet gathered as much from the financial press. That to ascribe the entrepreneurial function to the shareholders is absurd, is obvious enough once we have adopted the definition of enterprise as planning and decision-making activity in a world of change. Unfortunately this is far from being generally accepted, no doubt because so much of modern economics is still under the shadow of the static pattern of the classical school. In particular it has to be remembered that the theory of entrepreneurship has only gradually detached itself from the theory of profit, and to understand this problem we must therefore make a brief excursion into the history of economic thought.

The method by which the classical economists demonstrated the unity of the economic system was to design a theoretical pattern of symmetrical shape in which to each type of income – wage, rent, profit – there corresponded a 'factor of production' – labour, land, capital. When under the influence of J. B. Say and his school, profit came to be more clearly distinguished from interest, it became necessary, for the sake of symmetry, to invent a conceptual receptacle for this type of income; and thus the entrepreneur made his entry into economic theory. As the theory of profit developed it became evident that profit – unlike other forms of income – cannot exist in a stationary state, at least under competition. Then J. B. Clark showed that profit is a concomitant of economic change, and it seemed natural to conclude, as Professor Schumpeter did, that the entrepreneur is the man who engineers change. But unfortunately the main current of discussion turned in a different direction.

Professor Knight, discussing J. B. Clark, pointed out that 'the fatal criticism of this procedure of taking changes in conditions as the explanation and cause of profit is that it overlooks the fundamental question of the difference between a change that is foreseen a reasonable time in advance and one that is unforeseen'.[6] While this distinction and its corollary, the expectational nature of all action concerned with the future, have become the starting-point of most modern dynamic theory, it is to be regretted that it apparently has led Professor Knight to neglect another distinction, equally important, between man-made change and exogenous change, between change that is 'made' and chance that 'occurs'.[7] His argument, for all its incisive brilliance, runs almost exclusively in terms of knowledge and judgement; purpose and plan have no place in it. His is a world in which exogenous changes 'just happen' to men who, passively, react to them with varying degrees of foresight, the higher degrees of it giving rise to profit; it lacks the active element of change planned by man. For his own purpose, the analysis of profit, this may not matter much. It is just as possible to make profit by the correct anticipation of exogenous change (by speculation) as from change deliberately brought about (by enterprise). But this distinction, while possibly irrelevant to the theory of profit, is highly relevant to the theory of entrepreneurship. If, therefore, Professor Knight accords entrepreneurial status to the shareholders on the grounds that 'the final control is the selection of men to control in business organization, and this is inseparable from responsibility' while refusing it to the salaried manager because 'whenever we find an apparent separation between control and uncertainty-bearing, examination will show that we are confusing essentially routine activities with real control,'[8] he is, in our opinion, himself guilty of confusing the selection of persons to be entrusted with the task of carrying out changes with this activity itself. The mode of the latter is in no way determined by that of the former.

Enough, we trust, has been said to convince the reader that the location of entrepreneurship in modern joint-stock enterprise is as yet an unsolved problem. It is as a contribution to this problem that we have to look at the theory of finance capitalism. This theory avers that at a relatively late stage of the evolution of capitalism the active, planning and decision-making function in industry tends to devolve upon the representatives of financial interests. Prima facie it is not unplausible. Since the abdication of the modern shareholder there is a vacancy on the throne of joint-stock enterprise. It is not in conflict with economic theory, for economic theory has nothing to say about it. Whether it is not only plausible but true is the question to which we now have to address ourselves.

VERIFICATION

Any adequate empirical verification of the thesis under discussion would require nothing short of a comprehensive economic survey of the modern world. All we can do here is to examine a few facts from the recent economic history of the three industrially most advanced countries, Britain, Germany and the United States – the countries, that is to say, to which alone our thesis can apply – with regard to their relevance to our problem. The thesis under discussion, let us remember, is that in modern history the entre-preneurial, planning and decision-making function tends to shift into the hands of 'financiers', of the intermediaries of the capital market who specialize in directing capital flows. (This thesis will henceforth be referred to as 'the thesis' or 'the thesis under discussion.')

Wherever we may have to look for facts to bear out the thesis, British industry is not the place to look for them. On this point the strictures of the Macmillan Report[9] – especially in Part II, chapter IV – on the lack of contact between British finance and industry[10] are not yet forgotten. Nor can it be said that in this respect much has changed since 1931. It is certainly true that in the 1930s British industry has found the capital market far more accessible than before, but that has entailed none of the features of finance capitalism. A country to which an institution like the Bankers' Industrial Development Company came as a novelty, the terms of its intervention over the Ebbw Vale project in 1938 as something like a shock, and the resignation of Sir William Firth from the chairmanship of Richard Thomas & Co, and the events culminating in it as almost a financial sensation, is certainly no place to look for the manifestations of finance capitalism. All this, however, applies only to British home industry. Where British overseas enterprise is concerned the story is very different. As regards overseas mining enterprise, for instance,

> London has for many years been a great centre for the organization and finance of mining enterprise ... There has been slowly built up in England over the past 100 years or so a very efficient, very complex organization, financial, technical, industrial and commercial, which is spoken of as the London Mining Market. It is engaged in mining explor-ation in overseas countries, and in financing, developing and managing mining enterprises.[11]

As regards British industrial enterprise as a whole (both internal and overseas), the evidence for the existence of finance capitalism must therefore be regarded as inconclusive.

Prima facie the German case looks more favourable to our thesis. It is, of course, well known how much of German industry has been 'nursed' by banks. Moreover, Dr Hilferding and Lenin wrote with German examples in their minds. The prominent part played by the bankers of Cologne (like the A. Schaaffhausen'sche Bankverein) in establishing the industries of the Ruhr district is a notable example. But we have to remember that according to our thesis finance capitalism belongs to a late stage of capitalist evolution. Financial control over industry at the very beginnings of German industrialization is therefore no evidence for it. What evidence there is seems to point in the opposite direction.

In his careful and penetrating study of German banking (before 1930) Mr Whale observes that 'on the whole there was a tendency before the [last] War for the larger industrialists to become less dependent on the banks and to exercise greater initiative in their own sphere'.[12] This certainly applies to the 'heavy' industries of the Ruhr which about the turn of the century had reached economic maturity.[13] It is even more interesting to observe that the chemical and electrical engineering industries, which after 1900 were Germany's two outstanding 'young' industries, never fell under financial tutelage, even during the period of their economic immaturity.[14] In the chemical case this was most probably due to the high monopoly profits which allowed the industry to expand almost entirely out of its undistributed profits. But in the instance of electrical engineering it was due to the financial genius of Emil Rathenau,[15] who devised a special kind of holding company (*Finanzierungsgesellschaft*) for the financing of the public utilities on the development of which the process of his own company, the AEG, largely depended, thus retaining the central direction of the process of electrification while yielding to the bankers the control of the results of the process.[16] All this seems to bear out Mr Whale's conclusion:

> With regard to the question of leadership, it is always difficult to know how much is to be ascribed to personality and how much to circumstances. But it does seem significant that whereas in the period from 1850 to 1880, or thereabouts, the most outstanding men in business life were bankers –

Hansemann, Mevissen – in the following years they were industrialists – Rathenau, Kirdorf. In part at least this may be explained by the fact that the banks, having played their pioneer role, were now becoming more stereotyped in their business, and thus offered fewer opportunities to men of initiative.[17]

This conclusion, of course, openly contradicts the thesis. It must be added, however, that in the 1920s, after inflation and stabilization, there appeared certain phenomena which lend themselves to an interpretation in terms of it.

The United States is widely regarded as the Mecca of Finance Capitalism. On this point economists as different in background, sympathies and outlook as Thorstein Veblen[18] and the authors of the Macmillan Report are agreed.[19] More particularly, in the American mind our phenomenon is usually associated with that sphere of industrial influence which during the decades of economic expansion some prominent New York banking houses have been able to acquire and extend. It is hardly an exaggeration to say that to four out of five Americans Finance Capitalism is synonymous with the ascendancy of J. P. Morgan & Co. over a large field of American industry.

An exhaustive study of the relations between J. P. Morgan & Co. and the American Telephone & Telegraph Company (AT & T), America's largest industrial corporation (total assets over 4 milliard dollars), had been undertaken by the Temporary National Economic Committee (TNEC). In an investigation extending over several weeks, and in cross-examinations conducted by one of the ablest counsels of the Securities and Exchange Commission, nothing more germane to our problem came to light than attempts to monopolize the sale of AT & T bond issues. Even here Mr Whitney, a partner in J. P. Morgan & Co., was able to point out that whatever influence his firm may have had over AT & T financing was confined to bond issues, and to refer to

> the well-known fact that during that period [1906–39] they [AT & T] sold vast amounts of common stock, generally to their own stockholders, and a certain amount of convertible bonds during that period, all to their own stockholders, without any underwriting, and I think it is a fact that they increased the capital stock during this period something like 10 times without any relation to the bankers ... I think you

will find if you check the records ... that substantially more than half the total additional financing done from 1906 down to the present day was done through stock offered to their own stockholders, always at par and without underwriting of any kind.[20, 21, 22]

Practically all the bankers who gave evidence before the TNEC described their relationship to industry as the rendering of services in financial matters. Most of them emphasized the quasi-professional character of these services and added that the initiative lay invariably with their industrial clients. This point has found its classical formulation in the evidence which the late Otto H. Kahn gave in 1933 before the Pecora Committee:

> (A doctor) gets his clients by reason of his reputation for ability and for successful cures and for sound advice given. And so it is with the lawyer. So it is with the architect. And so in our case it has long been our policy and our effort to get our clients, not by chasing after them, not by praising our own wares, but by an attempt to establish a reputation which would make clients feel that if they have a problem of a financial nature, Dr Kuhn, Loeb & Co. is a pretty good doctor to go to.[23]

Testifying before the TNEC, Mr Whitney of J. P. Morgan & Co.[24] and Mr Mitchell, President of Bonbright & Co[25] used similar analogies between legal and financial advice. We must, of course, not forget that these are *ex parte* statements of the case.

But the TNEC investigation also revealed that the relationship between investment banker and industry is not always of the simple, quasi-professional type,[26] and that in fact there are cases in which bankers try to influence industrial management and managerial appointments. The case of the Cleveland-Cliffs Iron Company, on which the issuing bankers imposed fairly stringent conditions as to choice of officers, when in 1935 it converted a large bank debt into a bond issue, gave rise to the following exchange of views between the chairman, Senator King, Mr Leon Henderson (then) of the Securities and Exchange Commission, and the witness, Mr B. A. Tompkins, Vice-President of the Bankers' Trust Co.:

> *Chairman*: Would not a reputable investment house that sells its bonds to the public, even though it doesn't put up the

money itself but sells bonds and gets the money for its patron, be interested in having the company whose bonds it was selling or underwriting operated in a judicial manner and by persons competent to deal with the problems that would arise in the administration?

Mr Tompkins: Absolutely.

Chairman: Therefore, is there anything improper, in your judgement, and has it not been the practice not only with private individuals who are loaning money, but investment companies and banks, to inquire into the character of the business and who was in charge of it, and to desire to be satisfied as to the competency of the persons in charge to discharge their duties and obligations so as to make the business a success?

Mr Tompkins: That is always a very important consideration in handling money.

Chairman: So the investment company, I would suppose, would feel its honour was more or less involved when it sold securities to the public, though it did not advance its own money?

Mr Tompkins: Yes; it has a continuing responsibility to the people who buy the securities.

Mr Henderson: You get into a number of very delicate questions, do you not, when you get into the position of passing on management and its judgements. You get into what they call banker management once in a while, do you not?

Mr Tompkins: Yes. Management itself is a thing that a banker tries to avoid. He feels that his responsibility is to help select management, but wherever, in our experience, I have seen a banker as a banker try to operate an industrial company, the record of his management generally indicates that he ought to have stayed in the banking business.

Mr Henderson: That isn't always true, though. There are some examples where the bankers took over successfully.

Mr Tompkins: There are some examples.

Mr Henderson: But I think I would incline to agree with you that they ought to stick to their banking.

Mr Tompkins: In general.[27]

We may therefore conclude that the relationship between financial and industrial enterprises is of such a complex nature as to defy easy generalizations.

INTERPRETATION

Our attempt at an empirical verification of the thesis under discussion has not been successful. We endeavoured to 'let the facts speak for themselves' – and the facts said ever so many things, and said them in a somewhat ambiguous fashion. Some of the phenomena which we have observed bear an interpretation in terms of our thesis, others do not. Clearly, then, as our next step, we have to establish a criterion of distinction between the two classes of phenomena. Such a criterion has to satisfy two conditions. It must be sufficiently general to be of theoretical interest; unless it is on the same level of abstraction as economic theory in general we cannot fit it into our scientific edifice. But, secondly, it must not be purely formal; unless it helps us, not only to distinguish classes of phenomena, but *to understand why* the phenomena are different, it will make no contribution to the progress of our knowledge.

The thesis under discussion is a proposition about a social process. A social process consists of a number of mutually interrelated human actions. To analyse a social process means to explore the mode of this interrelationship, to dissect the process into actions. To understand an action means not only to know what it is 'for', its purpose, but also to know the plan behind the action, to reduce 'action' to 'plan'. In analysing a social process we have to start with the plans of the individuals, for it is their simultaneous attempts to carry out these plans – which may be inconsistent with each other and are to that extent bound to fail – which give rise to the process and determine its pattern. In analysing the process with which the thesis is concerned, we are studying the relationship between financial and industrial enterprise, and in tracing the pattern of financial action we shall learn what problems it sets out to solve.

The investment banker is a merchant of securities.[28] Being a merchant he tries to maximize his turnover. It is not, however, the total turnover of existing securities, but the number and magnitude of new issues forthcoming under his auspices that is of interest to him. And since new issues of securities will roughly (and with a few exceptions, one of which is important and will be discussed) represent new investment, it will usually be possible to say that the main source of the demand for his goods is saving, the main source of his supply new investment. A unit of production interests him solely in so far as it is, or is likely to become, a source of supply of those securities which he sells. Being, like every trader, by instinct a monopolist, he will try to secure for himself as large a number of supply sources as possible. But the efficacy of units of production as supply sources of securities depends on their capacity for expansion. Those that offer most extensive 'investment opportunities' will be most attractive to investment bankers.

Investment opportunities are never simply 'there'; they are the result of human action, the outcome of a process in which will-power and intensity of effort play a most prominent part. The number of them that can at each moment be regarded as 'data', waiting for a falling rate of interest to bring them into the limelight of industrial actuality, like pebbles on a beach which are exposed to the effects of light and air by the receding tide, is generally insignificant. Most investment opportunities owe their existence to innovations; they are creations of the human will, manifestations of enterprise. A 'lack of investment opportunities' will therefore indicate nothing so much as lack of enterprise. The innovations in which enterprise manifests itself may either take the form of changes in the combination of factors within a given unit of pro-duction (firm), or of the creation of new units, or of a modification of the relationship in which these units stand to each other, the 'structure of industry'. For fairly obvious reasons industrial enter-prise will find least difficulty in accomplishing the first, more in achieving the second, by far the most in the third kind of innovation.

Precisely at this point, where industrial enterprise falters, finan-cial enterprise enters the stage. In a progressive economy the financier has a function to fulfil. In order to describe this function we have to show, firstly, why it is a necessary function, secondly, why the financier is capable of fulfilling it, and thirdly, why it is in his interest to do so.

As to the first, it is obvious enough that a progressive economy is characterized by constant innovations which will frequently necessitate modifications of the industrial structure, the setting up of new industries, the reorganization of declining trades, etc. Confronted with such problems, industrial enterprise often fails, sometimes because they are beyond the reach of the management of a single firm, but sometimes for sheer lack of initiative, absence of strong business leadership, in short, for want of those human qualities which are indispensable to successful enterprise.[29] Secondly, in practically every instance innovation requires capital investment. (This is, of course, merely another way of saying that in a progressive economy innovation provides the main investment outlet for savings.) Now, the investment banker is a specialist in directing capital flows. By deflecting and withholding such flows he decides which investment opportunities will become actual innovations. Thirdly, since he is a merchant of securities, it is to his interest that savings do not run to waste, but find an outlet in investment and its financial counterpart, the flow of new securities. It is therefore to his interest to keep the flow of new securities on a level with the flow of savings, and to see to it that this level remains as high as possible.

To the rule that the source of new securities is new investment, there is an important exception, viz. the reorganization of businesses which have suffered capital loss. To this day economists have paid surprisingly little attention to the problems presented by bankruptcy and company reconstruction. The reason for their lack of curiosity has probably to be sought in their excessive preoccupation with the more spectacular (and measurable!) 'macrodynamic' aspects of capital. As long as changes in the amount of investment remain the only kind of capital change that can attract our attention, we are unlikely to discover the nature of the processes going on *within* that heterogeneous assortment of production goods with multiple uses. We shall have nothing to say, for instance, about *internal capital change*, or about the causes and consequences of malinvestment. It is precisely here that financial enterprise impinges upon our problem.

The reorganization of companies which have suffered capital losses is a kind of economico-surgical operation which requires the skilled hand of a specialist. The establishment of a business denotes the combination of various producers' goods (plant, equipment, raw materials, etc.) with a sum of money in such a way that the fixed resources, as it were (in the short run which here alone concerns us), form a receptacle for the circulating capital. Where this combination proves incapable of producing a net return over operating costs, the flow of circulating capital will be deflected from our combination of fixed resources, the receptacle will become empty, an example of 'excess capacity' presents itself. The solution of the dilemma evidently lies in transferring the fixed resources to some other use, 'to another industry', either bodily and 'as a going concern' (as, for instance, when an hotel with all its furniture and equipment is turned into a nursing home), or, perhaps, by partly dissolving the combination and changing its composition (as in the case of an unsuccessful theatre being converted into a cinema, where the stage settings become superfluous and can be disposed of by sale, but the combination has to be supplemented by the installation of a projector and screen). As error is a concomitant of rapid change, the recurrent necessity for such economic surgery is a regular and prominent feature of economic progress.

Such an economico-surgical operation requires the re-directing of the capital flow; somebody has to fill the new receptacle. The nature of the problem thus clearly points to a specialist in the directing of capital flows as the surgeon most likely to succeed.[30] Moreover, it is a task requiring a concentrated general knowledge of the whole economic system (such as one frequently finds in export merchants) surpassing that of the ordinary industrialist whose knowledge is necessarily specialized and restricted to *his* market, his plant, and to his industry. It is whenever problems of this kind have to be solved that the entrepreneurial function shifts into the hands of financiers. The *haute finance* is, as it were, the second line of defence of a free enterprise economy faced with problems of intersectional maladjustment. Where the task proves too intricate for ordinary industrial management the financier 'takes over'.[31] In the vernacular of Hollywood, he is the 'trouble shooter' of capitalism. This fact, once it is grasped, permits us to infer that a 'vanishing of investment opportunities' indicates nothing so much as a cracking of the second line of defence.

The criterion of distinction between cases in which the entrepreneurial function does, and those in which it does not, shift is therefore found in the appearance or non-appearance of problems with which industrial entrepreneurs are unable to cope. Finance capitalism, we may conclude, is not an epoch of economic history. It denotes the way in which a free enterprise economy adjusts itself to certain necessities when they arise, a type of response to problems, and a mode of solving them. There is no reason why we should not regard it as a recurrent phenomenon.

CONCLUSION

The thesis under discussion in this paper predicates the occurrence of a phenomenon as distinct in time from other phenomena. It suggests a view of economic history as a continuous succession of 'phases', each of which is more or less dominated and characterized by such a phenomenon and each of which is, by virtue of this fact, distinct from all other 'phases' preceding or succeeding it. In our particular case, the thesis asserts that the last phase of economic evolution in that part of the world that is industrially advanced and about which it is possible to generalize from experience – that is, roughly speaking, the half-century preceding the outbreak of the Second World War – was, in the sense mentioned, an age dominated and characterized by 'finance capitalism'.

What fragmentary evidence we were able to gather failed to support the thesis, at least in its historical aspect. A number of instances of 'finance capitalism' were found, but they did not conform to the time pattern postulated. In British industry, as late as for the 1930s, no such instances could be discovered, while in British overseas enterprise they could be traced back a very long time. In Germany instances were found at the very beginnings of industrialization and seemed to disappear later on. But we also noticed that in the 1920s, after inflation and stabilization, they showed a tendency to reappear.

We then applied to the phenomena observed the ordinary method of economic analysis which regards all events as the outcome of the pursuit of – possibly rival – human plans. It is true that in traditional static theory this method has hitherto only found a very limited range of application, confined to those cases in which the purpose pursued by individuals is to 'maximize' something. But it is readily seen that this is an entirely arbitrary restriction of the method, and that its potential range is co-extensive with all human activity which is conscious of its purposes, in other words, which is problem-solving activity and therefore capable of rational explanation; strategy is an obvious example where the method is in fact applied.

In studying the complex of phenomena described as 'finance capitalism' we were able to approach our subject from a new angle and to discover traits which thus far had gone unnoticed. We asked in the pursuit of what purpose it comes about that industrial entrepreneurship shifts into the hands of the specialists in directing capital flows, what problems present themselves to the minds of those concerned, what are the conditions of their successful solution. Finance capitalism, when seen from this angle, emerges as a type of action designed to meet a certain situation, an attempt to solve problems which for all we know about them need *not* be phenomena distinct in time but may well be recurrent phenomena.

We must leave it to the reader to judge whether in this way a deeper insight, a more satisfactory understanding of the problem has been achieved. But it is evident that his judgement will have an important bearing not only on the relative merits of 'methodological individualism' and 'methodological collectivism', but also on the issue which formed our starting-point in this paper viz. the mode of co-operation between economic theorists and historians. As Professor Hayek has repeatedly pointed out,[32] there is no inherent antagonism between those who evolve abstract patterns of human action and those who use them for the explanation of concrete events; the two methods are in fact complementary. There can, of course, be no historical narrative which is not at least an attempt at a rational explanation of the events narrated, for it is impossible to give any intelligible account of social phenomena in any other way. The greatest obstacle to closer co-operation between theorists and historians seems to lie in the fact that theorists find it difficult to produce models with time-dimensions, while historians cannot apply models which have no time-dimensions to the explanation of real processes which have. Moreover, one does not have to be a Bergsonian to feel some doubt whether the purely chronological concept of 'time' which historians seem bound to employ is necessarily the last word in the refinement of method which a social science is able to attain.

8

A NOTE ON THE
ELASTICITY OF
EXPECTATIONS [1945]

INTRODUCTION

In recent years the *Elasticity of Expectations* has come to occupy
a prominent place in dynamic theory. Economists, baffled by the
apparent intractability of expectations, which cannot be treated as
determined by other 'data' although it is clear that they are susceptible to economic experience,[1] were duly grateful for an analytical
tool which enabled them somehow to grapple with the matter. In
creating the concept Professor Hicks[2] has provided us with a
convenient criterion of classification of the modes of a relationship,
which we can use even though we may know nothing about the
causes and conditions of the various modes. More recently, Professor Lange, in his admirable investigation of the effects of flexible
prices on the volume of output and employment,[3] has made ample
use of the concept. Naturally, it has the defects of its virtues. As
the most elaborate thermometer can tell us nothing about the
causes of the fever from which the patient is suffering, so the elasticity of expectations, being a measure, can tell us nothing about
what causes the magnitude of our object of measurement.

But where, then, are we to turn for information about the factors
on which the magnitude of the elasticity of expectations depends?
Professor Hicks, it is true, has attempted to find an explanation
in 'the psychological condition of the individuals trading',[4] in the
greater or smaller 'sensitivity' with which different individuals
react to identical price changes. But this attempt to explain an
economic phenomenon by reducing it to one of 'group psychology' remains unconvincing, if for no other reason than that it
would commit us to the assumption that the same individual,
confronted at different times with price changes of equal magni-

tude, invariably reacts in an identical, and therefore predictable, manner. The causal explanation of the magnitude of the elasticity of expectations has to be sought elsewhere.

It seems to us that it can be found in an empirical fact quite familiar in the literature dealing with expectations that has sprung up during the last ten years, but which, for some strange reason, most authors treat as an obstacle to be overcome rather than as a potential element of their analysis. The fact we have in mind is the well known one that the object of our expectation is rarely one price expected with certainty, but usually a whole set of prices expected with various degrees of probability. Disregarding the most improbable prices we obtain what Professor Lange has called 'the practical range'.[5]

> Entrepreneurs and consumers need not, and usually do not, visualise an exact probability distribution of possible prices. For our purpose it is sufficient to assume that each person forms some idea about the most probable value and the 'practical range' of the expected price. For instance, an entre-preneur or consumer thinks that the price of some specified good at some given future date will be most probably $100, but in any case not less than $80 and not more than $150. He may believe that there is some slight probability that the price will turn out to be below $80 or above $150, but this is so small as to be negligible in practice and he takes the chances of disregarding such outcomes altogether. Such an assumption seems to be quite realistic.

Curiously enough, like most authors in this field, Professor Lange shows himself eager to discard this valuable discovery as soon as it is made, and the only use made of the 'practical range' is as a 'measure of the degree of uncertainty of price expectations'. He immediately proceeds to 'substitute for the most probable prices actually expected with uncertainty equivalent prices expected with certainty'. In this way the range is compressed to a point, a 'certainty-equivalent'.[6] This seems to be widely regarded as a gain, presumably because it is thought to facilitate comparison between actual and expected prices if both are brought to the common denominator of single values. By contrast, we shall try to show that by substituting single-value expectations for the uncertainty range of expected prices we stand to lose more than we gain, because reaction to price change will largely depend on the location of the prices affected within the scale of expected prices.

PRICE CHANGES WITHIN OR OUTSIDE OF AN 'INDIFFERENCE ZONE'

Let us assume that in Professor Lange's example in which expected prices range from $80 to $150, the actual market price was, to start with, $109.[7] Now, let the market price move, either rise above or fall below $109. It is readily seen that as the market price approaches the neighbourhood of the upper or lower limit, say, $140 or $90, expectations will tend to become inelastic. People will think that the price movement 'cannot go much farther', and anticipate a movement in the opposite direction, perhaps after a temporary stagnation; the narrower the uncertainty range the sooner expectations will become inelastic. On the other hand, as long as the market price moves between, say, $95 and $135, people's expectational reaction will not be affected by the actual movement and expectations will therefore be indifferent; the wider the range the larger is this 'indifference zone'. But as soon as the market price passes either the upper or the lower limit, a new situation arises. People, shocked out of their sense of normality, will have to readjust the basis of their predictions, and in the interval before forming a new, and probably wider, uncertainty range their expectations are likely to become elastic. A narrow range will thus at first, as we saw, cause inelastic expectations at an early stage of the price movement. But if in spite of them the movement continues, expectations will become elastic the sooner the narrower the range.

Two conclusions emerge from this reflection. In the first place, the existence of an uncertainty range gives a new significance to inelastic expectations. We can say that, as a rule, any price move-ment, if continued long enough, will sooner or later encounter inelastic expectations, because it will sooner or later touch the fringes of the range. Under anything like normal circumstances those inelastic price expectations of which Professor Lange has shown that 'given the monetary effect'[8] they 'always tend to stabil-ise the economy', will finally prevail. Within limits the economic system has a good deal more stability than appears.

Secondly, the degree of elasticity cannot be divorced from the kind of price change the reaction to which it measures. 'Explosive' price change is seen to be the main cause of elastic expectations, both in the sense of violent change, and in that it destroys the existing basis of expectations, the sense of normality, which provided a criterion of distinction between the more probable, the less probable, and the highly improbable. It does so by demonstrating that the highly improbable, which had been excluded from our range, is possible after all. Now, as we saw, a price will pass the limits of the range with difficulty. As it approaches them it encounters increasing pressure from inelastic expectations resulting in sales at the upper and purchases at the lower limit. To overcome the pressure of these stabilizing market forces the price movement will most probably have to be carried by a strong 'exogenous' force, i.e. one originating outside the market, unknown to it and therefore not taken into account when expectations were formed. Changes in the 'responsiveness' of the monetary system (only, of course, if they were not expected) are an obvious example.

An important objection may be raised against our method of analysis on the ground that to assume an uncertainty range invariant with respect to actual price change is to misinterpret the meaning of *Elasticity of Expectations*. The concept involves a relationship between an actual price change and an expected price change accompanying it. Are we, then, entitled to treat the range of expected prices as independent of actual change? When, in our example, we allow the market price to rise above, or fall below, $109, do we not have to assume a concomitant shifting of the range? It might even be argued that our conclusion about inelastic expectations in the neighbourhood of the limits follows merely from our assumption of an expectational range invariant with respect to actual change. Our reply to this is that we fail to see any plausible reason why the range should shift at all as long as the actual price moves within its limits, and that therefore the burden of proof is on the other side.

The objection mentioned raises, however, a fundamental issue in the theory of expectations. It vividly illustrates what is in our opinion the main defect of the 'elasticity of expectations', viz., the *purely mechanical* treatment of the relationship between actual and expected price change to which its use commits us. It compels us to interpret 'a given degree of elasticity' as meaning that every price change will lead to a proportionate shift in the range of expectations, irrespective of whether that price change was formerly regarded as probable, improbable, or whether it came as a complete surprise. That does not seem to us to be a sensible hypothesis, and we suspect that it would never have been made but for the fact that most economists, when they come to deal with the elasticity of expectations, have forgotten all about the uncertainty range and started to think exclusively in terms of a point-to-point comparison.

It seems preferable to base the relationship between actual and expected price change on a clear distinction between price phenomena which are consistent with the existing structure of expectations, fall 'within the range', and thus cause no disappointment – and phenomena inconsistent with the structure of expectations, which fall 'outside the range' a revision of which they necessitate. This vital distinction is apt to be concealed by the way in which the 'elasticity of expectations' is usually handled, even by so brilliant a performer as Professor Lange.

ELASTICITY DEPENDS ON INTERPRETATIONS

The reader might think it less than fair if we concluded these few critical remarks without at least giving an indication of a more positive point of view. We have criticized what we called the *purely mechanical* treatment of the relationship between actual and expected price change. By this we mean the treatment of the relationship as a mere 'reaction equation', which leaves no room for the *interpretation* of phenomena observed, an activity of the mind from which the relationship after all derives its meaning.[9] But what kind of treatment are we to substitute for it? We believe that progress in the theory of expectations is most likely to be made along lines like those to be described in what follows.

The formation of expectations is always incidental to the diagnosis of the situation in which we find ourselves; no prognosis without diagnosis. Such a diagnosis necessarily runs in terms of an analysis of forces. That we expect a certain event to take place at a future date τ_1 means that after a survey of what we regard as the major forces (obstacles included) likely to be operative in the period between 'now' and τ_1 we have arrived at the conclusion that their combined net result will be the event at τ_1. An expectation always implies a judgement on the character and strength of the economic forces producing change, believed to be major forces and operative in a situation. The *subjective* nature of expectations, due, in the first place, to divergences in individual interpretations of identical observable events, is thus seen to derive ultimately from divergent judgements on the strength of the economic forces believed to have caused them.

Now, expectations may be disappointed. When τ_1 becomes the present, our event may fail to happen, or an altogether different event may take place unexpectedly. We know then that our original diagnosis of the situation was wrong, that we had incorrectly assessed the strength of the various forces, or may have altogether ignored a major force, and we shall revise our diagnosis retrospectively.

In applying this reasoning to our uncertainty range we find that it offers a convenient framework for the testing of our diagnoses. A range extending from $80 to $150 means that people think they know enough of the nature and strength of the forces operative in their situation to allow them to predict that the price will be neither above $150 nor below $80. The width of the range expresses the degree of our uncertainty about the exhaustiveness of the information at our disposal. If we thought we knew everything relevant to the expected event about the forces, major and minor, which shape the situation, we could predict one price with certainty. An increasing range expresses an increasing uncertainty about the completeness of our knowledge.

The next point to grasp is that any price movement taking place between 'now' and τ_1, i.e. between the date at which the prognosis is made and the date to which it refers, can be regarded as a test of the diagnosis which forms the basis of our prognosis, throwing additional light on the nature and strength of the forces surveyed, and thus as adding to our information. As long as the price movement is confined to within the range, it does not provide relevant new information, but merely confirms the soundness of the diagnosis which found its expression in our range. That is why we said above that as long as the price moves within the middle reaches of the range, people's expectational reactions will not be affected by the actual movement and expectations will therefore be indifferent. But as soon as the price moves beyond the limits of the range, the inadequacy of the diagnosis on which the range was based becomes patent. A new situation has arisen which requires a new diagnosis.

We submit that if the objection mentioned above is valid, so that the elasticity of expectations has to be construed as implying that, with a given degree of elasticity, every actual price change, however people may interpret it, results in a corresponding shifting of the range, the concept would be deprived of all value as an analytical device. We should then reluctantly have to conclude that a formulation of the relationship between actual and expected price change, which refuses to seek the causes of expectational reactions in men's *interpretation* of observed phenomena, and compels us to substitute mechanical hypotheses for the logical analysis of a meaningful pattern of human action, cannot be regarded as a useful tool of economic analysis.

9

INVESTMENT
REPERCUSSIONS [1948]

INTRODUCTION

The modern theory of investment, set forth by Lord Keynes in the 'General Theory', has had its many triumphs these last twelve years, but it still has a number of gaps. Conceiving of investment as simple growth of a stock of homogeneous capital, it is ill-equipped to cope with situations in which the immobility of heterogeneous capital resources imposes a strain on the economic system. In particular, it can tell us little about the 'inducement to invest' in a world where scarcity of some capital resources co-exists with abundance of others.

At closer inspection, the theory of investment contains a micro-economic element, the theory of the investment decision, and a macro-economic element, exemplified in the multiplier. The former, modelled on the theory of the firm and on the analogy of the making of output decisions, explains how the individual investor arrives at his investment decision. The latter studies inter-relations between *aggregate investment* and other aggregate magnitudes, like consumption, incomes, and employment. The link between the two elements is provided by simple 'adding up'. The marginal efficiency schedule for the economic system as a whole is found as the sum of all the individual schedules in precisely the same way as the supply schedule of an industry is found as the sum of the supply schedules of individual firms. This, of course, is possible only where the individual schedules are determined independently of each other, that is to say under perfect competition; or, if under imperfect or monopolistic competition, then at least where individual schedules do not impinge upon each other. But under oligopoly such schedules can have no independent existence.

131

And as the largest and most interesting investment projects are likely to be found in fields such as railways and public utilities, where oligopoly is almost inevitable, it would appear that, at least over a wide field, there are no individual schedules sufficiently determinate to be woven into a ground design. Moreover, the effects of indeterminacy will not necessarily be confined to the oligopolistic 'industry'. The building of an additional blast furnace will affect investment decisions not merely in the oligopolistic steel industry but in many other branches throughout the economic system.

It would thus appear that there is scope for a study of the effects of investment decisions. How does investment affect the data on which other investment decisions are based? For these effects we propose the term 'investment repercussions'. The systematic study of these relationships is the task of the theory of investment repercussions. So far there is no such theory. Instead of a theory we have merely the dogmatic assertion that the effect of investment on further investment decisions is bound to be depressing; that over time, and in the absence of unforeseen change, the marginal efficiency of capital will decline.[1] Elsewhere we have endeavoured to show that this will be so only where all capital goods are more or less perfect substitutes, but that this absurdity is really inherent in the assumption of a homogeneous stock of capital.[2]

It is readily seen that mode and magnitude of the investment repercussions engendered by a given act of investment will depend on the power of the newly created capital good to add to or detract from the income-earning capacity of other capital resources, either existing or planned. And this effect will in its turn depend on the degree of complementarity or substitutability which exists between the new capital good and other capital goods, already existing or about to be created. In the one extreme case, where the new capital good is a perfect substitute for every other, the effect will be universally depressing. In the other extreme case of complementarity with all other capital resources, all incomes from capital will increase. Hence, the mode and magnitude of investment repercussions in any given situation depends on the shape of the capital structure in which the complementarity relations obtaining between all capital resources find their expression.

The theory of investment repercussions is thus seen to form an integral part of the theory of capital. In the present state of the latter, where the 'explanation of the rate of interest' in terms of a long-run equilibrium still takes precedence over all the more dynamic problems, our theory will, for its future development, clearly have to wait for a dynamic theory of capital, framed not in terms of equilibrium, but of process, which elaborates the various possible forms of structure. Theoretical development will have to be supported by a large number of empirical studies of the capital structure in modern industrial societies, both as regards the composition of the capital equipment of various industries, and as regards changes over time. In particular, the problems of capital *regrouping* in response to unexpected change call for special attention, both as to the technique employed and the consequences attending success or failure of such economico-surgical operations.

For these and other reasons the time for constructing a positive theory of investment repercussions, even in the shape of a first tentative model, is not yet. For the present we have to confine ourselves to the more humble tasks of preparing the ground and surveying the site. This chapter is in the main a critical examination of certain gaps in the current theory of investment. In the following section we shall examine the nature and consequences of the 'missing link' between the micro-economic theory of investment decisions and the macro-economic theory of aggregate investment. It will be seen that in order to forge the link we have to go beyond equilibrium analysis. In the final sections we shall consider three concrete economic problems, and endeavour to show that a theory of investment repercussions would be capable of throwing much needed light on each of them.

THE RELATION OF NEW INVESTMENT TO CHANGES IN THE USE OF EXISTING CAPITAL

The building of a railway, by making possible new types of intensive farming and other uses of adjacent land, engenders a land boom. Metallurgical research, financed by an engineering concern (investment in knowledge) leads to the discovery that, in certain circumstances, cheap low-grade ore can be substituted for expensive high-grade ore. As a result income from, and capital value of, the low-grade ore-fields rise considerably. Life in a sleepy seaside resort is stirred up by the opening of a casino, and capital values of hotels, antique shops, and restaurants soar. We are all familiar with such cases. What is their relevance to the theory of investment?

In each of the three cases mentioned new investment makes it possible to use certain existing capital resources *complementary to it* in a new and more profitable way. Hence, in each of the three cases investors could considerably enhance their profits by buying these existing resources *at the value they have in their present uses*. In fact, on the general postulate of profit maximization, this is what they are bound to do.

How does this fact, exemplified in our three cases, fit into the Keynesian theory of investment? At once we confront serious analytical difficulties. In the first place, in the Keynesian edifice there is no room for capital complementarity. Where the relationship between different types of capital is discussed, competitiveness is almost invariably taken for granted. This applies as well to the relationship between present and future investment, where it clearly rules out all but one type of investment repercussions, as to that between present investment and existing capital.[3]

Secondly, the marginal efficiency of capital, the chief motive-power of investment and the central concept of the theory, is explicitly defined with respect to 'not the market-price at which an asset of the type in question can actually be purchased in the market, but the price which would just induce a manufacturer to produce an additional unit of such assets.'[4] Prices of existing assets do not come within its scope. But if they do not come within its scope they cannot influence investment decisions, while in reality, undoubtedly, income and capital gains to be derived from the purchase of existing capital assets complementary to the new investment are a very strong incentive to invest.[5]

It might be thought that this dilemma could be overcome by relating the marginal efficiency of capital not to an asset, but to a group of assets. Could not a group of complementary capital assets, some of which exist and some of which are about to be produced, be regarded as a *unit of capital* with a marginal efficiency attached to it as a whole? Should not the total income to be derived from both classes of assets, old and new, be compared with the rate of interest on the capital laid out on purchase of the old and production of the new? The answer is here that if the degree of complementarity between old assets and new investment were fixed, so that the old assets formed a constant proportion of the asset group, the marginal efficiency might be thus redefined, but that in reality there is no reason to believe that this is necessarily so. And where it is not so, the marginal efficiency of capital thus redefined would not, in conjunction with the rate of interest, uniquely determine the amount of investment.

There is thus no escape from the dilemma that if we confine the concept of marginal efficiency to assets newly created, we leave out what we know to be in reality an important factor in investment decisions; while if we extend it to all assets, old and new, it will not tell us the amount of new investment. Behind this dilemma there loom even wider issues. In the three cases discussed, the root of all trouble lies in the impossibility of separating the effect of new investment from the effect of new uses of existing assets. And where such separation is impossible, traditional equilibrium analysis with its *ceteris paribus* assumptions becomes inapplicable. For where capital resources are diverted to uses other than those for which they were planned, the *cetera* are no longer *paria*. The value of capital assets in their new uses will no longer correspond to their cost of production, and it becomes impossible to speak of a 'given quantity of capital'. Equilibrium analysis, both of the long- and short-run variety, has to be superseded by some more appropriate method of analysis.

It is not difficult to see what this new method will have to be. Equilibrium analysis, in the broadest meaning of the term, provides a framework for testing the consistency of the plans of different people and classes of people, producers and consumers, investors and savers, employers and employees, etc. It cannot tell us why people make these plans, nor how they will 'react' to the disappointment suffered if their individual plan fails to pass the consistency test – if they become 'extra-marginal' buyers or sellers.

Even less can it tell us what happens where a production plan is interrupted by withdrawal of a resource *before* the final test, which is, of course, the case where a capital instrument is switched over from one use to another. Furthermore, in equilibrium analysis outside events cast their shadow by causing quantitatively measurable changes in data. An event that fails to register such a change is economically irrelevant. But a change in the mode of use of an existing capital asset is not a quantitatively measurable change, since it does not alter the quantity of capital. Hence, no change in data has taken place unless we include the capital coefficients, i.e. the proportions in which the various capital resources are combined, in our data.

All this points in the direction of the type of *plan* analysis expounded by Professor Lindahl[6] and illustrated by Dr Lundberg's model sequences.[7]

In a market economy capital resources are employed, in conjunction with labour services, in a number of productive processes, guided and co-ordinated each by a production plan, turning out output. These plans need not, in fact are unlikely to, be consistent with each other. But the market for output provides a consistency test for these production plans. Those plans which repeatedly fail to pass the test, i.e. to earn the profit in anticipation of which they were undertaken, will, sooner or later, have to be revised. The revision of plans is the function of the entrepreneur, as the carrying out of them is that of the manager. Now, in a market economy we shall also find a market for capital resources. Here demand will, of course, largely depend on expectations manifesting themselves in the new plans to be started, and so will the supply of *new* capital goods. The supply of *existing* capital resources largely depends on those discarded from plans that had to be revised. In fact we might almost say that their supply indicates the failure of past plans – as, in an ancient town, the merchants' palaces turned into hotels, the former stables now garages, and the old warehouses which have become modern workshops, remind us of the impossibility of planning for the remote future. The continual revision of plans, an inevitable concomitant of an uncertain world, will therefore affect the supply schedule of capital resources.

In reality, of course, the capital market here discussed consists of a network of markets for concrete capital goods, linked to each other by relationships of substitution and complementarity. It is important to realize that all services employed within the same plan are, as a means to the same end, necessarily *complements*, whilst factor substitution, whenever it does take place, is an incident of plan revision. In other words, for most of the time, the capital coefficients, i.e. the proportions in which the capital resources employed are combined within a given plan, are constant, but when the plan comes up for revision, some substitution may take place and the coefficients change. It is readily seen what these discontinuous changes in the production function must entail for the stability of the relative prices of capital goods. The prices of goods the relationship between which can and does turn from complementarity (in period P1) to some degree of substitutibility (at T1), to another mode of complementarity (in period P2) terminated by a new dose of substitution (at T2) etc., etc., will evidently be liable to violent fluctuations. There is here no question of stable supply and demand functions. All that can be said is that:

1 Supply of existing capital goods is the cumulative result of plan revisions necessitated by past failures rather than a function of any current mode of action.
2 Demand is largely shaped by expectations in general, and the demand for *new capital* will be particularly directed to those resources that can be used as complements to existing ones.
3 Supply of new capital goods, and particularly the concrete form they take, will largely depend on their complementarity to existing ones. Indeed it is hard to imagine any process in which only new and no old capital resources are employed.

Whilst equilibrium *over time* is thus practically ruled out, even equilibrium *at a point of time* could hardly be stable. Where so much of the supply depends on 'bygones', supply will be highly inelastic between an upper level, set by the cost of producing new resources, and a lower level set by scrap value. Demand, on the other hand, depends on individual expectations, which may diverge widely, and for which, in the absence of forward markets, there exists no test of consistency.[8] Moreover, the price one is willing to pay for a capital good will also depend on the prices at which its complements in the prospective combination have already been bought, or are expected to be available in the future. There is thus here no question of 'recontract'. In each market a highly erratic demand, depending on individual expectations and simultaneous events in other markets, confronts an inelastic supply and engenders price oscillations.

It remains to add that where it is possible to buy resources at prices corresponding to their value in their *present* uses, and turn them over to other, more profitable, uses of which the rest of the market is at the time ignorant, large capital gains can and will be made. In a dynamic world the successful performance of this function, based on realization of the effective possibilities of capital regrouping which are inherent in a given situation, is the real test of entrepreneurship. And these capital gains, which, of course, could not exist in a stationary state, converted into income flows by means of bonus shares and other financial devices, are the ultimate source of profits.[9]

To sum up, then, all new investment entails some change in the mode of use of existing capital. There can be no such change without some revision of plans. Investment decisions always entail such changes, and can therefore profitably anticipate them. This fact a theory of investment must not ignore.

A few remarks may be added on the role of the stock exchange in dynamic economics.

Most of what has just been said about markets for capital resources applies, with whatever degree of strictness is possible in such matters, to the stock exchange, the central market for capital resources. In a world of corporate enterprise it is hard to imagine any important act of capital regrouping that would not take the form of a deal in shares, such as the acquisition of majorities, formation of subsidiary companies, etc. On the other hand, capital resources and their structural relationships are not identical with the legal titles to them. Although a transfer of titles may indicate a change in the capital structure, it need not do so: at any moment we may observe shares moving from one investment portfolio to another without any consequent change in production plans.

But these 'purely financial' exchanges constitute merely a secondary phenomenon which, at least at our present level of abstraction, may be safely neglected. For these details in shares, even while not accompanied by production changes, are nevertheless *expectationally* linked to them. Nine times out of ten what impels shareholders to exchange shares are divergent forecasts of business plans. Thus, while such exchanges may have direct effects on production plans (except in the case of new issues), they are nevertheless oriented towards them, and are therefore of a derived nature. Entrepreneurs express their expectations by forming and reshuffling capital combinations; shareholders express theirs by forming and reshuffling investment portfolios based on their expectations of entrepreneurial success. We are here confronted with a secondary phenomenon which must not be allowed to obscure our field of vision while we are analysing our primary phenomenon, the factors causing the formation and disintegration of capital combinations. This is not to say that speculative movements may not help or hinder entrepreneurial planning by affecting the prices of existing resources required for new combinations. The point at issue is that, but for the anticipated results of such planning, these movements would not take place.

THE ANALYSIS APPLIED TO VERTICAL INTEGRATION

We shall now test the efficiency of the analytical tools we have forged by applying them to three concrete economic problems which have thus far proved somewhat impervious to theoretical analysis.

Vertical integration is an industrial phenomenon in the explanation of which economic theory has not been outstandingly successful. While horizontal integration, as a phenomenon of monopoly, is easily disposed of, vertical integration does not seem to fit into any particular pigeon-hole. It is readily seen that under ordinary competition no distinct advantage attaches to the possession of either sources of supply or market outlets,[10] and it is equally readily inferred that therefore vertical integration pays only in the absence of competition. It is true that the two most prominent instances, the coal–steel–heavy engineering and oil-refining–distributing combinations, are not examples of pure monopoly. But the general conclusion appears to be that then vertical integration is a phenomenon of oligopoly, a tactical device employed by oligopolists to hold their own in an area of unceasing economic warfare.[11]

That vertical integration is a phenomenon of oligopoly we do not seek to deny. It seems to us, however, that as a causal explanation this is a rather narrow view of the matter. The indeterminacy of equilibrium under oligopoly has in recent years been widely discussed. But it has never been sufficiently emphasized that the real cause of indeterminacy is here not the fewness of sellers, but the absence of static conditions and the necessity of action based on expectations most probably inconsistent with each other. Producers under oligopoly are in a position in no way different from that of any other producer under dynamic conditions. They have to act on guesses instead of on data, and their guesses will probably be, at least partly, inconsistent with each other. (Even were they perfectly consistent they may yet turn out to be wrong.) Without consistent expectations there can be no equilibrium. The conditions of business under oligopoly are thus incompatible with the framework of static theory, set by its objective data.

Seen from this wider point of view, vertical integration is a device for co-ordinating plans for successive stages of production in a world of uncertainty. The argument that under competition nothing is to be gained from it, is a half truth, for this is so only under static conditions. In an uncertain world the fact that a given material is available today at a given price does not entail that it will be so available tomorrow. By vertical integration we make sure that it will be. Once we substitute plan analysis for equilibrium analysis, vertical integration ceases to be an economic mystery capable of *ad hoc* explanations. We may add that vertical integration will probably be accompanied by capital gains. We noted above that as the capital value of any resource depends on the prospective profitability of the process in which it is employed and on the prices which have to be paid for the services of complementary factors, any transfer of resources from one process to another will result in a capital gain. Vertical integration is a device by which we fix the prices of complementary services, and thus reduce the aura of risk surrounding the determination of capital values.

THE ANALYSIS APPLIED TO DEVELOPMENT OF BACKWARD AREAS

The development of resources in 'backward areas' is a subject which has of late attracted a good deal of attention. Economists and others have pointed out that capital investment in 'underdeveloped' areas, financed out of the ample savings of industrial countries with high income levels, would confer benefits on all concerned. While raising the marginal productivity of labour, and thus the standard of living in 'backward' areas, such capital investment would at the same time enable the 'forward' areas of the globe to find profitable investment outlets for their potential surplus savings. In the absence of a full employment policy in industrial countries it would even be true to say that the social cost of such overseas investment programmes might be nil if those employed in them would otherwise be idle.

But such schemes are by no means universally welcomed by the inhabitants of these areas. There have been cases in which even offers of relief and rehabilitation by non-profitmaking international agencies, set up for this very purpose, had a cold reception, e.g. in some countries of south-east Asia. Suspicions of 'colonial exploitation' appear to be widespread. Some of this hostility to foreign-controlled investment and enterprise can, no doubt, like other forms of nationalism, be regarded as a manifestation of economically irrational, political myth-making. But there is undeniably some evidence for a belief that in the past the benefits of such investments have been somewhat unequally divided. The question we shall ask now is whether there exists an objective *criterion* of 'colonial exploitation'.

The usual explanation of such phenomena runs, of course, in terms of the monopsony for labour and other native services which the foreign entrepreneurs are said to enjoy, and which is said to enable them to reap unduly large profits. It is hard to see, however, how the entry of foreign entrepreneurs into the labour market could do anything but lessen the degree of monopsony. If this degree remains high, it must have been even higher before, and there is no reason to believe that without foreign intervention income distribution would have been any more equal. We believe that the explanation has to be sought along other lines.

The economics of colonial development is fundamentally simple. The apparent paradox of native poverty in the midst of seemingly abundant natural resources vanishes when we remember the necessary *complementarity* between natural and capital resources. Without the co-operation of capital in the form of transport, equipment[12] and, perhaps most important, knowledge of what to do with them, these natural resources would mostly lack economic character. Already Menger pointed out, and Professor Hayek recently reminded us, that one of the chief functions of the accumulation of capital is to create possibilities of economic use for natural resources for which so far there had been none, and thus to convert objects without economic value into economic resources.[13] Now, as we saw earlier, whenever a resource is taken out of one productive combination and inserted into another more profitable one, a capital gain equal to the capital value of the difference between the income it would earn in the former and in the latter will accrue to the owner. In our case therefore a capital gain equal to the *total capital value* of the natural resources in their prospective uses will accrue to entrepreneurs. It is these large capital gains which offer the glittering prizes of colonial enterprise. It is their disbursement in dividends and bonuses which is probably mainly responsible for the impression of 'exploitation'. And we may suspect that it is in rivalry for them, since they can only be made once, and not in any 'struggle for markets', that we have to look for the 'economic basis of imperialism'.

Complementarity is not, however, confined to the factors jointly employed, under a given plan, in one production unit. Throughout the economic system there exists some degree of complementarity of all resources. The capital investment in a Rhodesian copper mine, for example, is complementary to that invested in copper refining and processing industries in Europe and America. But it also is complementary to all, or most, other resources of the Rhodesian economy. With respect to the investment repercussions emanating from such investment we may therefore distinguish between those that are *external* to the country in which the investment takes place, and those that are *internal* to it. Now, there have been cases in the past where the investment repercussions of foreign investment in an undeveloped country were almost exclusively external. Chile, where foreign capital investment, concentrated in copper mines and nitrate fields, had very few effects on the rest of the economy, seems a case in point.[14] On the other hand, the building of the American railroads, by creating investment opportunities which in turn created new opportunities for further investment, engendered almost a wave of internal investment repercussions. It seems to us that it is possible to use the absence of internal investment repercussions from foreign-controlled capital investment in an undeveloped country as a criterion of 'exploitation'. From the point of view of colonial welfare economics, investment can be graded according to the investment repercussions, internal to the colonial economy, which emanate from it. The more new investment opportunities it engenders, and the more it enhances the value of native resources by opening up new types of uses for them, the more desirable foreign investment will be for the undeveloped country.

It is to be regretted that the growing interest of economists and others in the economic progress of underdeveloped areas, has not been matched by a more profound theoretical analysis of the factors and processes involved. Here, as in other branches of applied economics, the virtual non-existence of a theory of capital which could be applied to concrete problems, was bound to make itself painfully felt. For instance, much talk is now heard of 'planned regional development' of backward areas. While the implicit recognition of the complementarity of all resources in a region, and of the necessary simultaneity of their expansion, is welcome, the over-all complementarity of all resources in the world must not be ignored. It is clearly as impossible to preclude all external investment repercussions as it is undesirable that they should completely outweigh the internal ones. While there is a good deal to be said for TVAs in many parts of the globe, it must not be forgotten that the original version was made possible by the tax-payer in New York and Chicago. In a world of full employment, industrial countries cannot be expected to invest part of their savings overseas without any benefit to themselves, which benefit in this case means some complementarity to their own existing resources. In other words, not the region, but the world, would have to be planned.

It is time to remind the reader that we are here interested in colonial welfare economics only in so far as it serves to illustrate a purely theoretical argument about investment repercussions. Whilst proposals for the promotion of colonial welfare are defi-nitely beyond the scope of this chapter, it appears from what has been said that there is need for an international institution which, while encouraging foreign investment in underdeveloped areas, would supplement it with investment programmes of its own, designed to redress the balance between internal and external investment repercussions, whenever the former proved to be inadequate.

THE ANALYSIS APPLIED TO THE TRADE CYCLE

Finally, we shall test the significance of our newly gained knowl-edge by asking what light, if any, it sheds on the group of phenom-ena known as 'the trade cycle'. Most modern trade cycle theories regard fluctuations in investment activity as the main cause of the fluctuations in incomes and employment. If this is so, anything that affects investment must also indirectly affect these fluctuations.

Our argument in this paper has been two-fold. First, we endeav-oured to show that owing to the complementarity of all assets, existing and potential, in the production plan of an enterprise, a sharp separation between new and old capital assets is not possible, and the 'marginal efficiency of capital' based on this distinction is not a useful tool of analysis. Secondly, we argued that owing to the complementarity of all capital goods in an economic system, any investment project carried out would by itself modify the environment in which other investment decisions are made.

In this way every major investment engenders a wave of invest-ment repercussions, favourable or unfavourable to further investment decisions. The followers of Lord Keynes with remark-able unanimity have thus far stressed the unfavourable repercussions due to the substitutability of capital, while ignoring the favourable repercussions due to complementarity. The onset of economic depression is today almost universally ascribed to the 'exhaustion of investment opportunities'. It seems to us, however, that, in matters of the trade cycle, it would be prudent to adopt a more cautious and eclectic attitude. In fact, our waves of investment repercussions suggest nothing so much as the 'long waves' of economic expansion (Professor Schumpeter's 'Kondratieffs') witnessed between 1840 and 1870, or between 1895 and 1920.[15] Whether or not it is quite accurate to ascribe the whole momentum of these two phases of expansion to railway construction and electrification respectively, we should regard it as sufficient to find their historical origin there. All further developments could be interpreted as effects of investment repercussions. Railways and electrification did not merely offer favourable investment opportunities – they changed the world.

In any case, it is difficult to see how, say, the crises of 1847 or 1900 could be ascribed to 'exhaustion of investment opportunities'. Everyone knew they were not exhausted. The possibility that different explanations may have to be found for different types of disturbances, and that it may be wrong to think of the trade cycle as a one-model show, thus cannot be disregarded. In matters of the trade cycle the time seems ripe for a retreat from dogmatism and an advance in the direction of eclecticism.

Part III

DIAGNOSING THE AUSTRIAN SCHOOL'S 'GREAT DEPRESSION'

10

AUSTRIAN ECONOMICS UNDER FIRE

The Hayek-Sraffa duel in retrospect
[1986]

INTRODUCTION

When the history of economic thought in the twentieth century comes to be written, there is no doubt that the decade of the 1930s will occupy a very special place in it. The 'Keynesian revolution', the rise of new theories of competition such as those of Chamberlin and Joan Robinson, the beginnings of growth theory in Harrod's work, all belong to this decade. Prominent thinkers of the century, such as Hicks and Shackle, published their first writings during it. The 1930s were indeed 'years of high theory'.

For Austrian economics, however, this was a tragic decade. Owing to the political circumstances of the time many Austrian philosophers and economists were compelled to leave Austria. Some of the emigrants were successful in the countries of their adoption, others were not. Professor Hayek, having made a triumphal entry into the University of London in 1931 as Tooke Professor of Economics and Statistics, had become a rather lonely figure by 1939, when the London School of Economics was evacuated from its London premises for the duration of the Second World War. The decline in the fortunes of Austrian economics is usually attributed to the Keynesian revolution and the success of the full employment policy in Nazi Germany, its historical background, which made even liberal economists cast furtive glances at what they otherwise professed to abhor.

In 1967, in *The Hayek Story*, Sir John Hicks wrote

When the definitive history of economic analysis during the nineteen-thirties comes to be written, a leading character in the drama (it was quite a drama) will be Professor Hayek.

Hayek's economic writings ... are almost unknown to the modern student, it is hardly remembered that there was a time when the new theories of Hayek were the principal rival to the new theories of Keynes (Hicks, 1967, p. 203).

The Keynesian revolution is usually dated to 1936 as 'the new theories of Keynes' took shape in the *General Theory of Employment, Interest and Money* published in February 1936. In this chapter we shall be concerned with an episode four years earlier, in 1932, when the new Austrian theories to which Hayek gave provisional shape in *Prices and Production* (1931) incurred the wrath of Mr Piero Sraffa, who reviewed the book in an article 'Dr Hayek on Money and Capital' in the *Economic Journal* of March 1932. In the June issue Hayek wrote 'Money and Capital: a Reply'. His reply drew a brief two-page rejoinder from his opponent.

Sraffa's review was an onslaught conducted with unusual ferocity, somewhat out of keeping with the tone ordinarily adopted by book reviewers in the *Economic Journal*. It is significant that the altercation took place less than a year after Hayek's arrival in London. The new Austrian ideas had barely been presented by him when they were challenged by a scholar with an international reputation for incisive analysis, who, supposedly engaged in other fields, had gone out of his way to deliver the onslaught.

What was the ordinary economist of 1932 to make of all this? The feeling prevailing in London and other British universities was one of utter bewilderment. Hayek's ideas had been difficult to grasp. In Hicks' words, '*Prices and Production* was in English, but it was not English economics. It needed further translation before it could be properly assessed' (Hicks 1967: 204). Sraffa's review, however, was evidently not designed to provide such a translation. It appeared to proceed from assumptions no more familiar than were Hayek's. The more perceptive sensed that they were witnessing a clash of two irreconcilable views of the economic world. The less perceptive were just puzzled by what the two contestants were after. But nobody liked what he saw.

Here we have to remember that the possibility that these were the opening shots in a battle between two rival schools of economic thought was not one that would readily occur to the average Anglo-Saxon economist of the 1930s. The *Methodenstreit* was happily a matter of the past. The conviction of the unity of economic thought was a major article of the creed of the graduate schools.

School rivalries belonged to an unenlightened past one had fortunately left behind. When Keynes, in the *General Theory*, began to talk about 'classical economists', to denote his own thought by contrast to theirs, even some of his closest friends began to feel uneasy. This was to them a new and unfamiliar mode of discourse.

With the Austrian emigrés the conviction of the unity of economic thought was strong, and in the circumstances of their emigration naturally became stronger.[1] For Hayek Paretian general equilibrium was the pivot of economic theory, the centre of gravity towards which all major economic forces tended.[2] For him the task of trade cycle theory was to show how it came about that these major forces were temporarily impeded and their effects delayed, and since the cycle was supposed to start with a boom and end with a depression, he saw in the depression the ultimate triumph of the equilibrating forces.

His opponent took a very different view of the modern market economy. Equilibrium meant to him something quite different.

THE BACKGROUND TO SRAFFA'S ATTACK

Mr Sraffa's review of Hayek's book was his only publication in twenty-five years, from *The Laws of Returns under Competitive Conditions* (Sraffa 1926) to his Introduction to the Ricardo edition of the Royal Economic Society in 1951.[3] This fact in itself indicates the significance its author attributed to his review. In 1932 most contemporary economists missed this significance and, as we saw, were baffled by Sraffa's piece and Hayek's reply to it. Fortunately, in the 1980s we are in an altogether different position.

With the benefit of hindsight we are now able to understand that Sraffa's critique of Hayek's book marked the start of the neo-Ricardian counter-revolution. This is usually dated to 1960, the year in which Sraffa published his famous book *Production of Commodities by Means of Commodities* which bore the subtitle *Prelude to a Critique of Economic Theory*. We can now see that Sraffa's paper in 1932 was, as it were, a prelude to this *Prelude*. The aim of the neo-Ricardian counter-revolution is to undo the subjectivist revolution in economic thought which took place in the 1870s, led by Jevons, Menger, and Walras, in which it was shown that the value of economic goods depends on the (subjective) utility they have to different individuals, and not on their (objective) cost of production. And since Menger and his

Austrian successors were, among the assailants of the classical citadel in the 1870s, the most consistent subjectivists, while in the School of Lausanne the original Walrasian subjectivism of utility was soon sterilized in the shape of Paretian indifference curves, it is perhaps not surprising that a prominent Austrian economist became the first target of the new counter-revolution.

Seen from the perspective of today, it is not at all hard to understand why the readers of 1932 were so puzzled by this attack on Hayek: they never were told from what kind of a position it was made. For in this encounter Mr Sraffa wore a strange mask. He never informed his readers that the presuppositions of the views he presented to them, since they reflected an analytical creed which had fallen into oblivion sixty years earlier and was therefore bound to be unfamiliar to them, were, to them at least, 'new'. The reason for the disguise he chose to wear is obvious. Had he told the readers of the *Economic Journal* plainly that his criticism of the book under review proceeded from a Ricardian view of the nature of the economic system, he could not have hoped to carry many of his readers with him. The neo-Ricardian counter-revolution, in the circumstances of 1932, could not be expected to win adherents before its main articles of faith had been espoused in public, and this could hardly be done in a review article. As Sraffa's main aim evidently was to discredit Hayek in the eyes of the readers of the *Economic Journal*, who were brought up on a Marshallian view of the economic system, he had better not let them know how different were his views from theirs. For his polemical purpose it was better that they should be puzzled than that they might become suspicious.

Contemporary readers, by contrast, know the history of the counter-revolution and can turn their historical knowledge to good account. Moreover, they are enjoying the benefit of the writings of the post-Sraffa generation, such as those of Professor Garegnani (e.g. 1976), Dr Levine (1980) and Dr Milgate (1979). Having lived through twenty years of the 'revival of Classical Political Economy', whether or not impressed by the sheer verve and mental vigour of its proponents, if not by their achievements, we have learnt a good deal we did not know in 1932.

In only two brief passages of Sraffa's article do we catch a glimpse of his anti-subjectivist aim and Ricardian purpose. A footnote on p. 47 ends with the words 'Dr. Hayek, who extols the imaginary achievements of the "subjective method" in economics, often succeeds in making patent nonsense of it'. On p. 50, in discussing disequilibrium in the cotton market, he is compelled to define what he means by equilibrium. So we read: 'But if, for any reason, the supply and the demand for a commodity are not in equilibrium (i.e. its market price exceeds or falls short of its cost of production), its spot and forward prices diverge.' Here it becomes quite clear that to Sraffa equilibrium means 'classical' long-run cost-of-production equilibrium (that is, price equals cost of production), a norm from which market prices always diverge, while to Hayek equilibrium is 'neoclassical' market-clearing equilibrium in all markets (what neo-Ricardians nowadays call 'supply-and-demand equilibrium') with no particular regard being paid to the difference between the long and short run. And here, then, we have got to the bottom of our dispute and are provided with a clue to most of the other points at issue between the two contestants.

Hayek clearly perceived that the attack on him was conducted from (what in 1932 was) a somewhat unorthodox position and, we may guess, sensed that his opponent had something of substance to hide. So he issued a challenge to him. 'I should also like to ask him to define his own attitude to these problems more clearly than he has yet done. From his article one gains the impression that his attitude is a curious mixture of, on the one hand, an extreme theoretical nihilism which denies that existing theories of equilibrium provide any useful description of the non-monetary forces at work and, on the other hand, of an ultra-conservatism which resents any attempt to show that the differences between a monetary and a non-monetary economy are not only, and not even mainly, 'those characteristics which are set forth at the beginning of every textbook on money' (Hayek 1932: 238).

But he met with a flat refusal. Sraffa (1932b: 250) declined to say where he stood, for the less than cogent reason that Hayek's assumptions were altogether too fanciful to be taken seriously. 'After this Dr. Hayek will allow me not to take seriously his questions as to what I "really believe". Nobody could believe that anything that logically follows from such fantastic assumptions is true in reality.' Today we can appreciate the real reasons for his refusal to be drawn.

SRAFFA'S REVIEW

Sraffa starts his review with an attack on Hayek's monetary assumptions. While giving his blessing to an inquiry which 'would resolve itself into a comparison between the conditions of a specified non-monetary economy and those of various monetary systems', he feels that Hayek has failed to conduct it properly.

> But the reader soon realises that Dr Hayek completely forgets to deal with the task which he has set himself, and that he is only concerned with the wholly different problem of proving that only one particular banking policy (that which maintains constant under all circumstances the quantity of money multiplied by its velocity of circulation) succeeds in giving full effect to the 'voluntary decisions of individuals', especially in regard to saving, whilst under any other policy these decisions are 'distorted' by the 'artificial' interference of banks. Being entirely unaware that it may be doubted whether under a system of barter the decisions of individuals would have their full effects, once he has satisfied himself that a policy of constant money would achieve this result, he identifies it with 'neutral money'; and finally, feeling entitled to describe that policy as 'natural', he takes it for granted that it will be found desirable by every right-thinking person.
>
> (Sraffa 1932a: 43)

On the next page the attack is pressed while, suddenly, we become aware of how far away we are from the world of Ricardo and the classical quantity theory. Of Hayek we are told:

> The money which he contemplates is in effect used purely and simply as a medium of exchange. There are no debts, no money-contracts, no wage-agreements, no sticky prices in his suppositions. Thus he is able to neglect altogether the most obvious effects of a general fall, or rise, of prices.
>
> (1932a: 44)

While we cannot but admire the adroitness of a pose that enables Sraffa to stand with one leg in Ricardo's world and with the other in our world of industrial fix-prices, we cannot but reflect that in the latter world expectations, a manifestation of subjectivism, must surely carry some weight. On the same page we actually find a few words of praise for Hayek:

> Such a theory, according to him, ought simply to consider the influence of money on the relative prices of commodities – which is excellent, provided that money itself is one of the commodities under consideration; but Dr. Hayek goes further and rejects not only the notion of general price-level but every notion of the value of money in any sense whatever.

The conclusion of this part of the review is severe:

> The reader is forced to conclude that these alleged differences can only arise, either from an error of reasoning, or from the unwitting introduction, in working out the effects of one of the two systems compared, of some irrelevant non-monetary consideration, which produces the difference, attributed to the properties of the system itself. The task of the critic, therefore, is the somewhat monotonous one of discovering for each step of Dr. Hayek's parallel analysis, which is the error or irrelevancy which causes the difference.
>
> (1932a: 44–5)

We learn with some surprise that Sraffa, a prominent neo-Ricardian, regards those parts of Hayek's book devoted to Austrian capital theory as largely a waste of time. As the time dimension of production is a Ricardian theme its dismissal is rather unexpected.

> Dr. Hayek as it were builds up a terrific steam-hammer in order to crack a nut – and then he does not crack it. Since we are primarily concerned in this review with the nut that is not cracked, we need not spend time criticising the hammer. The part which its description plays in the book is little more than that of obscuring the main issue; a maze of contradictions makes the reader so completely dizzy, that when he reaches the discussion of money he may out of despair be prepared to believe anything.
>
> (1932a: 45)

Thus, in 1932 we did not learn what Sraffa thought of the Austrian theory of capital.[4]

After this, in the second part of the article, we encounter three issues which turn out to be major areas of contention between our Austrian author and his critic. These are: saving and invest-ment; the problem of malinvestment; and the meaning to be attributed to the notion of the natural rate of interest.

With the first of these we can deal fairly briefly here because it did not remain for long an issue between neo-Ricardians and Austrians, but after 1936 turned into one between Keynesians and their opponents. We have to remember that we are in 1932, half-way between *Treatise* and *General Theory*, and before the Myrdalian distinction between magnitudes *ex ante* and *ex post* became known outside Sweden. Keynesians, using the terminology of the *Treatise*, spoke of the divergence between savings and invest-ment (meaning *ex ante*) caused by the fact that in our society savers and investment decision-makers are typically different classes of people. Austrians like Mises and Hayek, by contrast, subscribed to the view, which at that time was a tenet of all mainstream economics, and nothing particularly Austrian, that saving deter-mines investment through the interest mechanism.

Sraffa, adopting the Keynesian view,[5] in a footnote attacks Hayek, who in his book had assumed that when banks grant increased credits all these are granted to producers (no consumer credit in the world of 1930).

> The essential contradiction is that Dr Hayek must both assume that the 'consumers' are the same individuals as the 'entrepreneurs', and that they are distinct. For only if they are identical can the consumers' decisions to save take the form of a decision to alter the 'proportions' in which the total gross receipts are divided between the purchase of con-sumers' goods and the purchase of producers' goods; and only if they are distinct has the contrast between 'credits to producers', which are used to buy producers' goods, and 'credits to consumers', which are used to buy consumers' goods, any definite meaning.
>
> (Sraffa 1932a: 45n)

Hayek's reply shows how unfamiliar he still is, in 1932, with Keynesian ways of thought.

> I do not understand why Mr. Sraffa should suggest that a consumer who is not an entrepreneur will not affect the proportion between the demand for consumers' goods and the demand for producers' goods by his decision to save. It

is certain that when he invests his savings by lending them
out at interest he is instrumental in directing part of his
money income to the purchase of producers' goods, without
himself becoming an entrepreneur.

(Hayek 1932: 241n)

Would anybody be so 'certain' about it today? We also must note
that Hayek here uses the verb 'to invest' in its ordinary financial
meaning which, since Keynes, is not the meaning in which economists use it today.

Today there appears to be fairly wide agreement that, in modern
industrial society at least, we had better refrain from saying either
that savings determine investment or that investment determines
savings. In the first place, there is no such thing as *a* rate of
interest, there is a structure of interest rates on a wide variety
of financial assets in a complex network of asset markets linked
by intermediation. The elements of this structure respond to a
large variety of influences prompted in part by divergent expectations about the magnitudes of rates of interest in the future. Put
briefly, it is impossible to say that the rate of interest brings savings
and investment into equality as such a statement would imply that
its function is confined to the market for new capital, while in
reality it extends to the markets for all existing assets on each of
which the rate of yield has to equate supply and demand. On the
other hand, as Hicks showed in *The Crisis in Keynesian Economics*
(Hicks 1974: 9–30), the Keynesian teaching that investment determines savings via the multiplier process is also untenable, at least
without considerable qualification.

THE COMPLEMENTARITY OF CAPITAL

We next have to turn to the problem of malinvestment which, in
the context of the controversy we are discussing, arises in connection with Hayek's assertion that capital resources brought into
existence in response to a money rate of interest below the level
of the natural rate cannot be maintained once credit inflation has
been stopped and monetary equilibrium is restored. Their owners
and their creditors suffer capital loss.

Sraffa demurs:

As a moment's reflection will show, 'there can be no doubt'
that nothing of the sort will happen. One class has, for a

time, robbed another class of a part of their incomes; and has saved the plunder. When the robbery comes to an end, it is clear that the victims cannot possibly consume the capital which is now well out of their reach. If they are wage-earners, who have all the time consumed every penny of their income, they have no wherewithal to expand consumption. And if they are capitalists, who have not shared in the plunder, they may indeed by induced to consume now a part of their capital by the fall in the rate of interest; but no more so than if the rate had been lowered by the 'voluntary savings' of other people.

(Sraffa 1932a: 48)

Hayek provides an effective retort.

That the physical quantity of these capital goods will, for some time, continue to exist unchanged does not mean that their owners have not lost the greater part, or all, of their capital. It is of very little use for the machine manufacturer to hold on tight to his capital goods when the producer who used to buy the machines is either unable, or finds it unprofitable at the higher rate of interest, to do so now. Whether he likes it or not, the actions of other people have destroyed his capital.

(Hayek 1932: 243)

Having described Sraffa's objection as 'surprisingly superficial' Hayek proceeds to ask him a couple of pointed questions.

Is Mr. Sraffa really unfamiliar with the fact that capital sometimes falls in value because the running costs of the plant have risen; or does he belong to the sect which believes in curing such a situation by stimulating consumption? And would he really deny that, by a sudden relative increase in the demand for consumers' goods capital may be destroyed against the will of its owners?

(Hayek 1932: 244)

The thought expressed in these two passages remains as significant today as it was in 1932. Nothing we have witnessed in twenty years of the 'revival of Classical Political Economy' is likely to still our misgivings. Neo-Ricardian thought appears to be unable to cope with the problem of capital resources which can undergo considerable changes in value while retaining their physical form.

Neo-Ricardians stand in need of a theory of capital, as without one they can have nothing to say about capitalism and its markets. In reality capital is concrete and heterogeneous, not abstract and homogeneous. Only certain forms of capital combinations, certain modes of capital complementarity, produce productive results, others do not. Hence there is always the danger that a capital resource may lose some of its complements. Moreover, capital values depend on future, not present, earnings. A theory of capital which takes no account of expectations can tell us little about the real world. The theory of capital, then, offers no promising ground for a return to classical objectivism in the theory of value.

In the face of these facts supporters of the 'classical revival' are unable to claim that all they are interested in is the process of reproduction of the economic system as a whole, and that they are entitled to abstract from such details as we have mentioned. For the maintenance of capital is a human art and a problematic endeavour, not an automatic occurrence, and he who chooses a level of abstraction too high to notice this fact can learn but little about our world.

INTEREST AND EQUILIBRIUM

We now come to the third of our contentious issues, the problem of the meaning of the Wicksellian 'natural rate of interest'. It gained some importance a few years later when Sraffa's argument on this issue provided the inspiration for the notion of 'own-rates of interest' in Chapter 17 of Keynes's *General Theory* (see Keynes 1936: 223n).

In *Prices and Production* Hayek stated the problem in these words:

> In a money economy, the actual or money rate of interest may differ from the equilibrium or natural rate, because the demand for and the supply of capital do not meet in their natural form but in the form of money, the quantity of which available for capital purposes may be arbitrarily changed by the banks.

(Hayek 1935: 23)

Sraffa objects. 'An essential confusion, which appears clearly from this statement, is the belief that the divergence of rates is a characteristic of a money economy.' He continues:

> If money did not exist, and loans were made in terms of all sorts of commodities, there would be a single rate which satisfies the conditions of equilibrium, but there might be at any one moment as many natural rates of interest as there are commodities, though they would not be equilibrium rates. The arbitrary action of the banks is by no means a necessary condition for the divergence; if loans were made in wheat and farmers (or for that matter the weather) 'arbitrarily changes' the quantity of wheat produced, the actual rate of interest on loans in terms of wheat would diverge from the rate on other commodities and there would be no single equilibrium rate.
>
> (Sraffa 1932a: 49)

On the next page he argues that on any forward market the ratio between forward and spot price implies a rate of interest. He goes on:

> In equilibrium the spot and forward price coincide, for cotton as for any other commodity, and all the 'natural' or commodity rates are equal to one another, and to the money rate. But if, for any reason, the supply and the demand for a commodity are not in equilibrium (i.e. its market price exceeds or falls short of its cost of production), its spot and forward prices diverge, and the 'natural' rate of interest on that commodity diverges from the 'natural' rates on other commodities. Suppose there is a change in the distribution of demand between various commodities; immediately some will rise in price, and others will fall, the market will expect that, after a certain time, the supply of the former will increase, and the supply of the latter fall, and accordingly the forward price, for the date on which equilibrium is expected to be restored, will be below the spot price in the case of the former and above it in the case of the latter; in other words, the rate of interest in the former will be higher than on the latter. It is only one step to pass from this to the case of a non-money economy.
>
> (Sraffa 1932a: 50)

Sraffa then shows the relevance of this argument to industrial fluctuations of any kind.

It will be noticed that, under free competition, this divergence of rates is as essential to the effecting of the transition as is the divergence of prices from the costs of production; it is, in fact, another aspect of the same thing.

He concludes: 'This applies as much to an increase of saving, which Dr. Hayek regards as equivalent to a shift in demand from consumers' to producers' goods, as to changes in the demand for or the supply of any other commodities' (ibid.).

In this argument four points call for our special attention. Firstly, we have here, in a few lines, a succinct sketch of the whole of classical theory and its *modus operandi*, with particular regard to the relationship between long-run equilibrium price, determined by cost of production, and market prices determined by supply and demand.

Secondly, this complex of relationships is given expression in a context of spot and forward markets. Forward prices, while evidently determined by expectations, are always nearer to equilibrium prices than are spot prices, though it is not suggested that they ever coincide. As forward markets without expectations are hardly conceivable, expectations are introduced, albeit in somewhat attenuated form: they are always orientated to equilibrium price. This raises a number of questions we shall have to return to later on.

Thirdly, the role of demand in classical theory is made articulate in a manner that serves the clarification of some baffling questions. Changes in demand affect market prices immediately, but they affect output quantities, and not equilibrium prices, in the long run.

Fourthly, the discussion explicitly concerns the relations between market prices and equilibrium price in the market for one commodity. Relationships between markets for different commodities are not discussed. This also is a matter requiring further discussion.

Hayek feels that in replying to Sraffa on this point (the natural rate of interest) he can deal with it much more briefly than on malinvestment 'since his confusion here must have been obvious to most readers. Mr. Sraffa denies the possibility of a divergence between the equilibrium rate of interest and the actual rate is a peculiar characteristic of a money economy' (Hayek 1932: 245).

To Sraffa's passage, quoted above, on what would happen if money did not exist and loans were made in terms of commodities, Hayek's reply is

> I think it would be truer to say that, in this situation, there would be *no single rate* which, applied to all commodities, would satisfy the conditions of equilibrium rates, but there might, at any moment, be as many 'natural' rates of interest as there are commodities, *all* of which would be *equilibrium rates*; and which would all be the combined result of the factors affecting the present and future supply of the individual commodities, and of the factors usually regarded as determining the rate of interest (emphasis in original).
>
> (ibid.)

Hayek continues: 'The inter-relation between these different rates of interest is far too complicated to allow of detailed discussion within the compass of this reply.'

One thing is clear: when Hayek and Sraffa use the word 'equilibrium' they use it to denote quite different things. For Hayek it means market-clearing demand-and-supply equilibrium, for Sraffa long-run cost-of-production equilibrium. Neither is ready to consider other kinds of equilibrium, for example, an inter-market equilibrium involving equality of interest rates in various commodity markets.

What is much less clear to us is to what extent Hayek was aware that by admitting that there might be *no single rate* he was making a fatal concession to his opponent. If there is a multitude of commodity rates, it is evidently possible for the money rate of interest to be lower than some but higher than others. What, then, becomes of monetary equilibrium?

Perhaps all Hayek meant to say was that no pattern of divergence of interest rates, whatever it be, would ever last long enough for it to have any permanent effect on capital investment. Perhaps this is what the emphasis on 'the factors usually regarded as determining the rate of interest' is meant to imply. As it was, Sraffa was able to end his *Rejoinder* to Hayek's *Reply* with a scoffing phrase:

> Dr. Hayek now acknowledges the multiplicity of the 'natural'

rates, but he has nothing more to say on this specific point than that they 'all would be equilibrium rates'. The only meaning (if it be a meaning) I can attach to this is that his maxim of policy now requires that the money rate should be equal to all these divergent natural rates.

(Sraffa 1932b: 257)

It is not difficult, however, to close this particular breach in the Austrian rampart. In a barter economy with free competition commodity arbitrage would tend to establish an overall equilibrium rate of interest. Otherwise, if the wheat rate were the highest and the barley rate the lowest of interest rates, it would become profitable to borrow in barley and lend in wheat. Inter-market arbitrage will tend to establish an overall equilibrium in the loan market such that, in terms of a third commodity serving as *numéraire*, say steel, it is no more profitable to lend in wheat than in barley. This does not mean that actual own-rates must all be equal, but that their disparities are exactly offset by disparities between forward prices. The case is exactly parallel to the way in which international arbitrage produces equilibrium in the international money market, where differences in local interest rates are offset by disparities in forward rates. In overall equilibrium it must be as impossible to make gains by 'switching' commodities as currencies.[6]

This overall equilibrium of interest rates constitutes a third type of equilibrium which is neither Sraffa's nor Hayek's. It need have nothing to do with costs of production, but neither is it entailed by the equality of demand and supply in commodity markets. It requires a vigilant and efficient arbitrage acting between markets, a special type of entrepreneurial action and institutions appropriate to it. What Hayek should have said is not that there might be as many rates of interest as there are commodities *all* of which would be equilibrium rates, but that only *some of them* would be. While overall equilibrium requires equality of demand and supply in each single market, the latter is not a sufficient condition of the former.

EXPECTATIONS EMASCULATED

At the beginning of this paper we said that in 1932 only the more perceptive sensed that they were witnessing a clash of irreconcilable views of the world. Half a century later, we know much more and can assign to this dispute its place in the history of economic ideas.

These, then, were the opening shots of the neo-Ricardian counter-revolution of our days. Its aim, as we said, is to undo the work of the subjective revolution of the 1870s. Austrian economics is the most consistent form of subjectivism among the schools of economic thought today. So, naturally, Austrian economics is under fire.

We learnt that our two authors have entirely different notions of equilibrium. These are naturally related to their attitudes to subjectivism. For Hayek equilibrium is an ever-present force. Equilibrium prices are primarily governed by demand. The proportions of capital and consumer goods in the gross national product are determined by the relative preferences of saver-consumers. It takes the arbitrary action of the banks to tamper with an otherwise firmly entrenched equilibrium.

For Sraffa real-world market prices are determined by supply and demand. But behind them, as a centre of gravity, there lies the equilibrium position. Equilibrium prices are determined by the objective, partly technical, conditions of production and distribution, while demand determines equilibrium quantities of goods produced. Sraffa has no need to assume interference by banks in order to explain disequilibria. To him they are an everyday occurrence.

Every counter-revolution has to incorporate a few of the achievements of the revolution it is directed against, but then must neutralise them in order to prevent them from affecting vital organs of the body politic. The same is the case with the neo-Ricardian counter-revolution. It has found a new role for demand, which once had a place of pre-eminence in the subjective revolution, in the determination of market price and equilibrium output. But its exponents resolutely refuse to ask any questions about what lies behind demand. The acts of human minds, the delineation of purpose, the making and carrying out of plans, which shape and impart meaning to demand, are all completely ignored. So the counter-revolutionaries have contrived to incorporate in their doctrine one of the achievements of subjectivism, albeit in a suitably emasculated form. It can do them no harm.

It seems that Sraffa is making an attempt to deal in somewhat similar fashion with expectations, the introduction of which into economic theory was another great achievement of subjectivism.

In the passage quoted above from Sraffa (1932a: 50) we are told that in the case of a shift in demand among commodities 'immediately some will rise in price, and others will fall; the market will expect that, after a certain time, the supply of the former will increase, and the supply of the latter fall, and accordingly the forward price, for the date on which equilibrium is expected to be restored, will be below the spot price in the case of the former and above it in the case of the latter'. What is introduced here is a 'market expectation' orientated to an equilibrium price known presumably to at least a majority of traders. What lies behind it, the configuration of divergent expectations of bulls and bears, without which trade in forward markets cannot exist, is ignored. By giving exclusive emphasis to expectations 'for the date on which equilibrium is expected to be restored' expectations are introduced into the argument in emasculated form. In an uncertain world no equilibrium position can be known with certainty.

This attenuation of expectations is a great pity. For Sraffa's argument, when slightly redesigned, lends itself to a subjectivist reinterpretation of the setting in which interest rates are determined.

A rate of interest requires a loan contract. A loan contract involves a combination of a spot and a forward transaction: A lends to B, B promises to return the amount lent at a later date to A. Such transactions become explicit in spot and forward markets. No forward market can operate without the divergent expectations of bulls and bears which every day give it its concrete shape. The forward price reflects a balance of bullish and bearish expectations. Daily fluctuations in it primarily reflect changes in the strength and determination of the two market parties. Hence changing expectations must affect interest rates via forward prices. In this way a gun originally designed to fire on the citadel of Austrian economics may be turned into a weapon in its defence. Why it was not done in the 1930s is a tale to be told another day.

The duel we have described did the reputation of Austrian economics a good deal of harm. Hayek's authority as an economic thinker of the first rank had been challenged with some vehemence in the august pages of the *Economic Journal*. Nobody knew what to make of it. Some of Hayek's recently gained supporters began to hesitate. When, four years later, the Keynesian revolution broke out, its assault forces encountered not a phalanx, but divided ranks.

11

THE SALVAGE OF IDEAS
Problems of the revival of Austrian economic thought [1982]

This paper is offered on his 70th birthday to Professor Terence W. Hutchison. All economists who care for origin and history of the ideas they espouse or oppose stand in his debt. His contributions to the methodology of economics have been many, and some of them have brought him fame.

The choice of our subject seems appropriate to the occasion. He has always taken a friendly interest in the work of the Austrian school of economics. His contribution to the Menger Centenary in 1971 is rightly remembered.

In his writings he has held up a mirror to the Austrians. Some of them have found encouragement in his appreciation of their work. Others have gained from his comments in other ways. Even those who found their faces distorted in the mirror drew some benefit from it. For even a mirror set at an angle which hurts our sensitivity is better than no mirror. None of us can do without one.

In recent years many economists, of all schools of thought, chastised by their experience, have come to take a new interest in the history and methodology of their discipline. Let us hope that for many years to come they will be able to read and enjoy the writings of one whose seminal thought has been an inspiration to so many of us.

THE 1930s: THE LOSS OF AUSTRIAN INTELLECTUAL CAPITAL

The 1930s were a tragic decade for many Austrians, economists and others, but the body of thought we have come to know as *Austrian Economics* suffered a fate all its own in it. Political

164

developments had something to do with it. Many Austrian economists were driven into exile and took Austrian economic thought with them to foreign shores. In some ways which are germane to our theme Anglo-Saxon economics, in particular, drew benefit from this transfer of ideas, while after the *Anschluss* Vienna ceased to be an important centre of economic studies.

In this chapter, however, our concern is with the reversal of fortune that attended the absorption into Anglo-Saxon economics of some Austrian ideas of the 1930s, and with certain consequences of these events which we perceive today. Our story starts about 1930, before the political disasters mentioned had had an impact, and extends to our day. In Hicks's words, we are interested in how it came about that, in the 1930s, the voices of the Austrians were almost drowned in the fanfare of the Keynesian orchestra, and in some consequences of this fact (Hicks 1965: 185).

At this time, Mises and Hayek were the most prominent Austrian economists.[1] In January 1931 Hayek made his triumphal entry on the London stage with his lectures on 'Prices and Production', soon to be followed by his appointment to the Tooke chair. When I arrived at the London School of Economics in the spring of 1933, all important economists there were Hayekians. At the end of the decade Hayek was a rather lonely figure, even though he remained editor of *Economica* throughout the war.

When the decade started, Mises, a figure of some weight in the Chamber of Industries in Vienna, presided over his famous *Privatseminar*. In August 1940 he landed in New York as a refugee from Europe. These facts illuminate the vicissitudes of Austrian economics in the 1930s.

Schumpeter's comment is noteworthy:

The theory has been sketched by Professor von Mises, who while extending critical recognition to Wicksell, described it as a development of currency school views. It was fully developed by Professor von Hayek into a much more elaborate analytic structure of his own, which, on being presented to the Anglo-American community of economists, met with a sweeping success that has never been equaled by any strictly theoretical book that failed to make amends for its rigors by including plans and policy recommendations or to make contact in other ways with its readers' loves or hates. A strong critical reaction followed that, at first, but served to underline

the success, and then the profession turned away to other
leaders and other interests. The social psychology of this is
interesting matter for study.

(Schumpeter 1954: 1120)

Our concern here is, by contrast, with the consequences of these
calamitous events for other Austrian economists and for the body
of ideas we may call Austrian economics. These were disastrous.
It is true that in the 1940s Hayek acquired new fame with such
essays as 'The Use of Knowledge in Society' and 'The Meaning
of Competition' (Hayek 1949: 77–106) in which a devastating
critique of neoclassical theories of knowledge and competition was
presented, while Mises made his mark in the Anglo-Saxon world
in 1949 with *Human Action*. But when in 1950 Hayek left the
London School of Economics to join the distinguished Committee
on Social Thought in Chicago and devote himself entirely to political philosophy, Austrian economists lost their most inspiring
leader. For them, the next twenty-five years or so were years in
the wilderness. Only Mises's seminar at New York University
remained as an active centre of Austrian economic thought. In the
rest of the world it fell into oblivion or was, at best, regarded as
an appendage of neoclassical orthodoxy. In 1967, in the opening
passage of *The Hayek Story*, Sir John Hicks had this to say:
'Hayek's economic writings ... are almost unknown to the modern
student; it is hardly remembered that there was a time when the
new theories of Hayek were the principal rival of the new theories
of Keynes' (Hicks 1967: 203). Although Professor Shackle, the
most eminent subjectivist of our time, rose to fame in the 1960s
it was not easy to see how his subjectivism was related to that of
the Austrian tradition.

As is usually the case, it is difficult to give a date to the recent
revival of Austrian economic thought. Hicks's *Hayek Story*, mentioned above, was probably no more than a harbinger of better
things to come. We are perhaps on firmer ground in choosing the
early 1970s as the turning point, when Professor Shackle (1972)
in *Epistemics and Economics*, subtitled *A Critique of Economic
Doctrines*, started an attack on neoclassical orthodoxy on a broad
front and from a subjectivist standpoint, and Professor Kirzner
(1973) in *Competition and Entrepreneurship* laid bare the pretences
of neo-classical 'growth theories' which offered no scope for entrepreneurship.

166

But it is hard to restore to life a body of thought once the threads that link its various parts are torn. It is even harder to do it in a rapidly changing world in which the vocabulary of economists is notorious not only for the flow of innovations but for sudden shifts in the meaning of terms long in use. There is a danger that Austrian ideas of the 1930s may not be understood today because they were stated in terms which to the present generation of economists no longer have their original meaning. There is a problem of the storage of ideas which of course affects all schools of thought, but in the Austrian case is of particular significance.

In the circumstances ordinarily surrounding the existence of schools of thought the storage of ideas, the carrying over of those that have not been fully utilized in one period to the next, has proved to be a feasible activity, at least where these ideas have once been made generally accessible by publication. Such intergenerational transfer, most easily visible of course, but also most needed, where short bursts of original thinking are followed by long periods of drought and academic mediocrity, is part of our normal intellectual life. What is needed of course is the patient work of skillful editors devoted to their task. The storage of ideas, by keeping thought alive through a sequence of generations and enabling scholars to examine new developments in the light of old ideas, plays thus an essential part in the life of all schools of thought and in the maintenance of their traditions. Even without the splendour of the *Collected Writings of J. M. Keynes* and the *Max Weber Gesamtausgabe* to remind us of what can be achieved by single-minded and well-organized effort, the storage of ideas remains a necessary task.

It is here that the revival of Austrian economic thought encounters formidable problems. The years around 1930 were for Austrians years of fertility and promise. The *Zeitschrift für Nationalökonomie* was started in 1929 in order to give expression to this abundance of ideas, but all this was nipped in the bud by the events of the 1930s. During the years in the wilderness the storage of ideas was impossible. Most of the earlier Austrian achievements were simply forgotten.

Where the storage of ideas failed we must at least make an attempt at their salvage. In what follows we shall try to rescue from oblivion some earlier Austrian ideas germane to what are important issues today. We shall start by reconsidering some of

Hans Mayer's views on the inadequacy of functional price theories. We shall, secondly, examine some implications of Professor Hayek's views on the role of knowledge in economics. Finally, we shall cast a glance, from the perspective of 1982, at the fierce controversy on capital between Knight and the Austrians which 50 years ago aroused so much interest.

MAYER'S CRITIQUE OF FUNCTIONALISM

In our attempt to revive and re-examine Austrian economic thought of the past we encounter another problem which, though germane to that of changing terminology, has much deeper roots: the change of conceptual tools used by successive generations. The various conceptual tools we use constitute 'a set', i.e. they require a unity, a central principle enabling us to allocate to each its proper place in our tool-box. As a result the extent of our ability to grasp aspects of the world around us is limited by the reach of our set of conceptual tools. Attempts to take a concept out of one tool-box and put it into another may succeed, but of course invite the risk of misunderstanding. The centre of orientation of the new set will probably differ from that of the old. The comparative study of different schools of thought, or of successive generations of the same, has to be undertaken with some circumspection. Needless to say, this applies in particular to a case such as ours in which the temporary eclipse of Austrian thought gave rise to the loss of numerous conceptual tools.

In 1932, in the face of the sweeping success of Neo-Walrasian thought, the Austrian economist Hans Mayer issued a warning. In his *Erkenntniswert der funktionellen Preistheorien* he examined the thought of advocates of the general equilibrium model from Cournot to Cassel, with particular attention to Walras and Pareto. His main conclusion was that 'functional price theories', i.e. general equilibrium theories, are incapable of explaining how prices are actually formed in real markets, and, by implication, that Austrians had no reason to give up their own analytical efforts and accept the conclusions of the School of Lausanne.

Eine Klassifizierung der modernen Preistheorien nach den ihnen eigentümlichen Erkenntnisaufgaben und diesen adäquaten Erkenntnismitteln wird die Klarstellung ihrer Vorzüge und Mängel und der Grenzen ihrer Leistungsfähigkeit erleichtern. Es lassen sich als Haupttypen feststellen:

I. Genetisch-kausale Theorien mit dem Ziele, durch Erklärung der Preisbildung ein Verstehen der Preiszusammenhänge vermittels der Gesetze ihres Entstehens zu geben.

II. Funktionelle Theorien mit dem Ziele, das Entsprechungsverhältnis der bereits bestehenden Preise im Gleichgewichtszustande durch exakte Fixierung der Bedingungen des Gleichgewichtes zu beschreiben.

(Mayer 1932: 148)

In the Anglo-Saxon world, to our knowledge, Lord Kaldor almost alone took notice of Mayer's effort.[2] He had this to say:

It seems to be this problem of the effects of experience with which the 'causal-genetic' approach of the Austrian School has been mainly concerned. The aim of the latter is to exhibit not so much the conditions of equilibrium under a given situation (the task assumed by the 'functional' theories), but to show how, in a given situation, a position of equilibrium is reached – the problem of how prices come into being rather that what system of prices will secure equilibrium. It is, however, only under our present very rigid assumptions that a causal-genetic theory can reach the same conclusions concerning the nature of equilibrium, as are evolved, by using a different method, by the 'functional' theories. In the absence of these conditions it is only by means of a 'theory of the path' (a theory showing what determines the actual path followed) that a causal-genetic approach can arrive at generalizations concerning the nature of equilibrium – and such a theory has not hitherto been forthcoming, although the necessity for it has frequently been emphasized by writers of the Austrian School.

(Kaldor 1960: 21. Originally in *Review of Economic Studies*, March 1934)

Not much appears to have changed here since 1934. The 'theory of the path' remains an item on the Austrian agenda.

Most of the criticism of general equilibrium theory in recent years, so it seems, did not follow Mayer's line, was not couched in causal-genetic language, but mostly based on the incompatibility of human action in an uncertain world with the determinism of prices and outputs. But there were exceptions. Professor Pasinetti, no mean critic of the Walrasian system, had this to say: 'As against the attitude ... that "everything depends on everything else", Keynes (as Ricardo) takes the opposite attitude that it is one of the tasks of the economic theorist himself also to specify which variables are sufficiently interdependent as to be best represented by one-way direction relations' (Pasinetti 1974: 44). He adds in a footnote that the term 'causal ordering' we might use in this context 'is here used simply in the sense of an asymmetrical relation among certain variables, namely as indicating a one-way direction in which, in a formal sense, the variables of the system are determined' (ibid.). No doubt Professor Pasinetti knew nothing of Mayer's effort forty years earlier, and the latter may not have relished the company in which he is thus seen, but it is clear that the causal-genetic approach has its uses in our time.

Looking at the position Mayer took up in 1932 from the perspective of 1982, we are able to discern lines running backward and forward from it, linking it to the classical past as well as to some major issues of our own day. By price formation Mayer means the formation of market prices, not equilibrium prices. This to the classical economists never was a problem. Market prices, to be sure, depended on supply and demand in the short run, but in the long run tended towards a position indicated by a cost of production, the classical value equilibrium. But with the decline of classical doctrine after the 'subjective revolution' the problem arose in a new form. All that Austrian economists of the first generation had to say was that market prices depended on the marginal utilities of market participants. Mayer in his polemic against Cassel makes it clear that in his view a price theory not embedded in a theory of value would be impossible.

> Hat man einmal den instrumentalen Charakter der Wertlehre für die Preislehre erkannt, dann kann man nie zu der Forderung Kommen, das Instrument zur Erreichung eines umfassenderen Zweckes durch einen weniger umfassenden Zweck, der dieses Instrument nicht benötigt, zu ersetzen.
>
> (Mayer 1932: 225)

In neoclassical equilibrium theory the relationship between value and price becomes problematical in a way it was not for classical economists. The difference is one of the knowledge we may attribute to market participants. In the classical world it was reasonable to assume that every trader in a market knew the long-run cost of production of the product traded and was able to make use of this knowledge in dealing with day-to-day price fluctuations. But neoclassical equilibrium rests on a complex interplay of demand and supply in thousands of markets. In the absence of 'The Auctioneer' nobody can 'know' an equilibrium price until the system as a whole has attained this position. Traders are unable to compare current prices with a 'long-run normal price' as they do not know the latter. The problem of price formation arises in a new form. The day-to-day conduct of traders requires a new form of explanation.

It is therefore not surprising that a fairly straight line links Mayer's position to contemporary discussions of fixprice and flexprice markets, two terms we owe to Sir John Hicks. Once we realise that in our world all prices are disequilibrium prices, the problem mentioned above arises on many levels. It was to be expected that post-Keynesians would seek guidance in the writings of Keynes who, in any case, distrusted neoclassical theory. Chapter 29 of the *Treatise on Money* may be said to contain a rudimentary theory of price formation in conditions of disequilibrium. A few years ago Professor Davidson made a notable attempt to take Keynes's thought on price formation in different markets a little further by distinguishing between 'produce-to-market' and 'produce-to-contract' entrepreneurs (Harcourt (ed.) 1977: 313–17).

In different markets prices are formed in different ways. Not all price-fixing agents have the same interests. Here historical change plays its part. The decline of the wholesale merchant, whose dominating role Marshall took for granted, for instance in textile markets, and who naturally aimed at setting such prices as would permit him to maximize his turnover (a short-run consideration), reduced the range of markets with flexible prices. The rise of the industrial cost accountant as a price-fixer, with his interest in 'orderly marketing' (a long-run consideration) and his aversion to frequent price changes, has made most prices of industrial goods in our world Hicksian fixprices. In all markets dominated by speculation of course prices must be flexible. On the other hand, all bureaucracies, including those concerned with production planning in large industrial enterprises, naturally abhor flexible prices. Since Mayer wrote little progress has been made towards understanding these phenomena. Causal-genetic explanation comes into its own when we turn from the construction of models to an endeavour to understand the course of real events.

EPISTEMICS IN ECONOMICS

When Professor Hayek, in November 1936, in presenting 'Economics and Knowledge', suggested that the most important task of economics as an empirical science consists in explaining how men come to acquire knowledge of the 'data' governing the markets in which they operate, he found his audience (the London Economic Club which at the time contained an unusual number of distinguished economists) in a humble no less than an inquisitive mood. The inescapable conclusion that all was not well with a discipline, not to say science, in which such fundamental questions, hitherto neglected, could be raised with no prospect of answers readily forthcoming, baffled most of his listeners and, later on, readers.

We cannot say that today these questions have been forgotten. Questions concerning the knowledge we may ascribe to economic agents do play a part in contemporary discussions. Walrasian *tâtonnement*, after all, was an attempt to explore problems germane to this sphere, even though it was not successful. The various theories of search that have become popular in recent years, may be regarded as attempts in the same direction. If they tell us little about how agents decide what to search for and in what area, they have, by this very failure, at least helped us to understand the existence of problems of complementarity in the field of knowledge: we must have some knowledge before engaging in a search for more.

In Hayek's original presentation the whole problem was stated in equilibrium terms. When stressing 'the admittedly fictitious state of equilibrium' he nevertheless insisted that 'the only justification for this is the supposed existence of a tendency toward equilibrium. It is only by this assertion that such a tendency exists that economics ceases to be an exercise in pure logic and becomes an empirical science' (Hayek 1949: 44). After what has happened in economics in the last thirty years we are today inclined to look askance at the whole notion of equilibrium, and even more so at the Hayekian version of 1936 in which we were told 'It can hardly mean anything but that, under certain conditions, the knowledge and intentions of the different members of society are supposed to come more and more into agreement' (ibid: 45). But even if we discard the equilibrium terms in which the problem was first stated, it nevertheless remains. In a stationary world, we might hold, time will in the long run, 'hammer logic into brains' and teach its human pupils what they must do to achieve success and stave off failure. Why this should be so in a changing world is by no means clear. In such a world there may always be speculators who believe that yesterday's success may not be much of a clue to tomorrow's, and who try to gain from knowing better than the rest of the market what the future will bring. Speculative markets require divergent, not convergent, expectations. They cannot exist without bulls and bears.

Our problem, then, is in reality not an empirical one. It consists rather in how to formalize an experience all members of modern industrial societies share. We all know quite well how consumers gain knowledge about the variety of goods, and their prices, on which they might spend their incomes. Nor is there much of a mystery about the corresponding conduct of producers. The problem arises when we formulate theories, analytical 'models', which are supposed to reflect some features of the real world while we are entitled to abstract from others. Seen in this light, what Hayek said in 1936 amounted to the demand that, when economists formulate empirical generalizations about how markets operate, they must not abstract from the process by which knowledge is gained. In other words, we must not dwell on too high a level of abstraction when studying markets. In view of the opinion which appears to be widely held, that any theorist is entitled to choose his own level of abstraction, this is a wholesome lesson. In judging a theory we must ask about how many phenomena of the real world it has something interesting to say. In our case, we should begin by distinguishing between different kinds of knowledge.

In the 1940s Hayek, in several essays, returned to the subject of knowledge. We thus may say that it is an essential ingredient of Austrian economics. But we also encounter some difficulties. On the one hand, the dissemination of knowledge plays a prominent part in the process of competition. 'We must look at the price system as such a mechanism for communicating information if we want to understand its real function' (ibid: 86), and 'Competition is essentially a process of the formation of opinion: by spreading information, it creates that unity and coherence of the economic system which we presuppose when we think of it as one market' (ibid: 106). On the other hand, we also find emphasis on 'the dispersed bits of incomplete and frequently contradictory knowledge which all the separate individuals possess' (ibid: 77). How can knowledge be both, dispersed and diffusable? Hayek faces the problem in the following passage

> We need decentralization because only thus can we insure that the knowledge of the particular circumstances of time and place will be promptly used. But, 'the man on the spot' cannot decide solely on the basis of his limited but intimate knowledge of the facts of his immediate surroundings. There still remains the problem of communicating to him much further information as he needs to fit his decisions into the whole pattern of changes of the larger economic system.
>
> (ibid: 84)

So the decision-maker stands in need of various kinds of knowledge, some disseminable, some not. Our next step in reviving this Austrian subject will have to consist in classifying them and relating them to other parts of our economic experience. At a first glance it is perhaps tempting to identify our distinction with that between technical and market knowledge: useful technical knowledge will spread throughout the world while business knowledge in a narrower sense is confined to the markets in which it is acquired. A moment's reflection shows, however, that it is impossible thus to link our two pairs of knowledge. The existence of international trade and finance shows that world-wide diffusion of market knowledge is possible, while in conditions of rapid technical progress the dissemination of each bit of technical knowledge may be impeded by fear of early obsolescence.[3]

In recent years the importance of 'learning by doing' as a cause of technical progress in modern industrial society has aroused some interest among economists. Unfortunately this has happened during the decades of Austrian eclipse. Viewed from a macro-economic perspective, 'learning by doing' was widely regarded as relevant to the existence of the 'neoclassical production function'. What is far more important is that we appreciate the contribution a subjectivist interpretation of these phenomena may make to our understanding of how technical progress operates in a market economy. What really matters here is, surely, that from experience with identical technical processes every producer in his workshop learns a different lesson. In this way a form of 'product differentiation' comes into existence. While in the end the scale of this variation will be reduced again when the market, acting as the final arbiter, decides which product is preferable to which, what we can learn from this process is, how the subjectivism of technological ingenuity, manifesting itself in the width of this scale of variation, provides the material on which ultimately the subjectivism of preferences can be brought to bear. Here technical knowledge which is specific to its place of origin and thus not diffusable makes possible the diffusion of market knowledge.

Behind these phenomena there lies the important fact that in a changing world business knowledge may become out of date and thus has to be continually monitored. To business men it is often as important to 'unlearn' knowledge of the past as to acquire new knowledge. Large parts of their 'stock of knowledge' have to be renewed as regularly as their stock of capital. This applies in the first place to market knowledge, in a world in which market constellations shift every day, but, in the economically relevant sense, technical knowledge may also become out of date. What then happens is not of course that the technical processes to which such knowledge pertains become impossible, but that it is no longer profitable to perform them. While we must retain the distinction between technical and market knowledge, all knowledge is in a sense like capital in that without any observable physical change it may suddenly lose its value.

While to an economist all this may be obvious (and slightly commonplace), to an epistemologist it would be rather shocking. Here we have to remember the difference between propositional and practical knowledge, between *knowledge that* and *knowledge how*. We mean the latter, and not the former, when we speak of the knowledge consumers and producers need. While to the logician all knowledge must be certain, consumers and business men know that theirs never is. Even though all technical knowledge is of course scientific knowledge applied to concrete circumstances, and as such its validity unaffected by market change, its economic significance is affected. Problems are apt to arise here only, however, when, like Hayek and Shackle, economists innocently introduce practical knowledge with all its defects into analytical models of a fairly high level of abstraction, and strict logicians then misunderstand them and take them to refer to certain knowledge of propositions instead.[4]

The relevance of what we said to the present position of Austrian economics is perhaps seen more clearly if we contrast it with the view of technology and technical progress we encounter in neo-Ricardian writings descended from the Sraffa model.

For neo-Ricardians there always is in existence a *best* technique. Competition enforces its universal adoption. Technological change here comes about gradually as each new generation of craftsmen producers absorbs techniques reflecting the latest stage of knowledge. Such change is here an exogenous force impinging on the economic system from outside and gradually absorbed by it. In the Austrian view, by contrast, technological progress is the product of human minds. It is the result of a social process in which individual producers learn different lessons in workshop and market and then try to gain by making use of what they have learned. If in the end one method is universally adopted, which need not be the case, this happens as the ultimate result of a process of interaction, and events taking place during this process will affect the final result.

The world of the Sraffa model is a pre-industrial world in which technical knowledge is to craftsmen producers simply a 'social datum', to be absorbed like all other data. Such states of knowledge change only gradually, and while they prevail nobody ever thinks of a better method. The simultaneous existence of several, perhaps experimental, methods of production is of course incompatible with neo-Ricardian equilibrium. It is, however, a commonplace experience in an industrial society.

What needs salvage here is not of course the notion of technological change and its impact as such, but the Austrian variant of this notion which had little chance of a hearing during the decades of Austrian eclipse. Technical knowledge as a weapon in the competitive struggle is a subject to which, since Schumpeter's day, economists have paid far too little attention.

A CAPITAL CONTROVERSY NOT SO ANCIENT

When in the 1930s Frank Knight launched a series of vehement attacks on the Austrian theory of capital, this meant to most Austrian economists, exasperated as they already were, another challenge to be met and another fortress to be defended. To some, however, like Professor Hayek, Knight's assault essentially meant the revival of an old controversy in which Böhm-Bawerk and

J. B. Clark had been engaged in the early years of this century, and which concerned the notion of 'true capital' as a 'fund', a quantity of value.[5] Professor Hayek chose his strategy of defence accordingly (Knight 1933, 1934, 1935; Hayek 1936).

In 1937 Lord Kaldor, then widely regarded as an exponent of Austrian views, provided a useful summary of 'The Recent Controversy on the Theory of Capital' (Kaldor 1937). He summarized Knight's criticism of the Austrian theory of capital under three headings:

> First, that it is impossible to distinguish between permanent and nonpermanent resources (or 'original' and 'produced' means of production) or between the services of these resources. Second, that it is irrelevant, and in many cases impossible, to distinguish – analytically or physically – between expenditures incurred in 'maintaining' resources and those incurred in replacing them. Third, that there is no necessary correlation between the 'period of production' and the quantity of capital.
>
> (ibid: 203)

Kaldor rightly pointed out that Knight's critical arguments directed against the Austrian position are hard to appreciate unless we keep in mind his vision of the economic world from which they are flowing. It is therefore necessary to have

> a general picture of the world as Professor Knight sees it. It consists of a collection of resources, which, like heavenly bodies, emanate light and absorb light. All these resources have to be 'maintained', i.e. they all absorb a quantity of services at every unit period which is the absolute condition of their continuing to radiate another stream of services, which is this 'output'. No distinction can be made between maintenance and replacement, or even between production for immediate consumption and production for 'maintenance' or future consumption . . . It is impossible to say how much of the input served to produce the immediate output, and how much served to maintain the resource itself.
>
> (ibid: 215)

As regards permanent resources like labour and land, we face another problem which makes it hard for us to define capital by contrasting it with them. It stems from the fact that in Knight's view such permanent resources 'cannot be thought of except as a rate of flow in time: like light or electricity (but unlike water) they flow but cannot exist as a stock, or have their use transferred to any other period. Just as one cannot "bottle up" sunshine... today's labour hours cannot be deferred until tomorrow: they must be used immediately or lost' (ibid: 203). Hence the stock of capital has to be given a conceptual form other than one which would correlate it to so elusive an entity. To speak of 'nonpermanent resources' is meaningless when permanent resources cannot exist. The way is open to a conception of capital which abstracts from all physical properties of capital resources and regards the capital stock of society as nothing but a value aggregate. The accountant's view of capital is extended to a social aggregate. This idea, as we shall see, has far-reaching consequences.

Austrian economists of the 1930s, whose vision of the economic world differed from Knight's, were of course bewildered by his assault on them. That there is no such simple thing as a 'period of production' for the economic system as a whole did not come as a surprise to most of them. But what were they to make of statements such as 'All capital is, in a growing society, inherently immortal, and we need not speculate as to what would happen if society as a whole decided to "liquidate"' (Knight 1933: 328), when daily proceedings in the bankruptcy courts showed that there were fairly regular exceptions to such immortality? They were puzzled to learn of capital that 'its replacement has to be taken for granted as a technological detail' (Knight 1934: 264), when in reality it is only too often a matter of painful necessity. Moreover, since it is hard to tell reinvestment from new investment, did it follow that all investment 'has to be taken for granted as a technological detail'?

Hayek reacted rather strongly to the Knightian strictures. He saw in them the revival of an ancient fallacy. 'This basic mistake – if the substitution of a meaningless statement for the solution of a problem can be called a mistake – is the idea of capital as a fund which maintains itself automatically, and that, in consequence, once an amount of capital has been brought into existence the necessity of reproducing it presents no economic problem' (Hayek 1936: 202).

At the same time he dissociated himself from certain parts of Böhm-Bawerk's theory.

In my opinion the oversimplified form in which he (and Jevons before him) tried to incorporate the time element into the theory of capital prevented him from cutting himself finally loose from the misleading concept of capital as a definite 'fund', and is largely responsible for much of the confusion which exists on the subject; and I have full sympathy with those who see in the concept of a single or average period of production a meaningless abstraction which has little if any relationship to anything in the real world.

(ibid.: 199–200)

In other words, Hayek rejected not merely Böhm-Bawerk's measure of the time dimension of production but also his notion of the subsistence fund. For the former he later on substituted the 'investment periods' of individual capital resources, but for the latter there could be no substitute. We had to 'cut ourselves loose' from this misleading conception.

By the 1970s, this whole controversy had been completely forgotten. To what extent this was the case can be seen from the fact that when in 1973 Sir John Hicks, in *Capital Controversies, Ancient and Modern*, classified capital theorists as 'fundists' or 'materialists' he had no doubt where to put Hayek. Evidently quite oblivious of what Hayek had said of Knight in 1936, he wrote

Hayek of course was a Fundist, but a very sophisticated Fundist, deeply preoccupied with the problems of ignorance and uncertainty which come to the fore as soon as one thinks of capital value as being determined by expectations of the future. It was the omission of this aspect which set him against the Materialism of Pigou.

(Hicks 1977: 163)

With the notable exception of Professor Kirzner, who pointed out at once that Hicksian fundism was obviously not the same thing as Knightian fundism, as the former was forward-looking and the latter not, nobody found Hicks's classification strange. Nor did it strike anybody as odd that, in addition to describing Hayek as a fundist, Hicks also told us that 'Jevons and Böhm-Bawerk kept the Fundist flag flying. But most economists, in England and in America, went Materialist' (ibid.: 153). From the

179

passage quoted above it would appear that Hayek might have preferred it if they had lowered that flag!

What are we to make of all this? And why do the ideas at issue in this particular controversy deserve salvage? The answers to these two questions are not unconnected.

In the 1930s, when blow after blow fell upon the Austrians, the Knightian blow was felt to be a severe one. The tone of Hayek's reply to Knight testifies to that. While few economists today may have heard of this controversy, a revival of Austrian economics without at least an attempt at clarifying the issues that were at stake in it seems hard to imagine. On the other hand, in part no doubt as a result of the methodological pluralism of our day, we have become more sensitive to the intellectual roots of economic ideas. Such pluralism has not merely taught us that the economic world looks different when viewed from different perspectives. In part as a result of the neo-Ricardian counter-revolution, we know a classical idea when we see one!

It now seems clear that Hayek and Knight looked at the world of capital from two different perspectives, and that this was the main reason why they were unable to understand each other. Knight's perspective is classical and plutological. What interests him is the meaning and functions of the capital stock as an aggregate, a macroeconomic entity.[6] What individuals may or may not do with their capital goods does not really interest him. Hayek, as an Austrian, has entirely discarded the classical perspective in favour of a catallactic one. What interests him is the co-ordination of the activities of millions of individuals in a multitude of markets, and the decisions they have to face. Stocks, funds and other such entities are of no interest to him. He is indeed apt to regard them as meaningless. His approach is of course microeconomic. Hence he is almost compelled to disavow those elements of Böhm-Bawerk's thought, like the subsistence fund, which belong to the classical tradition. To Hayek all such notions are relics of a rather embarrassing past which are best forgotten.[7] The theory of capital has to be reconstructed from the basis of individual decision-making.

Perspectives such as those here displayed by our two contestants are of course forms of thought and not matters of experience. Facts are inserted in them and then derive their meaning to the individuals concerned from them. Hence the same facts in different perspectives may come to have altogether different significance.

Which level of abstraction we choose and which facts we abstract from has also something to do with our perspective which is thus 'prior' to such decisions. It was therefore beside the point for Hayek to call Knight's concept of capital 'a mystical quantity' and to say of it in his concluding passage, 'It has the somewhat questionable advantage that there is no way of deciding whether any statement about this quantity is true or false' (loc cit.: 228). Whatever it may be, it is not an empirical generalization, but neither is Professor Hayek's own conception.

In assessing the merits of our two perspectives we have to judge by the facts on which they cast light and by the significance of these facts to us. If we are interested in certain facts which in one of the perspectives are either abstracted from or given low status, we shall of course not adopt it, but this gives us no right to condemn it as an analytical device.

Knight's strong point was an important practical conclusion his analytical scheme, however dubious in other respects, permitted him to reach: that in modern industrial society disinvestment for society as a whole, as distinct from what is the case with individuals, is possible only on a limited scale. Any sustained attempt to consume working capital or stocks of finished products would rapidly lead to disaster. It would then become clear to the owners of fixed capital that this latter, so far from having the 'investment period' they embodied in their plans, was lost. In other words, the Austrians seemed unable to understand that the social process of accumulation of capital is bound to give rise to certain forms of complementarity between capital resources belonging to different owners which, once in existence, cannot easily be reversed. A multitude of plans has here been so well co-ordinated that it is virtually impossible to change any one of them. How, then, can we speak of 'investment periods' for each of them? As Austrians are committed to the tracing of unintended results of deliberate action it seems odd that this particular instance of the complementarity of different capital resources (e.g. fixed and working capital) which different capital owners planned for investment periods of different length should have eluded them.

On the other hand, from the perspective of 1982, Austrian reluctance to embrace fundism in any of its various forms other than Böhm-Bawerk's (and, as we saw, Hayek's reluctance extended even to his) seems vindicated. In order to turn the heterogeneous stock of capital into a homogeneous value aggregate, such as a 'fund', we need either a coherent and constant price system which no market can offer us or the unity of an evaluating mind. When a firm draws up its balance sheet we find such unity of an evaluating mind. But how can we extend this principle to the capital stock of society as a whole? As Professor Kirzner pointed out in 1974,

> A forward-looking measure of Jones's capital stock and also of Smith's must presume plans on the part of Jones and of Smith, but Jones's plan and Smith's plan may be, in whole or in part, mutually exclusive. Perhaps Jones expects rain and builds a factory to produce umbrellas, whereas Smith expects fine weather and builds a factory to produce tennis racquets ... What is significant is that it is already NOW meaningless to add a valuation of Jones's factory to a valuation of Smith's factory when each valuation depends on the expectation of one that the expectation of the other will prove erroneous.
>
> (Kirzner in Dolan 1976: 141)

The classical notion of the capital stock as 'an entity capable of maintaining its quantity while altering its form' (Pigou 1935: 239) is thus hard to sustain. It can have meaning only where the minds of different capital owners are in concurrence. What has happened here is similar to what happened in the case of equilibrium: in both cases concepts which are meaningful, and indeed indispensable, in the case of the individual have been torn up by their roots and transplanted to an alien soil. In both cases the results were calamitous. The controversy between Knight and the Austrians offers a good example of such calamity. Perhaps in an era in which philosophers would not let us say that men have minds but societies do not, economists and other social scientists were predisposed to commit such blunders. Probably the metaphorical use of terms such as 'social accounting', where entirely new terms should have been invented, contributed to confusion and misled even Sir John Hicks. We also have to remember that in the early 1930s, when Knight launched his assault, the distinction between macroeconomists and microeconomists had not yet come into general use.

The Austrians therefore have good reason to look askance at fundism in all its varieties. At the same time it might be better to refrain from making statements such as that capital 'can be nothing but' the totality of nonpermanent resources at our disposal, and from referring to 'a separate substance of capital apart from its manifestations in concrete capital and goods'. To speak thus would be, once again, to confuse what is meaningful and legitimate at the microlevel with that which is not at the macrolevel.

Capital resources, after all, exist in the minds of agents as well as in physical reality. They have a value dimension in addition to their physical dimensions. Indeed in most cases it is the former which is the economically relevant. To speak here of 'duplication' and 'mythology' is to ignore some of the most important problems in the theory of capital. Value as a common denominator is something we need in order to compare means and ends. That capital values may change without any concomitant physical change is hardly to be denied. If so, we have to allow for it in our analytical models and must coin appropriate terms.

The theory of capital lacks a simple dimension for the measurement of its subject matter. To some minds this makes it all the more attractive.

12

JOHN MAYNARD KEYNES
A view from an Austrian window [1983]

INTRODUCTION

By tradition, ancient and cherished, the hundredth birthday of a thinker who has made his mark provides an occasion for reconsideration of his work and re-examination of his thought. We may find justification for doing so in the hope that the distance history provides and the cooling of passions will permit us to arrive at judgements more settled and mature, if not more acute, than was formerly possible. Indeed, unless we are ready to believe that as time goes by our state of knowledge changes, there would be little point in such centenary reflections.

In Keynes's case we encounter a number of difficulties. In his life-time his work was the subject of a number of controversies not all of which have subsided since. From the enormous literature that has grown up we may conclude that there must have been 'many Keyneses' rather than one Keynes, and Keynes's well-known pragmatic inclination seems to support this conclusion. It is hardly an exaggeration to say that today almost every reputable economist holds and cherishes his own view of 'what Keynes really meant'. Moreover, there is the ancient problem of the relationship between the master and his disciples, emerging today in the form of 'Keynes and the Keynesians'. We have no reason to expect that on the occasion of the centenary all these views will suddenly begin to converge. What perhaps we might hope for is that, gradually and to some extent, most of these divergent views will become tempered by the wisdom of history.

As the years go by, such a state of mind should become easier to attain. Economists may even learn to distinguish between 'Keynesian' economic policies and Keynes's (authentic?) economic thought. Keynes, to be sure, was a pragmatist, but it is hard to see how anybody can be held responsible for events occurring more than thirty years after his death. In any case, as the world changes and the circumstances in which decisions on economic policy have to be made come to resemble less and less those Keynes envisaged in his own time, all these disputes on which of these policies have to be regarded as 'Keynesian' and which not, are bound to become less and less relevant to any practical pursuits. Their contribution to the elucidation of his thought has always been meagre.

In the 1930s, in Britain and Germany at least, money wage rates in industry showed a tendency to remain constant even· in the face of very strong fluctuations in output. So Keynes based his recommendations for an economic policy designed to raise levels of employment and output in industry on this empirical generalization. Who would do it today?

Assessing Keynes's contribution as an economic thinker from an Austrian point of view is an endeavour in which we encounter additional problems, in some respects even more formidable than those mentioned. It is to them that we have to turn next.

KEYNES'S UNEASY RELATION TO THE AUSTRIANS

Keynes's relations with the Austrian school of economic thought, and in particular with Mises and Hayek, its most prominent representatives from the late 1920s onwards, were never cordial, and at times they were really bad. Although this unhappy state of affairs fully emerged only in the 1930s with their clashes and misunderstandings, Keynes's aversion to the Austrian school can be documented for a period much earlier.

In September 1914 Keynes reviewed Mises's *Theorie des Geldes und der Umlaufsmittel* in the *Economic Journal* together with a volume of essays on questions of monetary policy by Friedrich Bendixen, an economist from Hamburg who was a supporter of Knapp and his *State Theory of Money*.[1]

Keynes wrote

Dr von Mises' treatise is the work of an acute and cultivated mind. But it is critical rather than constructive, dialectical and not original. The author avoids all the usual pitfalls, but he avoids them by pointing them out and turning back rather than by surmounting them. Dr Mises strikes an outside reader as being the very highly educated pupil of a school, once of great eminence, but now losing its vitality ... One closes the book, therefore, with a feeling of disappointment that an author so intelligent, so candid and so widely read should, after all, help one so little to a clear and constructive understanding of the fundamentals of his subject.

When this much has been said, the book is not to be denied considerable merits. Its lucid common sense has the quality, to be found so much more often in Austrian than in German authors, of the best French writing ... The book is 'enlightened' in the highest degree possible.

(*Economic Journal*, September 1914, p. 417).[2]

At the end of the review Keynes compared the authors of the two books reviewed. 'Dr von Bendixen is without the cultivated subtlety of Dr von Mises, but his practical wisdom is of a higher order. Hamburg's mind is not so clever as Vienna's, but more comes of it' (ibid.: 419).

We can all understand why Mises hated Keynes after that. The remark about the 'school, once of great eminence, but now losing its vitality' shows how early in his career Keynes had formed an unfavourable view of the work of his own generation of the Austrian school.

The clash with Hayek occurred in 1931, when the latter reviewed Keynes's *Treatise on Money* in two long articles in *Economica* (August 1931 and February 1932). Without even waiting for the publication of the second of these Keynes wrote a reply ('The Pure Theory of Money: A Reply to Dr Hayek') which was published in the November issue of *Economica* and in which he stated that Hayek had completely misunderstood him.[3] Moreover, in defiance of all traditional rules governing such replies, he went over to the offensive and began to criticize Hayek's own *Prices and Production* which had just been published.

The book, as it stands, seems to me to be one of the most frightful muddles I have ever read, with scarcely a sound proposition in it beginning with page 45, and yet it remains a book of some interest, which is likely to leave its mark on the mind of the reader. It is an extraordinary example of how, starting with a mistake, a remorseless logician can end up in Bedlam. Yet Dr Hayek has seen a vision, and though when he woke up he has made nonsense of his story by giving the wrong names to the objects which occur in it, his Khubla Khan is not without inspiration and must set the reader thinking with the germs of an idea in his head.

(*Economica*, November 1931: 394)

In the words of Keynes's biographer Harrod: 'Professor Hayek replied with a powerful and dignified protest against this kind of behaviour. These polemics temporarily caused a widening of the gulf between Cambridge and London. It may be recorded, however, that at a later date Keynes and Professor von Hayek achieved a happy relation of friendship' (Harrod 1951: 436).

Whatever improvement there was, was, however, halted when in the *General Theory*, in the appendix to chapter 14, Keynes accused Mises and Hayek of a confusion of terms. 'As a result of confusing the marginal efficiency of capital with the rate of interest, Professor von Mises and his disciples have got their conclusions exactly the wrong way round' (Keynes 1936: 193).

In reality, however, the Austrians were merely following Wicksell in drawing a distinction between the 'natural rate of interest' and the money rate, and Keynes's own distinction between marginal efficiency of capital and the latter is exactly parallel to it. Keynes might justifiably have accused his Austrian opponents, as Myrdal did, of neglecting the strong expectational ingredient of the incentive to invest, a fact of which Wicksell's Swedish pupils proved well aware when they interpreted their master's 'natural rate of interest'. But this is quite a different matter. The charge of simple confusion of terms is groundless.

The real turning point in Austro-Keynesian relations arrived when Hayek published *The Road to Serfdom* in 1944. In the midst of his strenuous war-time work Keynes, on 28 June 1944, found time to write Hayek an enthusiastic letter. 'In my opinion it is a grand book. We all have the greatest reason to be grateful to you for saying so well what needs so much to be said. You will not expect me to accept quite all the economic dicta in it. But morally and philosophically I find myself in agreement with virtually the whole of it, and not only in agreement with it, but in deeply moved agreement' (Harrod 1951: 436).

Even this endorsement was not unqualified. 'I should say that what we want is not no planning, or even less planning, indeed I should say that we almost certainly want more. But the planning should take place in a community in which as many people as possible, both leaders and followers, wholly share your own moral position. Moderate planning will be safe if those carrying it out are rightly orientated in their minds and hearts to the moral issue' (ibid). He added 'Dangerous acts can be done safely in a community which thinks and feels rightly, which would be the way to hell if they were executed by those who think and feel wrongly' (ibid.: 437).

We may note that the reconciliation took place on the level of political philosophy rather than of economic theory. Why was the controversy so fierce? What exactly were the issues at stake in it? Looking out from our centenary watchtower we should be able to discern some features of the landscape beneath us that have hitherto remained undetected and might be of some help to us in attempting to find answers to our puzzles.

The dispute, as we saw, was not a political one. Nor will it do to impute 'hidden political motives' to our contestants. Hayek, Keynes and Mises were all pretty outspoken in expressing their political views. On the other hand, the fundamentals of economic theory, its scope and methods, were not at issue either. In such matters as the rejection of the methods of the natural sciences for economics and other social sciences our contestants were, as we shall see, to a remarkable degree in full accord. What, then, was the quarrel about?

It seems to us that the source of this vehement dispute is to be found on the empirical, and this is to say historical, level. Keynes and the Austrians made different, and as it happens exactly opposite, assumptions about the typical constellation of market forces in twentieth-century industrial society. Keynes assumed that in our world the majority of markets for industrial goods, both capital and consumption goods, are what Sir John Hicks has called *fixprice* markets, not, in the short run, susceptible to the pressure of supply and demand. The price fixers in each industry take their orientation largely, though not exclusively, from the level of money wage rates in it. Interest rates are determined in financial markets which, by the same token, are *flexprice* markets, most sensitive to changes in demand and supply and, indirectly, to the expectations prompting these market forces. The Austrians, by contrast, made exactly the opposite assumptions. For Hayek, in *Prices and Production*, prices of capital and consumption goods, immediately responding to changes in demand, are flexprices, while the banks determine the money rate of interest. In other words, for him the prices of financial assets are fixprices, with the banks acting as price fixers, while the markets for most ordinary goods, both capital and consumption goods, are flexprice markets. No wonder the two protagonists in our controversy were talking at cross purposes and unable to understand one another.

In Professor Streissler's apt phrase, we have to 'note that this Hayekian vision is exactly, so to speak, the reflected image of the Keynesian system, where the financial markets, though somewhat differently conceived, are price-equilibrating, all other markets being Q-markets' (Streissler 1977: 107).[4]

If it is true that the source of the controversy has to be found on the empirical level, in the divergence of generalizations about the typical constellation of market forces in our world, the centenary appears to offer an auspicious occasion for an attempt to surmount it by taking a new view, other than those that 50 years ago were within the field of vision of either of our contestants. We shall return to the matter in the last section.

COMMON GROUND

Peering from our centenary watchtower we can clearly make out two areas of broad agreement between Keynesian and Austrian economics, of which one concerns monetary disturbances and the other the foundations of economic science. These are the areas of inflation and methodology. In the light of all we know about their differences, in particular as regards the different perspectives on market forces, we shall hardly expect to find here agreement on matters of detail. But broad agreement on matters of principle does exist.

In 1919, in a famous passage of *The Economic Consequences of the Peace*, Keynes wrote

> As the inflation proceeds and the real value of the currency fluctuates wildly from month to month, all permanent relations between debtors and creditors, which form the ultimate foundation of capitalism, become so utterly disordered as to be almost meaningless, and the process of wealth-getting degenerates into a gamble and a lottery.
>
> Lenin was certainly right. There is no subtler, no surer means of overturning the existing basis of society than to

debauch the currency. The process engages all the hidden forces of economic law on the side of destruction, and does it in a manner which not one man in a million is able to diagnose.

(JMK, vol. ii, p. 149)[5]

Professor Hayek has, on several occasions, quoted this passage with approval. When doing so in 1975 he added about Keynes, 'His political judgment made him the inflationist, or at least avid anti-deflationist, of the 1930s. I have, however, good reason to believe that he would have disapproved of what his followers did in the post-war period. If he had not died so soon, he would have become one of the leaders in the fight against inflation' (Hayek 1975: 18).

So there is agreement that inflation is an evil and the fight against it is, for economists, a pursuit of virtue. This said, we may note that Hayek and Keynes are inclined to trace the evil effects of inflation in different directions and tend to take a different view of the main danger zones. Rather more than a difference of perspectives is involved here.

For Hayek what matters most is the effect of inflation on relative prices and their 'signalling' function. In an inflation the distortion of relative prices from their equilibrium values causes malinvestment and thus leads to dislocation of the capital structure. We note that what matters here is not the primary effect of inflation on all money prices, but the secondary effect on relative prices, and also the underlying assumption that without inflation relative prices would tend towards their equilibrium values and the capital structure towards the state of an integrated whole.

Keynes is not interested in this. Perhaps the Marshallian teaching that in the short run the structure of capital is unalterable has led him to infer that inflation cannot affect it. His interest in the effects of inflation concerns the institutional basis of market society, in particular its effects on existing contracts between debtors and creditors 'which form the ultimate foundation of capitalism'. In an inflation all debtors make capital gains at the expense of their creditors. Keynes sees in this fact merely the outer expression of the danger facing a society which cannot exist without money contracts when the latter begin to lose their original meaning.

For Keynes money is much more than the medium of exchange. Even apart from its other functions, it forms the substance of money contracts, the foundation of capitalistic society. The institutions of society are all parts of an organic whole. When one is corrupted, the others cannot remain unscathed. For Keynes and Keynesians this truth has an important application: Of all money contracts the money wage contract is today perhaps the most important. Autonomous changes in it hold perils for society as a whole. There always is a danger that an inflationary process that may have started outside the industrial sphere (e.g. by budget deficit) may acquire a momentum of its own once it affects money wage settlements. Hence Keynesians are inclined to regard the 'indexation' of wages and salaries with misgivings.

In the field of methodology Keynes and the Austrians agree that economics is a social science to which methods that have proved successful in the natural sciences should not be applied without careful inspection, and that, in particular, all attempts to 'give numerical values' to the parameters of economic models ignore the essential meaning of economic theory. It is hardly surprising that even here we find differences of accent and perspective, but, with the area of agreement so broad and significant, they do not amount to much.

In his Nobel Memorial Lecture *The Pretence of Knowledge* Professor Hayek was eager to dispel the impression that he rejected the mathematical method as such. 'Without this algebraic technique we could scarcely have achieved that comprehensive picture of the *mutual interdependencies* of the different events in a market. It has, however, led to the allusion that we can use this technique to determine and predict the *numerical values* of those magnitudes, and this has led to a vain search for quantitative or numerical constants' (Hayek 1975: 35). We may note here the implicit endorsement of the Walrasian general equilibrium model.

Hayek sees the main problem of the social sciences in the complexity of the facts to which they refer.

> The chief point we must remember is that the vast and rapid advance of the physical sciences took place in fields where it proved that explanation and prediction could be based on laws which accounted for the observed phenomena as functions of comparatively *few* variables – either particular facts or relative frequencies of events.... The difficulties we encounter in essentially complex phenomena are ... due to the chief problem which arises when we apply our theories

to any particular situation in the real world. A theory of essentially complex phenomena must refer to a *large* number of particular facts, all of which must be ascertained before we can derive a prediction from it, or test it.

(ibid.: 40).

Keynes concurs with Hayek's misgivings about numerical values. In his letter to Harrod of 16 July 1938 we read

In chemistry and physics and other natural sciences the object of experiment is to fill in the actual values of the various quantities and factors appearing in an equation or a formula; and the work when done is once and for all. In economics that is not the case, and to convert a model into a quantitative formula is to destroy its usefulness as an instrument of thought. Tinbergen endeavours to work out the variable quantities in a particular case ... and he then suggests that the quantitative formula so obtained has general validity. Yet in fact, by filling in figures, which one can be quite sure will not apply next time, so far from increasing the value of his instrument, he has destroyed it. All the statisticians tend that way.

(JMK, vol. XIV, p. 299)

But Keynes's mind also moves in another direction.

I also want to emphasize strongly the point about economics being a moral science. I mentioned before that it deals with introspection and with values. I might have added that it deals more with motives, expectations, psychological uncertainties. One has to be constantly on guard against treating the material as constant and homogeneous. It is as though the fall of the apple to the ground depended on the apple's motives, on whether it is worthwhile falling to the ground, and whether the ground wanted the apple to fall, and on mistaken calculations on the part of the apple as to how far it was from the centre of the earth.

(ibid.: 300)

Keynes sees in social facts manifestations of the human mind. While to Hayek it is the complexity of these facts, their multitude and diversity, that defies the attribution of numerical values to social concepts, to Keynes it is their mental character ('mistaken calculations on the part of the apple') that does so. Rather to the surprise of some of us, Keynes emerges as being more deeply committed to subjectivism than is his Austrian opponent.

AUSTRIAN CRITICISMS OF KEYNES

In the previous section we have been concerned with regions of congruity between Austrian and Keynesian thought. As, looking out from our centenary vantage point, we turn our glance to another part of the landscape, however, we also find large areas of disagreement. With some of them we have been acquainted for many decades, others came into view more recently in the course of the incessant battles between Keynes's faithful disciples and their critics. Still other features of Keynesian theory, which from the Austrian point of view have to be regarded as weaknesses, have thus far failed to attract the attention they deserve.

Austrian and non-Austrian critics of Keynesian economics share many an argument. There is no need for us to deal here at length with such cases. This applies in particular to the impressive array of critical work Sir John Hicks has presented in *The Crisis in Keynesian Economics* (1974). Austrians will wholeheartedly endorse what Sir John has to say about Keynes's view of investment.

> The trouble lies deep in his version of short-run macro-economics, in which one form of investment appears as good as another. Only investment expenditure is taken into account; the productivity of the investment is neglected. (One remembers those pyramids!) Once one accepts that one form of investment is not as good as another, it follows that it is socially productive that the form of investment should be wisely chosen. It cannot be wisely chosen if it is too much hurried. The social function of liquidity is that it gives time to think.
>
> (Hicks 1974: 57)

The same applies to Austrian approval of Hicks's misgivings about multiplier theory: 'It was not right to give the impression – the impression that one so easily gets from the *General Theory* – that the only obstacle to expansion, even to fast expansion, is scarcity of labour. There are other problems too' (ibid.: 29).

It will not surprise us to learn that Austrian descent from Keynesian teaching is strongest in the field of capital. Keynes, giving Marshall's doctrine that 'in the short period the stock of capital may be regarded as given' (in itself an ambiguous phrase) a rather too literal interpretation, appears to have persuaded himself that, if output and employment in the short run are the objects of our inquiry, no human action concerning existing capital could possibly affect these. While investment matters, replacement, maintenance and repair of existing capital equipment do not. Even if this were true for each short period, their total effects over a sequence of short periods might not be negligible.

In the *General Theory* we are given to understand that in the modern capitalistic market economy a state of full employment is rarely achieved and some unemployment the normal state of affairs. In the book Keynes advocates the pursuit of full employment policies by governments. The question whether the magnitude of the capital stock of society under conditions in which some unemployment has to be regarded as normal would permit the pursuit of such policies is never asked.

Under such circumstances each capital owner would maintain a capital stock of such size as he can expect to be in permanent use. Why should he bother to maintain those of his capital resources which, experience teaches him, yield income only intermittently? He would scrap them and put the proceeds into financial assets. If all capital owners do this, capital goods constituting excess capacity will disappear and the size of the capital stock normally maintained will correspond, not to full employment, but to normal employment. This means that full employment cannot be attained in such a society before the capital stock has been increased to a corresponding level.

Another Keynesian notion, the expectation that capitalistic society would at some future time face a state of 'capital-saturation' is open to similar doubts.

Keynes tells us that on two assumptions, viz., that

> steps are taken to ensure that the rate of interest is consistent with the rate of investment which corresponds to full employment [and] that State action enters in as a balancing factor to provide that the growth of capital equipment shall be such as to approach saturation-point ... I should guess that a properly run community equipped with modern technical resources, of which the population is not increasing

rapidly, ought to be able to bring down the marginal efficiency of capital in equilibrium approximately to zero within a single generation.

(Keynes 1936: 220).

If capital resources were to yield no net return to their owners, why should these maintain and replace them? Moreover, we notice how the macro-economic notion of *the* marginal efficiency of capital here serves to conceal a fundamental fact with which all theory of captial has to reckon: that the capital stock of society is a heterogeneous aggregate, not a homogeneous mass. Different capital resources yield different rates of return, and capital losses suffered by owners of fixed resources in shrinking industries, in which they are indeed abundant, in no way affect the high rates of return available to investors in new and expanding industries.

Today most economists, including Austrians and Keynesians, agree that outside a state of long-run equilibrium, capital cannot be measured. A capital resource constitutes the present embodiment of an expected future income stream. Different capital owners hold different expectations. There is no objective criterion to tell us which expectation will in the end prove right.

Keynes's definition of his *current investment*, however, rests on the assumption of a measurable capital stock. 'For we must mean by this the current addition to the value of the capital equipment which has resulted from the productive activity of the period' (Keynes 1936: 62). If we are unable to measure the capital stock, how can we know what constitutes an addition to it? Keynesians will have to look for another definition of current investment which does not link it to the magnitude of the capital stock, and should put this task on their centenary agenda.

Before we descend from our watchtower we once more have to turn to the disputes and misunderstandings of the 1930s. As we saw earlier, these were in large part due to different assumptions about the typical constellation of market forces in different sectors of the modern market economy. The task facing us, especially on this centenary occasion, is to prevent the occurrence of similar misunderstandings in the future. How is this to be done?

It is tempting to think of surmounting such disputes by means of finding a 'more general' theory comprehensive enough to 'cover' both, Austrian and Keynesian doctrines, as special cases, but this is not the way out. Economists expect to find different constellations of market forces in different markets. As regards our particular case, for one thing, as we saw, the dispute did not really arise on the level of abstract theory. For another thing, although the concepts of fixprice and flexprice markets as analytical categories did not exist in the 1930s, and Keynes and the Austrians were thus not aware of them, we may doubt whether it would have made much difference if they had been. What was lacking on both sides was a serious endeavour to grasp the empirical presuppositions of one's opponent's conclusions.

As we said above, the dispute arose on the empirical level. It concerned the interpretation of (in the 1930s) contemporary facts, not theories. Many people believe that facts are 'objective' and that disputes about them should be settled by applying tests to them. However this may be, whenever we confront very large numbers of facts, it is in any case impossible to know all of them and we have to 'stylize' what we regard as a representative selection of them.[6]

The situation confronting agents, in which they have to take action and make plans guiding such action, consists almost entirely of such stylized facts. In this regard those who act and those who formulate generalizations about such action face the same problem. Needless to say, in this activity, as in so many others, everybody has his own style reflecting the subjectivism of a choosing mind.[7] As each situation is made up of a multitude of facts only a fraction of which can be known to anybody, nothing is less surprising than that different men facing what to an outside observer may look like the same 'objective situation' should form different pictures of it and reach different conclusions. (Subjectivists should be the last to be puzzled by this phenomenon.) We see no reason to believe that in this respect social scientists are different from other men, but they do shoulder a duty of their own.

This particular extension of the sphere of subjectivism imposes upon all those studying real situations in which men have to act the duty to pay heed to the variety of perspectives from which they may be viewed. *Verstehen* as the method of enquiry specific to the social sciences may be said, like charity, to begin at home. Scholars unwilling or unable to practise towards each other's work what they profess to practise towards the objects of their studies can hardly complain if we lose confidence in them.

Economists, like others, when engaged in a dispute seen to be related to the facts of a situation, must make an effort to understand the point of view from which their opponents see these facts. In particular, they should acquaint themselves with the style that informs the stylized facts that, in their opponents' minds, make up the situation in question. In the controversies of the 1930s these rules were almost entirely ignored by both sides. Austrians and Keynesians stylized the facts of their contemporary situation each in their own way, and neither would recognize that it might be done otherwise.

Standing on our watchtower, glancing at Keynes's work from the perspective of history, this is perhaps the most important lesson for us to learn on this centenary occasion. It is to be hoped that it will be taken to heart on other occasions as well.

13

REFLECTIONS ON HAYEKIAN CAPITAL THEORY [1975]

INTRODUCTION

The student who, more than thirty years after its original publication in 1941, turns to Hayek's *Pure Theory of Capital* cannot but be baffled by the wayward nature of the progress of economic thought, the sudden turns and twists he finds in the discussion of most economic problems, and the futility of much learned dispute. We know of course that most ideas are likely to become transformed as they are being absorbed by a growing number of minds. We have even heard of thinkers who prospered more when they were misunderstood than they otherwise might have done. But these facts account for little of what has happened to the theory of capital in recent years.

Today's reader of Hayek's book is struck, no less than was the reader of three decades ago, by the profusion of ideas and the depth of the level of comprehension the author attains. He will also be intrigued by the thought of how many of these ideas have turned up in recent controversies, though mostly in a shape noticeably different from the one they were here given originally. Yet, for all the fertility of these ideas, the theory of capital as originally set out by Hayek has made little progress in three decades. 'Our main concern will be to discuss in general terms what type of equipment it will be most profitable to create under various conditions, and how the equipment existing at any moment will be used, rather than to explain the factors which determined the value of a given stock of productive equipment and of the income that will be derived from it.' (Hayek 1941: 3) A theory of capital in this sense can hardly be said to exist today. What goes by the name of 'capital theory' in our days is still mostly concerned with the source and magnitude of income derived from capital. How do we explain the striking contrast between the evident failure of the main aim of Hayek's book and the undeniable influence of so many of its main ideas? This seems a question worth asking even though we may be unable to answer it.

WHAT HAPPENED TO HAYEK'S CAPITAL THEORY?

Three of Hayek's ideas appear to have proved most fertile in the discussions of recent years:

1 The stock of capital does not constitute a measurable quantity.
2 The notion of 'intertemporal' or 'dynamic' equilibrium.
3 The reinterpretation of the 'higher productivity of roundabout methods of production' as the process in the course of which 'as investment proceeds, more and more of those natural forces which before were only potential resources are utilized and gradually drawn into the circle of scarce goods'.

(Hayek 1941: 64)

1 Everybody seems to agree today that the stock of capital cannot be measured outside equilibrium, viz. outside entirely artificial conditions. But there are two reasons for it of which we may call one the 'Ricardian' or 'objectivist', the other the 'Austrian' or 'subjectivist' reason. We may also say that the one is 'backward looking', the other 'forward looking'. The former rests on the fact that any change in the mode of income distribution, in rate of profit or wage rate, will affect relative prices and thus deprive us of any solid yardstick. It is particularly germane to any view of capital which links the present value of capital resources to their current cost of reproduction, a 'backward looking' view.

The second reason rests on the fact that the purpose of all capital, hence also of the current maintenance of existing capital goods, is to secure a future income stream. But the future is unknowable, though not unimaginable, and men have to use knowledge substitutes in order to evaluate future income streams, viz. expectations. Experience shows that different persons will typically hold different expectations about the future income to be expected from the same resource, and that the same person may hold different expectations about the same future event at different points of time. The inevitably subjective nature of all 'forward looking' views renders the measurement of capital impossible.

In the 'Cambridge controversies' of recent years most of the emphasis has been on the former argument, though the latter is mentioned on occasion.[1] But in none of the numerous writings devoted to these controversies, to our knowledge, is the fact ever mentioned that Hayek presented the 'Austrian' argument why capital cannot be measured in 1935 in 'The Maintenance of Capital' (*Economica*, August 1935). It is repeated in chapters XXII[2] and XXIII of the *Pure Theory*. Meanwhile an impious legend has grown up that our inability to measure the stock of capital in the real world was discovered in the Cambridge of the 1950s.

2 Hayek's notion of an equilibrium that is not stationary but 'intertemporal' or 'dynamic' has now blossomed into the 'growth equilibrium' or 'steady-state growth' of recent theory. But the role it plays here is not that it plays in Hayek's construction. He introduced it 'For it is only by contrast with this imaginary state, which serves as a kind of foil, that we are able to predict what will happen if entrepreneurs attempt to carry out any given set of plans.' (Hayek 1941: 23) We are warned 'To make full use of the equilibrium concept we must abandon the pretence that it refers to something real' (1941: 21). Modern macroeconomics, however, treats certain macro-magnitudes as though they were real, and actual changes in incomes, consumption, etc. as though they were changes from one (short-run) equilibrium to another. Hayek, by contrast, expresses 'serious doubt . . . whether the concept of short-period equilibrium, if applied to an economic system as a whole, has any definite meaning. The question is whether there is any such interval of comparative rest between the moment when the more mobile factors have been adjusted and the time when the more rigid elements of the structure can be effectively adjusted'. (1941: 20) For Keynes the rigidity of money wage-rates provided just such an 'interval'. Hayek, by denying it, deprives modern macroeconomics of its indispensable basis in Keynesian short-period equilibrium analysis. The notion of intertemporal equilibrium which, as we just saw, is a long-period equilibrium of the economic system as a whole, occupies a central place in Hayekian capital theory. All analysis of the capital structure conducted in the 'Pure Theory' is such equilibrium analysis. But Hayek also regards it as a means to an end, viz. causal analysis, and we shall

have to raise the question whether it is an adequate means to this end. To this question we return in our next section.

3 For Hayek, as for Menger, the cause of the 'productivity' of capital lies in the complementarity between mobile investible resources and certain potential natural resources which, until the capital required for their exploitation has come into existence, were not 'scarce' and thus had no economic value. Mineral deposits require investment in mining equipment and railroads to turn them into actual resources. The oceans of the world provided a vast unused transport resource when, at the beginning of the modern age, the maritime nations of Europe began to invest what surplus resources they had in ships, mobile resources complementary to the oceans.

In this way Hayek, by reinterpreting the extended time dimension of capital as an increasing degree of complexity of the pattern of complementarity displayed by the capital structure, succeeds in meeting the attacks of Knight and the Chicago School. As the stock of capital increases relatively to other factors of production the downward pressure on the marginal rate of return is temporarily eased as these potential resources become actual resources and begin to make a contribution to output.

An extension of this argument to the case of 'embodied technical progress' appears to be called for, though it would defy the limits set to it by Hayek when he denied that lengthening the period of production had anything to do with technical progress (1941: 72). We might say that in a world in which technical progress is taking place all the time some potential capital goods (machines) will always exist in the brains of the inventors which require complementary capital in which to be 'embodied', and that an increase in investment will primarily take this direction. We have to remember, however, that within the capital structure relations of substitutability coexist with those of complementarity, and that, as the rate of return on mobile resources increases when new complements came into view, that on old complements may diminish, or disappear altogether. In the case of technical progress this is, of course, well known but the case of potential resources drawn into the network of the structure of production is not altogether different. There just is no such thing as *a* rate of return uniform throughout the economic system. Output from resources which until yesterday were unused must compete with some existing output. Strictly speaking, of course, we should rule out all such cases as involving the failure of some plans and thus falling outside equilibrium analysis. But by the same token we then rule out the possibility of investment in equilibrium, or at least of its having any repercussions. The real difficulty here is that of conceiving of any major change, like investment, while the consistency of all plans remains unimpaired. It is hard to avoid the conclusion that the notion of a state of intertemporal equilibrium which allows for capital change, but only such change as will upset no single individual plan, is hardly less open to objections than the Keynesian notion of general short-period equilibrium.

The theory of capital as we find it in Hayek's writing did not come into existence as a result of deliberate endeavour but as a by-product of an effort that had a different aim. Böhm-Bawerk, in many respects more a Ricardian than an Austrian, attempted to answer the Ricardian question how, in a competitive economy, the owners of augmentable material resources can succeed in drawing a permanent income from them. In the course of his quest he introduced the notion of a 'structure of production' which permits us to classify capital resources according to their 'distance from the consumption end'. He had to rely on the (intertemporal) heterogeneity of capital resources in order to account for the productivity of investment. He made use of a certain property of capital resources in order to solve a problem in the theory of distribution, a means to an end. But the idea of the heterogeneity of the capital stock was no sooner born than it was seen to call for development in its own right, partly because the criterion of classification Böhm-Bawerk chose is evidently not the only possible one, but largely because most economic theory had simply ignored it and treated the stock of capital as a homogeneous fund. It is true that the difference between fixed and circulating capital had always been known to hide problems and that, at least since Ricardo's chapter 'On Machinery', these had been discussed. All the same, Hayek's main contribution to the theory of capital has been the endeavour to initiate its modern development.

Alas, this development has made little progress since 1941. The very idea of a theory of capital pursued for its own sake seems lost under the sands of time. In 1963, in his De Vries lectures, Professor Solow, in this as in other matters the most articulate spokesman of the neoclassical hierarchy, told his audience 'Capital theory ... has a technocratic and a descriptive side. I believe that the easiest and safest route to a simple but rigorous view of the subject is to begin technocratically.'³ And 'Thinking about saving and investment from this technocratic point of view has convinced me that the central concept in capital theory should be *the rate of return on investment*. In short, we really want a theory of interest rates, not a theory of capital' (ibid.: 16. His italics).

In this way the clock was put back. In the common parlance of economists today capital theory means the theory of interest (or profit). A few efforts have been made to keep the theory of capital alive among which Professor Kirzner's *An Essay on Capital* (New York 1966) has been outstanding. It is also true that in the Cambridge controversies of recent years the subject of the heterogeneity of capital and some of its implications has repeatedly come up for discussion. But nobody, to our knowledge, has suggested that one of these implications is the need for a morphology of the capital stock. The present situation of the theory Hayek initiated in 1941 is as dismal as we described it.

We thus find Hayekian capital theory in the paradoxical position that while, as we saw, it has inspired a number of variations on some of its themes which have left their mark on the economic thought of the last thirty-five years, its own continued existence is today by no means assured. To secure a new lease of life for it is one of the most urgent tasks facing us today.

TOWARDS AN ORIENTATIVE PROCESS ANALYSIS

We have heard the suggestion that Hayek, at some time during the 1940s, and before devoting most of his efforts to political philosophy, turned from an adherent into a critic of equilibrium analysis and became an exponent of process analysis in general and the market process in particular. This view finds little support in Hayek's writings. He makes it quite clear that the *genetic-causal* method of the Austrians⁴ is his method and says that

> it refers to an explanation of the economic process as it proceeds in time, an explanation in terms of causation which must necessarily be treated as a chain of historical sequences. What we find here is not mutual interdependence between all phenomena but a unilateral dependence of the succeeding event on the preceding one. This kind of causal explanation of the process in time is of course the ultimate goal of all

economic analysis, and equilibrium analysis is significant only in so far as it is preparatory to this main task.

(Hayek 1941: 17)

There is no contradiction; equilibrium analysis is a necessary first step on our way to causal explanation, a means towards an end.

But the kind of social process in which the 'unilateral dependence of the succeeding event on the preceding one' provides the prototype of explanation is not the only kind of process of which we might think. We also have to ask whether it is consistent with the Austrian theory of the market as process, as evolved by Hayek and Kirzner,[5] or even with the Austrian argument against the measurement of capital.

There are at least two possible types of social process. (There may be more). We may describe the first as 'mechanical', the second (for want of a better term) as 'orientative'. In the first, whatever men do within a period depends on the position they have reached. A 'feedback' mechanism in which each subsequent step depends on 'distance from equilibrium' is a special instance of it. Actors, when in disequilibrium, plan to take their next steps in the direction of equilibrium. This is what Hayek must have had in mind. 'The direction in which an entrepreneur will have to revise his plans will depend on the direction in which events prove to differ from his expectations. The statement of the conditions under which individual plans will be compatible is therefore implicitly a statement of what will happen if they are not compatible' (1941: 23). But in a footnote to this passage we are warned 'This is strictly true only if we are thinking of a single deviation of a particular element in a situation which is otherwise in equilibrium, that is on the assumption that all other expectations are confirmed. If more than one element turns out to be different from what was expected, the relation is no longer so simple.'

Experience shows that in the real world of disequilibrium different persons will typically hold different expectations about the same future event. If so, at best one person's expectation can be confirmed and all other expectations will be disappointed. Hence the 'assumption that all other expectations are confirmed' cannot possibly hold. Nobody can take his equilibrium bearings if he does not know how others will act. In such a situation, which we have every reason to regard as normal, his equilibrium, as Hayek admits, cannot serve as a source of a 'feedback mechanism'. The beacon that had been designed to keep entrepreneurs from straying from the narrow path of convergent expectations turns out, on most nights, to be rather dim.

The other kind of social process, by contrast, leaves ample scope for divergent expectations. In it men's actions are neither determined by what happened in a past period nor by the distance of their present position from an imaginary equilibrium. No doubt, in making and revising their plans they will take account of these facts. But the latter serve them as points of orientation, and not as determining forces.

This, second, kind of process offers scope for the exercise of the autonomy of the human mind. Real inceptive action inspired by new knowledge is here possible. The source of such new knowledge may well be past experience, but the latter requires interpretation by a discerning mind, and optimists will interpret it differently from pessimists. The human mind is a filter of experience, but each individual's filter is different from every other filter. Divergent expectations are thus as 'natural' a feature of the social landscape as are divergent tastes. Changes in the constellation of knowledge are an inevitable concomitant of the passing of time, and changes in the constellation of expectations are bound to follow them.

This second, kind of 'spontaneous' or 'orientative' process does not lend itself any less to the method of causal analysis than does our first. To be sure, we can no longer 'predict' what will happen in future periods. But if we accept that we have to seek the causes of human action in ends pursued and the constraints operating in such pursuit, causal analysis in terms of the orientation of the various actors at various points of time during a course of action appears quite possible.

It seems to us that such orientative process analysis is much more companionable to two of Hayek's major achievements as an economist than mechanical process could be. When Austrian economists, following Hayek, conceive of the market as a process, and not a state of affairs, they conceive of it as implying not merely the co-ordination of knowledge presently existing in various parts of the economic system, but also the continuous digestion of new knowledge entailing the obsolescence of some old knowledge. For in the absence of the latter the market as process must evidently come to an early end as soon as all existing knowledge has been co-ordinated. What keeps the market process in continuous motion thus is the continuous dissemination of new knowledge. No state of uniform knowledge ever exists, and divergent expectations seem a natural concomitant to divergent knowledge.

Furthermore, when Hayek attributes our inability to measure the stock of capital to divergent expectations about future income streams to be derived from it, the permanent nature of such divergence appears pretty well assumed. Should we not acknowledge its ubiquitous presence?

LESSONS OF HAYEKIAN CAPITAL THEORY FOR TODAY

Economics has declared these public values [prices] to have the force and meaning of such physical attributes as length or mass, and to be able to support a vast structure of aggregative calculations. Economics has veritably turned imprecision itself into a science: economics, the science of the quantification of the unquantifiable and the aggregation of the incompatible. It has followed this road at so violent a gallop, that much which is of significance and influence has been trampled on, much territory has been claimed which cannot be held.

(G. L. S. Shackle *Epistemics and Economics*,
Cambridge 1972: 360)

What lessons does Hayekian capital theory hold for us today? The first lesson is clearly to distrust all macroeconomic magnitudes. 'If the stock of capital which will be required in a changing society to keep income constant at successive moments cannot in any sense be defined as a constant magnitude, it is also impossible to say that any sacrifice of present income in order to increase future income (or the reverse) will necessarily lead to any net change in the amount of capital' (1941: 335). If capital cannot be measured, neither can investment. This corollary of their own doctrine 'neo-Keynesian' economists appear to have overlooked. It is incumbent on Hayekians to bring it to their attention. Moreover, if 'we cannot determine the size of either saving or investment by any reference to changes in the quantity of capital' then 'with the abandonment of this basis for the distinction there must go the economists' habitual practice of separating out the part of general investment activity which happens to leave the capital stock in some sense constant, as something different from activities which add to that stock. This distinction has no relationship to anything in the real world.' (1941: 336)

The same applies to 'aggregate profits', as Sir John Hicks has recently shown. 'Only in the steady state can we unambiguously determine the size of profits. Out of the steady state the profit that is allocated to a particular period depends on expectations, such as are in practice expressed by conventions about depreciation. There is no such convention that is unambiguously right.'[6] Outside the steady state questions about the mode of the distribution of incomes appear to lose their meaning, and much recent dispute about 'the rate of profits' becomes pointless.

Next, we have to consider some implications of the divergence of expectations. Divergent expectations may be as common a feature of our economic landscape as are divergent tastes, but they are more important for asset markets than for ordinary commodity markets. The central asset market, the Stock Exchange, is the distinguishing characteristic of a market economy. A socialist economy may leave room for a 'private sector' of some size, but it cannot have a Stock Exchange. Economists of the Austrian persuasion have thus good reason to take more interest in asset markets and the circumstances surrounding them than (with the distinguished exception of Professor Machlup) they have done.

Divergent expectations are of significance in asset markets for (at least) two reasons: firstly, because the securities traded in them embody titles to future income streams which involve long-term expectations, while the annual flow of potatoes does not; secondly, because in asset markets the stock held is large in relation to the annual flow of new assets, and the willingness to hold an existing stock involves expectations in terms of 'bullishness' and 'bearishness'. In fact, asset markets can operate only as long as 'bulls' and 'bears' hold divergent expectations. The function of the asset market consists in dividing its participants into two equal halves of 'bulls' and 'bears'. Prices must move until such a state is reached, and the (market day) equilibrium price thus reflects a balance of divergent expectations. As we all know, prices formed in such asset markets, speculative by their very nature, are most volatile. These markets generate every day capital gains and losses which Hayek in Chapter XXIII described as 'the effects of unforeseen changes'.

Two consequences of the volatile nature of these asset markets, and the divergent expectations to which they lend daily expression, call for notice. In the first place, these daily capital gains and losses produce a continuous redistribution of wealth in a market economy. Those who advocate another redistribution of wealth by means of taxation for egalitarian purposes must learn that whatever desirable state of the distribution of wealth they may hope to attain one day, the market will modify it in the days that follow. Secondly, it is hard to see how general equilibrium in a market economy, which must comprise both, asset and commodity markets, could ever be established. The mode of distribution of resources in a 'datum' of general equilibrium, but a datum that is affected every day by capital gains and losses in asset markets.

Finally, scepticism about equilibrium need not deter us from appraising the relative strength and weakness of the equilibrating forces in various situations. In fact, it must encourage us to do so. To make confident use of the notion of equilibrium means to imply that the equilibrating forces will always be of sufficient strength to triumph over all obstacles. A sceptic might readily admit that such situations may exist, but he will probably doubt whether they occur with sufficient frequency to warrant our treating them as the norm. The more sceptical we are about general equilibrium as the central notion of economic analysis, the more incumbent on us it becomes to examine each situation individually with respect to the balance of strength of equilibrating and disequilibrating forces.

These general considerations are germane to a problem we encounter when, in the spirit of Hayek's theory of capital, we begin to ask questions about the concrete forms of the capital structure. Capital structure implies complementarity of various capital resources. Within each firm the complementarity of its capital combination is of course planned, envisaged in and vouchsafed by its production plan. But are market forces of sufficient strength to generate an over-all complementarity of capital resources in different firms and industries? We can show that a tendency to it does exist, we can indicate the equilibrating forces, but must not ignore the obstacles they encounter.

Capital goods which fit into no existing capital combination will evidently have to be scrapped as they are of no use to their owners. On the other hand, where 'gaps' in the capital structure ('bottlenecks') arise it will be profitable to fill them. The equilibrating forces operating in the direction of an integration of the capital structure are readily seen. But of course unforeseen change may overtake them. It remains true that in a market economy what it is profitable to do depends on the actions of others.

The time dimension of the integrating forces appears to be here a matter of some importance. In our instance these forces will in most cases belong to the short period. Surplus capital equipment may be kept in existence by speculative hopes for the future, but this can happen only for a short while, while the 'filling of gaps' requires new investment which by definition belongs to the short run. The faster the equilibrating forces can do their work, the more they are likely to succeed. It remains true of course that certain obstacles to the over-all complementarity of all capital resources are inherent in the character of a market economy: the capital resources of competing firms can hardly be said to be complementary to each other. All the same, it seems to us that, without prejudice to whatever scepticism about the value of the notion of general equilibrium we might entertain, it is permissible to assert with some confidence the existence of a strong tendency towards the integration of the capital structure. A theory of capital in Hayek's sense may evolve along these lines.

Part IV

SUBJECTIVISM AND THE INTERPRETATION OF INSTITUTIONS

14

CARL MENGER AND THE INCOMPLETE REVOLUTION OF SUBJECTIVISM [1978]

I have to start by dispelling misunderstandings to which my title may give rise. In the first place, it is not suggested that Menger, if anybody, has to bear the blame for the incompleteness of the subjectivist movement, and there are few pioneers in the history of thought to whom it is given to witness the completion of what they have set in motion. Secondly, I have to confess that I know of no criterion that would permit us to decide whether a movement of thought has reached its 'end' and is thus 'complete'. Subjectivism has in this century been extended from human preferences to expectations. In years to come it may be extended to the interpretation of so-called information. What, then, does its incompleteness at Menger's time signify?

In this paper I am concerned with certain features of Menger's work which appear to have prevented him from carrying his subjectivist intentions quite as far as, in the light of the later development of the train of thought he set in motion, might have been possible; in other words, with certain obstacles to his subjectivist mode of thought that he failed to surmount.

At the Menger Symposium in 1971, Professor Hayek characterized the style of Menger's subjectivism in a memorable passage:

> Menger believes that in observing the actions of other persons we are assisted by a capacity of *understanding* the meaning of such actions in a manner in which we cannot understand physical events. This is closely connected with one of the senses in which at least Menger's followers spoke of the 'subjective' character of their theories, by which they meant, among other things, that they were based on our capacity to

213

comprehend the intended meaning of the observed actions. 'Observation,' as Menger uses the term, has thus a meaning that modern behaviorists would not accept, and it implies a *Verstehen* [understanding] in the sense in which Max Weber later developed the concept.

(Hicks and Weber 1973: 8)

In other words, even though Menger never uses the word, 'subjectivism', this is the essential meaning of his teaching.

There are, however, important parts of Menger's work which do not seem to fit into this pattern. Let us take his famous definition of value:

Value is thus nothing inherent in goods, no property of them, nor an independent thing existing by itself. It is a judgment economizing men make about the importance of the goods at their disposal for the maintenance of their lives and well-being. Hence value does not exist outside the consciousness of men.

(Menger 1951: 121)

To be sure, value is here subjective, it resides in the 'judgment economizing men make', but at the same time such judgements are oriented to something Menger seems to have regarded as objective, i.e. the nature of human needs. In what sense is a drug addict interested in the maintenance of his well-being? Perhaps in a purely formal sense, but in his classification of wants Menger appears to have a more solid, 'objectivist' orientation in mind. He says,

The maintenance of life depends neither on having a comfortable bed nor on having a chessboard, but the use of these goods contributes, and certainly in very different degrees, to the increase of our well-being. Hence there can also be no doubt that, when men have a choice between doing without a comfortable bed or doing without a chessboard, they will forego the latter more readily than the former.

(Menger 1951: 123)

From this example we have to infer that there exists a universal order of wants in all men, as part of the human condition, which permits us to predict what choices men will make. Menger tells us, to be sure, that men frequently misjudge the order of their wants. But as we can only *mis*-judge that which exists objectively, the subjectivism of our conscious minds contrasts sharply with the objective, almost physiological, nature of our wants. There seems little scope here for changes of taste or fashion, for instance, from beds to chessboards. It is a long way from Menger's theory of wants to Mises's doctrine of ends and means.

For a long time students of Menger have been puzzled by the precise meaning of his notion of 'exact laws'. He regards it as the prime task of economic science to formulate such laws. In Appendix V of the *Untersuchungen* we are told that 'in the field of human phenomena exact laws (so-called 'laws of nature') are attainable under the same conditions as in that of natural phenomena.' In this regard, then, there is no difference at all between social and natural sciences. On the other hand, Menger distinguishes sharply between these 'exact laws', i.e. 'laws of the phenomena which are not only valid without exception but which, according to the laws of our thought simply cannot be thought of in any other way but as without exceptions' (Menger 1963: 42), and 'empirical laws' which rest on observation and admit of exceptions.

Menger uses the 'law of demand' as an example for this distinction. According to him the exact law tells us not merely that a rise in demand will lead to a rise in price, but that, under certain conditions, the extent of this price rise is quantitatively exactly determinable (*'dem Masse nach genau bestimmbar'*). But he goes on to warn us that these conditions require not only that all participants maximize their satisfaction in the pursuit of which they must be free of all external coercion, but also the absence of error and ignorance. Hence we must not expect to find instances of the exact law in the real world. It is

> unempirical when tested by reality in its full complexity. But what else does this prove than that the results of exact research do not find their criteria in experience in the above sense? The above law is, in spite of everything, true, completely true, and of the highest significance for the theoretical understanding of price phenomena as soon as one looks at it from that standpoint appropriate for exact research. If one looks at it from the point of view of realistic research, to be sure, one arrives at contradictions . . . but in this case the error lies not in the law, but in the false perspective.
>
> (Menger 1963: 57)

These views will no doubt strike many of us as odd, but the main reason for it is that we have come to take it for granted that ours is a world of relentless positivism. There will be few natural scientists today ready to acknowledge that their prime task is to find exact laws of the kind Menger describes. For the most of us 'laws of nature' are empirical laws, in principle falsifiable. But we have to remember that Menger was an Aristotelian for whom the quest for 'essence' constituted the central task of the human intellect, and that he wrote before Mach and Poincaré revolutionized the philosophy of science after the turn of the century. It is also not unlikely that Menger allowed the mathematical form of most theoretical work in the natural sciences to deceive him about the logical nature of its content.

On the other hand, we may find in Menger's emphasis on the need for exact laws the origin of what Hayek has described as the 'pure logic of choice'.

Finally, we have to ask how Menger faced the issue of subjectivism *versus* determinism. In a world governed by exact laws, how much room is there for individual choice and decision? Menger, it appears, did not see any irreconcilable contradiction. In the Preface to the *Principles* we learn

> Although reference to freedom of the human will may well be legitimate as an objection to the complete predictability of economic activity, it can never have force as a denial of the conformity to definite laws of phenomena that condition the outcome of the economic activity of men and are entirely independent of the human will. It is precisely phenomena of this description, however, which are the objects of study in our science.

(Menger 1951: 48–9)

It seems legitimate to interpret this statement to mean that while men are free to choose their ends, the means they have to employ are subject to many limitations, and that economic laws ultimately inhere in the scarcity and specificity of means. In the *Untersuchungen*, on the other hand, we are told in the title of Appendix VI 'that the starting-point and the final objective of all human economizing is strictly determined.' But the vigour of this pronouncement is subsequently modified.

> Arbitrary judgment, error, and other influences can, and actually do, bring it about that acting men take different roads

216

from a strictly given starting-point to a just as strictly determined goal of their action. It is nevertheless certain that, in
the above circumstances, only one road can be the most
efficient.

(Menger 1963: 264)

Let me draw attention to two aspects of this passage. On the one
hand we may well ask how a 'strictly determined goal of action'
is to be reconciled with freedom of the human will. On the other
hand, however, the emphasis on ignorance and error as obstacles
to the determinateness of the outcome of action points beyond
Menger's own times, to the subjectivism of the twentieth century,
as it finds expression in the teaching of today's Austrian school,
and even in the work of Keynes and Shackle. Menger's readiness
to take the human mind with all its limitations as his starting point
is what really distinguishes Menger from Jevons and Walras. As
Professor Jaffe put it so well:

Man, as Menger saw him, far from being a 'lightning calcu-
lator', is a bumbling, erring, ill-informed creature, plagued
with uncertainty, forever hovering between alluring hopes
and haunting fears, and congenitally incapable of making
finely calibrated decisions in pursuit of satisfactions. Hence
Menger's scales of the declining importance of satisfactions
are represented by discrete integers. In Menger's scheme of
thought, positive first derivatives and negative second derivatives of utility with respect to quantity had no place; nothing
is differentiable.

(Jaffe 1976: 511–24)

Menger, a man between two worlds, an Aristotelian who had to
live in an age of triumphant positivism, was a nineteenth century
subjectivist who was unable to rid himself of his reliance on objective wants and his quest for 'exact laws'. But at the same time his
work points beyond itself and beyond his day to important issues
with which we are today intensely concerned.

15

VICISSITUDES OF SUBJECTIVISM AND THE DILEMMA OF THE THEORY OF CHOICE [1978]

INTRODUCTION

The social world consists of facts and the perspectives in which we see them. The number of possible perspectives is always very large; the number actually in use in the models presented by social sciences at any time is bound to be relatively small. All the social sciences have passed through periods of consensus during which one 'paradigm' seemed paramount, and subsequent periods of controversy characterized by a multitude of paradigms espoused by rival schools. Nevertheless the number of paradigms in actual use is always an exiguous proportion of those possible.

All analytical thought requires abstraction, but the more inclined we are to concede this need, the more apt we become to forget that that which has been abstracted from may become important, if not at present, perhaps at a later stage of our enquiry. In the economic thinking of our age this tendency has been greatly strengthened by the well known proclivity of model builders to 'close' their models and thus to impart to the relationships described in them, which in reality, often are relationships between contingent facts, an appearance of 'necessity' that seems to lend them a higher methodological status. This is usually done by introducing an array of restrictive assumptions.

Some methodologists believe this to be a necessary, indeed a welcome, step in expanding and unifying knowledge. 'A lot of effort is expended to assure that the theorems proposed will be "necessarily true" once the language is only used "correctly".' (Leijonhufvud 1976: 8). It is not surprising that the apparent necessity of the theorems proposed in our models soon begins to

218

'rub off' on the concepts used in constructing them and tends to lend them a spurious respectability. We forget by what artifices of abstraction the necessity that dwells in our models was obtained and refrain from asking awkward questions about what other forms the contingent relationships here appearing in the guise of necessary ones might in reality assume. We no longer question the set of concepts used. The potential range of experience mirrored in our theorems shrivels.

In this paper we argue that a certain view of human action (hereafter, for brevity, referred to as 'subjectivism') which commands wide assent as soon as presented and might even be described as the 'natural view', a view which once found expression in Lord Robbins' famous definition of economics,[1] has been entirely ignored when the foundations of modern microeconomics were laid; in fact, that the 'theory of choice' which came to occupy the place of such a foundation is incompatible with this 'natural view' of human action. In other words, we contend that, as economic thought developed in this century, subjectivism, again and again, has been thwarted.

SUBJECTIVISM OF MEANS, OF ENDS, AND OF EXPECTATIONS

We can best understand human action in terms of means and ends since our own experience of it has been made in these terms. Means must exist in the present, or at least be regarded as likely to come within our reach in the foreseeable future, while ends necessarily lie entirely within the future, near or remote. When we look at means and ends we look at them, therefore, within a perspective which contains several layers of time. These, it is now widely agreed, can constitute no continuum. Time is irreversible. The present is always a solitary instant. The various layers of our perspective of the future exist only at a given moment. As time passes and we move from one solitary instant to the next, these layers cease to exist and their contents appear in the shape of new layers composing a new perspective.

Acts of choice, though made in the present, always concern future objects. We never are able to choose between present objects. It is always 'too late' for that.

The plan of action, its 'blueprint' or scheme of intended action comprehends means and ends (or purposes) as envisaged by the actor before any observable action is taken. It is within the framework of the plan that means and ends take firm shape. We may therefore say that the plan, as its mental scheme, 'guides' the course of action, or that the latter may be 'explained' by the former as its 'cause'. It is the separate existence of these terms that permits us to juxtapose *ex ante* with *ex post*, the plan with the outcome of the course of action guided by it.

The ends denoted in some plans may be intermediate ends, means to further ends. At any moment the actor is engaged in carrying out a whole bundle of plans which he has to co-ordinate in his mind. We almost invariably find that within this comprehensive scheme the ends of some plans serve as means in other plans.

This whole scheme of action exists within the actor's mind at any moment of time, but finds its external manifestation in an observable course of action that gradually unfolds over time. Over time, alas, circumstances change and plans have to be revised and adapted to such change. Unexpected obstacles may impede the planned course of action. Some means are found to be inadequate to the tasks allotted to them in the original plans; other objects, originally not thought of as means, turn out to be within the compass of a plan in which they might serve as such. Above all, ends are reconsidered as the generations succeed one another, but often enough sooner than that. The revision of plans occurs as experience is made over time, but all experience has to be interpreted, and different men will interpret the same experience in different ways. In attempting to understand human action we must take account of the subjectivism of interpretation no less than of the subjectivism of ends.

This is most relevant to our appreciation of the role of knowledge in action. Even where different actors possess identical knowledge about the same objects, they will not make the same use of it, as such knowledge exists for each of them within a different frame of relevance. Also, in a changing world a good deal of our practical knowledge (how to use means to obtain ends) is continuously exposed to a threat of obsolescence while new knowledge is only gradually acquired. For purposes of action there is no such thing as a constant or expanding stock of knowledge. All our practical knowledge is always problematical.

All human action, of course, takes place in a world of uncertainty. The future is unknowable though not unimaginable. In this regard two important facts call for our attention. In the first place, future events, whether pertaining to means or ends, typically appear in plans in the form of *expectations*. But different actors will typically hold divergent expectations about the same future event. The regular appearance of 'bulls' and 'bears' on markets in which transactions concerning future events are concluded proves it. Expectations are the more important the more strongly they diverge.

Secondly, in an uncertain world in which the success of plans must depend on future events unforeseeable at the time of planning it becomes necessary to make alternative plans against various contingencies. For practical reasons only a limited number of them can be made in each case. An unlimited number of alternative plans in a given situation is an obvious impossibility.[2]

SUBJECTIVISM IN MICROECONOMICS

A 'change in methods of production in a given state of knowledge' is, strictly speaking, a contradiction in terms.

(Robinson 1952: 54)

When we ask how much of the subjectivist view of human action, sketched briefly, if inadequately, in the last section, has been absorbed into the main body of modern economic thought, it will be best to distinguish, as regards the latter, between micro- and macro-economics. For the relationship between the subjectivist view and macroeconomics, and in particular the treatment it received at the hands of Keynes, is a matter we will have to take up in the following section. Its relationship to microeconomics, on the other hand, can be summed up in one brief sentence: it suffered complete neglect.

We will have to examine the consequences of this neglect in three instances of which one concerns the microeconomic framework of so-called 'data' while the other two belong more strictly to the theory of choice. In each case we will attempt to demonstrate that neglect of the circumstances surrounding action, as we described them above, has not merely led economic thinkers who, from Pareto onwards, were in this century responsible for laying the foundations of modern microeconomics to make a number of highly questionable and unrealistic assumptions, but also that, given their methodological predilections, they had little choice in the matter. It will be seen that as the neglect of action compelled them to regard forms of action as though they were forms of something else, they were driven to adopt a perspective so restrictive that in it action could have no place. With such a perspective once adopted it is perhaps inevitable, but in any case most likely, that an outcome of action should appear in the guise of the product of a mechanism that contingent events are made to look as though they were 'necessary' and that a whole range of important practical problems vanishes from view. A determinate outcome of an act of choice is, of course, a contradiction in terms.

We are often told that tastes, resources and technical knowledge constitute three classes of 'independent variables' which together determine the 'price vector' and 'output vector' of the economic system. As resources and knowledge serve the satisfaction of wants, this sounds odd to us if we view the matter from the perspective of subjectivism. How can means exist independently of ends? How can a sudden and sustained fall in the demand for automobiles fail to destroy the resource character of much of the capital equipment of the automobile industry and to affect the economic value of a good deal of its technical knowledge? Where, then, is the independence of these variables?

The answer is of course that, looking at these matters from the neoclassical perspective, we would never be able to 'see' these events happening. We conduct our thinking at a level of abstraction at which all resources are homogeneous and knowledge exists in a form sufficiently universal to make it useful to satisfy any tastes, however rapidly changing.

Such an assumption of a homogeneous stock of resources and a completely variable, and hence non-descript, 'stock of knowledge' is not merely unrealistic. It also hides a whole range of problems that deserve study: to what, if limited, extent resources are in fact mobile, and to what extent in reality knowledge exists in sufficiently abstract form to permit multiple applications. It is, for instance, obvious that the growth rate of an economy must to some extent depend on the degree of mobility of its resources. What most interests us, however, in this connection is that the assumption of complete mobility ignores the distinction between means and ends and conceals an important insight we owe to the subjectivist view: that means are means only within a given plan, an existing scheme of intended action, and that, though some alternative uses always exist, and a number of alternative plans usually has to be made before any action is taken, an infinite number of alternatives never exists.

We now have to consider the position of the theory of choice currently in fashion *vis-à-vis* subjectivism. For our purpose it will be most useful to consider together its two basic tenets: 'revealed preference' and the assumption of the existence of a comprehensive preference field for each individual. Without the latter the former has little cogency.

The principle of revealed preference asserts the existence of such a close degree of correspondence between the preferences and the overt actions of an individual that we as observers are able, for each individual observed, to infer the former from the latter. Evidently this presupposes the existence of a consistent, and hence comprehensive, field of preferences for each individual. It also requires the persistence of such preference fields during periods of observation. All 'changes of tastes' must take place between periods of observation; they evidently must take place instantaneously. These are perhaps rather stringent requirements already.

Seen from the perspective of subjectivism, however, the fact that individuals simultaneously pursue different plans, albeit coordinated on a higher level, means that we can say nothing about consistency of market action observed without knowing these plans. If, for instance, we observe a woman shopper, who on her weekly visits to a store has never bought a bottle of wine, purchasing three one week, we are not entitled to infer inconsistency or that she must have changed her tastes. She may have bought them for a dinner party for a couple of friends at which she herself may not drink a drop of it. Identical objects may serve as a means for different ends. We are unable to understand what happens during a course of action we observe without knowledge of the plan that guides it.

From Pareto onwards, the comprehensive set of indifference curves as geometrical expression of the individual's order of preferences became the basis and a major dogma of microeconomics, a dogma the scribes and typesetters of the textbook industry proclaimed the more readily the less they were able to understand its hidden perils. Recently, however, Sir John Hicks has openly expressed doubt.

> It is immensely convenient, in economics, to suppose that 'the consumer' (as we call him) has a fully formed scale of

preferences, by which all choices that are available to him on the market can be ordered. I am still of the opinion that there are many purposes (including, very probably, the most important purposes) for which that assumption can be justified. But it is itself a very odd assumption; to take it, as many economists do, as being justifiable for all purposes, must, I now believe, be wrong.

(Hicks 1976: 137)

These, to be sure, are modest doubts. But in view of the well known seismographic quality of his mind, Sir John's pronouncement may mark a turning point. The time may have arrived for a critical examination of the dogma from the point of view of subjectivism.

The main source of such criticism has already been mentioned and is illustrated by our example of the woman shopper. Means derive their meaning from the ends they serve. Outside the context of given plans the facts of preference or indifference have no meaningful existence. Market 'data' observed require interpretation in terms of the actor's scheme of action.

To put this matter differently, the existence of a comprehensive preference field means that the combinations of goods denoted by each point in our positive quadrant are simultaneously present to the mind of the actor, an evident impossibility. It means, furthermore, that an infinite number of alternative plans against any possible relative price change has been made beforehand and can instantaneously be set in motion. In reality we are not dealing here with action, which means a sequence of acts of the mind, but with mere reaction by mindless mechanisms made up to look like human actors. To speak here of 'choice' is gross misuse of language. With a given set of comprehensive indifference curves and given prices, what is there to 'choose'? With the result already inherent in the assumptions, a theory of action is indeed redundant.

Choice is an activity. A theory that refuses to concern itself with activity but nevertheless proposes to make use of its results must rest on the assumption that what happens during an activity does not matter to its result. It is therefore incompatible with any view which ascribes significance to states of mind and forms of action.

What would happen if we gave up the notion of a comprehensive preference field? We would then be confronted by the possible existence of patches of indecision, areas in which some actors would at first be unable to act. If, say, as a result of violent price movements many people suddenly find themselves in the midst of such areas, they will, wherever possible, defer making decisions, but where not, may be compelled to make decisions other than those they would have reached had they had time to ponder the new situation. Men are not equal, and different agents require periods of different length to make up their minds. Hence in the real market economy there will always be some agents who are not in equilibrium because they require more time to put their preferences in order – a conclusion of some significance which the theory under discussion conceals from us.

By the same token, we now understand why this 'very odd assumption' became the basis of the general equilibrium model that dominates microeconomics: there can, of course, be no general equilibrium without equilibrium of each agent, and the 'odd assumption' serves to ensure that this always exists. In other words, the theory under discussion sacrifices realism and a proper regard for the facts of human action, along with a good deal else, for the sake of ensuring the existence of a determinate general equilibrium position. Yet this aim cannot be achieved since, as long as we permit 'tastes' to change, no equilibrium position, of course, remains determinate for long. Sooner or later such change is bound to happen. It is the tragedy of the neoclassical model that the independence of its independent variables (tastes, resources, technical knowledge) destroys its principal objective for the sake of which so much had to be foregone, and that the very reason for which the theory of choice, its base, had to be given such an odd shape proves in the end as futile as the whole attempt to ignore the forms and meaning of action in the construction of a model ostensibly devoted to a description of the interaction of market forces. The dilemma of the theory of choice is to be found in this fact.

The sad tale of the vicissitudes of subjectivism, however, is not yet at an end.

SUBJECTIVISM IN MACROECONOMICS

It might be thought that if our attempt to trace subjectivist influences in microeconomics has proved abortive, we are unlikely to fare any better with macroeconomics since the former is ostensibly concerned with individual action while the latter is not. The matter is, however, more complex than it seems. This is largely due to the prominent, if unsatisfactory, place expectations have come to occupy in macroeconomics and to the arbitrary manner in which Keynes handled them when modern macroeconomics was in its infancy.

We have emphasized the importance of expectations for the subjectivist view of action. It is well known that in the *General Theory*, Keynes's main aim was to establish the possibility of unemployment equilibrium and that everything else he had to say was made to serve this purpose. The introduction of expectations was thus to him a means to an end. He brought them into his argument when it suited him[3] and left them out when it did not.[4] Sir John Hicks has recently noted the fact.

> He [Keynes] has (very skillfully) divided his theory into two parts. There is one, that concerned with the Marginal Efficiency of Capital and with Liquidity Preference, which is unquestionably *in* time; it is basically forward-looking; time and uncertainty are written all over it. But there is another, the multiplier theory (and indeed the whole theory of production and prices which is – somehow – wrapped up in the multiplier theory) which is out of time. It runs in terms of demand curves, and supply curves and cost curves – just the old tools of equilibrium economics. A state of equilibrium, by definition, is a state in which something, something relevant, is *not* changing; so the use of an equilibrium concept is a signal that time, in some respect at least, has been put to one side.
>
> (Hicks 1976: 140)

It would be easy to add other examples of Keynes's arbitrary use of expectations. The speculative demand for money arises only in the markets for financial assets. Commodity speculation apparently does not exist. Moreover, in order to make expectations amenable to the requirements of his macroeconomic framework, Keynes had to transform individual expectations into a 'macro-proxy', viz. his 'state of long-term expectation'. In this way the crucial importance of the divergence of individual expectations, of 'bullishness' and 'bearishness' he had himself stressed in chapter 15 of the *Treatise* was lost. In liquidity preference, on the other hand, the divergence of individual expectations is allowed to play a crucial part.

So subjectivism was once again thwarted. Yet, for all this there is today a ray of hope. The present position of economics with its two separate realms of macro- and microeconomics is not likely to last. Attempts at co-ordination and unification are sure to be made. If the first attempts are likely to fail, we may expect renewed efforts at a higher level of sophistication and, one hopes, penetration.

In the course of these endeavours, expectations will have to be introduced into microeconomics, since in macroeconomics they already have a part, however unsatisfactory and stunted. They could not be introduced purely formally, for instance, by assuming that every commodity market includes a forward market in which expectations find expression and are co-ordinated. For the importance of expectations clearly varies between different markets. In a pure flow market, like the Marshallian fish market, they matter little. Expectations are the more important the greater the proportion of transactions from and for stock in a market. The difference between asset and commodity markets here calls for notice. Without divergent expectations the former cannot continue to exist.

Purely formal assumptions can vitiate economic theories. The assumption, for instance, in monetary theory, that the market chooses 'at random' one of its goods to serve as a *numéraire* contrasts with the plain fact that the precious metals were so chosen for very good reasons, and not at all 'at random'. It is to be hoped that when expectations are brought into microeconomics, where, as elements of individual action, they properly belong, the instruments of formalism will, even by their addicts, be handled with restraint.

In fact, it will then become apparent that expectations are deeply embedded in the view of human action we tried to adumbrate in the section on subjectivism of means, of ends, and of expectations (pp. 219–21) and can no more be divorced from it than can a passage be torn from its context without losing its meaning. All expectations derive their economic meaning from the plans they guide. Their presentation within an analytical framework requires, therefore, a full view of action, and of the network of plans as guided by acts of the mind. It will prove impossible to introduce expectations into microeconomics without adopting the natural view of human action we set out above.

When this has been done, subjectivism will at long last come into its own.

16

FROM MISES TO SHACKLE

An essay on Austrian economics and the kaleidic society [1976]

INTRODUCTION

A delicate task faces the historian of thought whenever an established doctrine, what in the language of current fashion is called a paradigm or, more recently, a 'research programme', is challenged. He has to trace the genealogy of the challengers. To this end he must pick up threads covered by the sands of time, dust them, and try to connect them with the new skein of thought.

His task is all the more difficult, but also the more urgent and rewarding, since history of thought is almost invariably written from the point of view of the reigning orthodoxy. For Schumpeter, Walras's system is the crowning achievement, hence every earlier economist is either a predecessor or belongs to a lost tribe. From such a perspective most unorthodox strands of thought appear as blind alleys if they are mentioned at all. By the same token the challengers must seem 'rootless' iconoclasts. Nevertheless, the historian cannot rest or claim to have completed his task until he has unearthed at least some of the historical roots of the ideas of the challengers of his day.

Professor Shackle's *Epistemics and Economics* (1972) is a case in point. His bold challenge to neoclassical orthodoxy, with its determinism borrowed from the natural sciences and with its bland assumption of a world sufficiently tranquil and restful to provide us with a set of supposedly constant 'data', is bound to have far-reaching repercussions. Although neoclassical orthodoxy is the main target of his attack, the subtitle of his book *A Critique of Economic Doctrines* (we may note the plural) indicates a wider scope. Some economic doctrines of our time, we may surmise, invite more trenchant criticism than do others.

In what follows we attempt to show that the body of economic thought that has come to be known as 'Austrian', and in particular that part of it which found expression in the seminal work of Ludwig von Mises (1949), is not only less vulnerable to Shackle's attack than the main body of current orthodoxy, but that to a striking extent Mises and Shackle share a common outlook on the foundations of our discipline. In the light of this circumstance, we then examine the position of Austrian economics with regard to Shackle's *kaleidic society*, a society in which sooner or later unexpected change is bound to upset existing patterns, a society 'interspersing its moments or intervals of order, assurance and beauty with sudden disintegration and a cascade into a new pattern' (Shackle 1972: 76).

SHACKLE'S CRITIQUE

Shackle has attacked the neoclassical citadel just where it is most vulnerable. The assumptions made by general equilibrium theory about nature and scope of the knowledge possessed by economic actors have never been stated with much precision. All economic action is of course concerned with the future, the more or less distant future. But the future is to all of us unknowable, though not unimaginable. Shackle strongly contends that our ignorance of the future invalidates any theory attributing knowledge of the future to economic actors engaged in providing for it. To defend a theory against this criticism, we evidently have to know exactly what assumptions are made about knowledge. With the modern neoclassical model this move is anything but easy.

We are often told that knowledge is to be included among the equilibrium 'data' along with tastes and resources, so that changing knowledge entails changing prices and output quantities. But 'data' must be measurable and knowledge is not. How do we determine that change of knowledge that would be required just to offset any given change of tastes or resources in such a way as to maintain an existing vector of prices?

Moreover, how can tastes and resources be of any economic relevance without being known? The independent datum 'knowledge' evidently cannot refer to them. Perhaps we should take it to refer to technological knowledge only, knowledge about how to turn input into output, about feasible 'coefficients of production' in Walras's terminology. If so, what do we have to assume about market knowledge, the knowledge of tastes and resources without which nobody can operate in a market? Do we assume that all market actors know all the tastes and resources in all markets in which they, actually or potentially, do or might operate? But if so, equilibrium should at once be attained in all markets. If we were to make this assumption, there could be no disequilibrium, no dealings at 'false prices', Walras's 'auctioneer' would become superfluous. If, on the other hand, we do not make it, how do we delimit the extent of each actor's knowledge at each point of time, and how do we deal with the flow of knowledge between actors over time?

It is perhaps only another aspect of this dilemma that it has never, to our knowledge, been made clear whether a 'state of knowledge' means a state of affairs in which everybody shares the knowledge everyone else has, or whether it merely denotes an existing 'pattern of knowledge' that permits differences in knowledge between individuals. If the former, we should be told how it could come about and how, in a world of change, it could ever be maintained. If the latter, and knowledge as a datum means just any existing pattern of knowledge, evidently not a day can pass without some change in this interindividual pattern of knowledge. As it seems to be widely agreed that some constancy of the data is necessary for general equilibrium theory to be of much relevance, daily changes in the pattern of knowledge, quite inevitable in a world of change, must be fatal to it. Whatever assumptions about knowledge we may attribute to it, general equilibrium does not seem to stand up well to a critical inquiry into them.

In modern Austrian economics, by contrast, we find the problem of knowledge to be a matter of fundamental concern. In 1937 Professor Hayek divided the subject matter of economics into the pure logic of choice and the enquiry into the dissemination of knowledge.[1] In 1946, in criticizing most modern theories of market forms, he pointed out that competition is a process, not a state of affairs, and that it reflects continuous changes in the pattern of knowledge.[2] In Mises's *Human Action*, the market process kept in motion by the flow of events is a major theme (1949).

New knowledge may originate 'exogenously' by technical progress or discovery of new resources or markets by alert minds. Some new knowledge, however, is generated 'endogenously', within the market, every day by equally alert minds observing and exploiting profitable changes in the pattern of relative prices. Old knowledge may unexpectedly become obsolete in similar ways.

The world of the market economy is thus a kaleidic world, a world of flux in which the ceaseless flow of news daily impinges on human choice and the making of decisions. We shall trace some consequences of this important insight in the work of Mises and Professor Shackle. But we can hardly expect to find more congruence between the thought of two such highly individualistic minds than the kaleidic nature of our world permits. It may be worth our while to ask to what extent, and in regard to what, Shackle in his latest work 'made progress' beyond the common ground he shares with Mises.

SIMILARITIES

It might sound rash to say that in Mises's work on praxeology in the opening chapters of *Human Action*, in which he gathers and examines the elements of a logic of successful action to serve as the basis of a methodology of the social sciences, Austrian economics attained a level of methodological self-awareness it had never previously enjoyed. But those who will be most reluctant to agree with this statement are likely to be identical with those who object strenuously to the principle of apriorism Mises expounds in the same pages, and there may be several Austrians among them. Such objections, to be sure, are largely due to a misunderstanding, a confusion between form of thought and its empirical content, which Mises attempted to clarify e.g. 1949: 38, 66. But whatever our attitude to this particular controversy, it seems to us that a good deal remains to be said for our statement about methodological self-awareness.

Before Mises, Austrians, by and large, took little interest in methodology. Carl Menger in 1883, to be sure, published his *Untersuchungen* (1883). However, what he defended in it against the attacks of the German Historical School was the Ricardian method rather than any kind of subjectivism. Moreover, this defence occurred in 1883, before the age of Poincaré and Mach. When, in 1908, Schumpeter applied Mach's positivistic methodology to economics, most Austrians felt shock and revulsion, but they lacked the firm methodological basis from which they could have attacked him (see Schumpeter 1908).

Mises drew his inspiration from a different source, the neo-

Kantian philosophy that dominated academic Germany in the first decade of this century. Max Weber can hardly be called an Austrian economist, but he made a contribution of fundamental significance to what in the hands of Mises became Austrian methodology. In 1909 Weber wrote

> The rational theory of price formation not only has nothing to do with the concepts of experimental psychology, but has nothing to do with a psychology of any kind, which desires to be a 'science' going beyond everyday experience... The theory of marginal utility, and every other subjective value theory, are not psychologically, but, if one wants a methodological term, 'pragmatically' based, i.e. they involve the use of the categories 'ends' and 'means'.[3]

Here, then, we have the origin of the Misesian *praxeology*, the Hayekian 'pure logic of choice'. As Mises put it, 'If Weber had known the term 'praxeology' he probably would have preferred it' (1949: 126, fn 5).

In all essentials the views on the nature of human action, the character of the world in which it takes place and the methods appropriate to its study, which we find in the work of Mises and Shackle are virtually identical. Action is thought. For Mises 'economics is not about things and tangible material objects; it is about men, their meanings and actions. Goods, commodities, and wealth and all the other notions of conduct are not elements of nature; they are elements of human meaning and conduct' (1949: 92). For Shackle '[e]conomics, concerned with thoughts and only secondarily with things, the objects of those thoughts, must be as protean as thought itself' (1972: 246). Action is guided by plans, i.e. by thought, and all action has to be interpreted as the outward manifestation of such plans, which must be coherent if they are to have a chance of success. In fact all economic phenomena are intelligible only as the outcome of planned action.

For both our authors the world in which thinkers and actors have to move is one of ceaseless change. Shackle describes it as a kaleidic world. For Mises '[t]here is in the course of human events no stability and consequently no safety' (1949: 113). He points out that consistency of plans does not entail constancy of observable action in a world of change. 'Constancy and rationality are entirely different notions.... Only in one respect can acting be constant: in preferring the more valuable to the less valuable. If the valuations change, acting must change also' (1949: 103).

In each plan means and ends are riveted by choice. In a world of change plans have to be revised, but such revision is also always a matter of choice of ends and means. Both our authors thus regard choice as the 'pure' type of action and reject determinism along with the other paraphernalia of positivism. Two of Shackle's statements make that quite clear. '[I]f the world is determinist, then it seems idle to speak of choice' (1972: 122), but [c]hoice is always amongst thoughts, for it is always too late to choose amongst facts' (1972: 280). According to Mises, 'What counts for praxeology is only the fact that acting man chooses between alternatives. That man is placed at crossroads, that he must and does choose is ... due to the fact that he lives in a quantitative world and not in a world without quantity' (1949: 126–7).

Both our authors emphasize that the mathematical notion of time as a continuum, a dimension in which events take place, does not fit the requirements of a science of human action. According to Mises, 'Time as we measure it by various mechanical devices is always past, and time as the philosophers use this concept is always either past or future. The present is, from these aspects, nothing but an ideal boundary line separating the past from the future. But from the praxeological aspect there is between the past and the future a real extended present. Action is as such in the real present because it utilizes the instant and thus embodies its reality' (1949: 100). He quotes from Henri Bergson, 'What I call my present is really my attitude to the immediate future, that is to say, my imminent action.'[4]

Shackle refrains from stressing the Bergsonian affiliation of his thought, but makes the same point. 'We cannot have experience of actuality at two distinct "moments". The moment of actuality, the moment in being, "the present", is *solitary*. Extended time, beyond "the moment", appears in this light as a figment, a product of thought" ' (Shackle 1972: 245).

Both authors emphatically reject the calculus of probability as a tool for dealing with human conduct in a world of uncertainty. Shackle devotes his chapter 34 ('Languages for Expectation') to this matter. He sums up his view in the heading of section 34.40: 'Probability concerns groups of events, not single critical choices' (1972: 400). Mises makes the same point by distinguishing between class and case probability.

Case probability has nothing in common with class probability but the incompleteness of our knowledge. In every other regard the two are entirely different... Case probability is a peculiar feature of our dealing with problems of human action. Here any reference to frequency is inappropriate, as our statements always deal with unique events which as such – i.e. with regard to the problem in question – are not members of any class... Case probability is not open to any kind of numerical evaluation.

(Mises 1949: 110–13)

To sum up, then, in their emphasis on the spontaneous, and thus unpredictable nature of human action, in their rejection of mechanistic notions of time and probability, our two authors are completely at one. They also agree that a science of human action requires a methodology *sui generis*.

DIFFERENCES

One is not surprised to find differences alongside similarities between two such original minds. With such striking identity of outlook and methodological approach, however, as we have just encountered, any differences in conclusions must be due to differences in what Schumpeter called 'vision', in the interpretation and evaluation of facts in the world around us. In theoretical argument these are then reflected in the form of 'subsidiary assumptions', which have to be elucidated and weighed for the degree of insight into the social world they afford us. Once we have done this, we may say that the more comprehensive vision, if it affords us a deeper insight into the world and does not merely encompass more facts, has advanced our understanding of the phenomena in question.

It is in this sense that we now have to ask how far Shackle may be said to have widened the scope of the enquiry beyond the common ground of praxeology we outlined above. In what ways, then, does his recent work differ from that of Hayek and Mises? In this regard three aspects of it call for our particular attention.

In the first place, Shackle has extended the scope of subjectivism from tastes to expectations. It is a curious fact that, when around 1930 (in Keynes's *Treatise on Money*), expectations made their appearance in the economic thought of the Anglo-Saxon world, the Austrians failed to grasp with both hands this golden opportunity to enlarge the basis of their approach and, by and large, treated the subject rather gingerly. Professor Hayek, to be sure, dealt with expectations in 1933 in his Copenhagen lecture on 'Price Expectations, Monetary Disturbances and Mal-investments' (1939) and in 'Economics and Knowledge' (1948), but not with the causes and consequences of their divergence. In fact, expectations were here regarded as being of analytical interest only to the extent to which they converge.[5] They were, on the whole, treated as a mode of foresight, a rather unfortunate but inevitable consequence of imperfect knowledge. Mises hardly ever mentions expectations, though entrepreneurs and speculators often enough turn up in his pages. Thus from 1939 onwards Shackle had to take on expectations more or less single-handedly without much benefit of support from the Austrian side.[6]

Secondly, there is a sense in which Shackle's emphasis on action without knowledge poses an even stronger challenge to Austrians than to neoclassical equilibrium theory. In the work of Hayek, I. M. Kirzner (1973) and Mises the market as process, not as a state of rest, is of fundamental importance. Its main economic function here is to co-ordinate existing knowledge scattered over many parts of the economic system and to disseminate the market knowledge thus gained. Nobody can profitably exploit his knowledge without conveying hints to others. But can the market process diffuse expectations in the same way as it diffuses knowledge where this exists? This is by no means obvious. The dissemination of superior knowledge is entailed by the fact that men can judge it by success. But how successful an expectation is we can know only when it is too late for others to embrace it. Moreover, in a kaleidic society in which there is always some hope that better knowledge will be available tomorrow if only we wait, and nobody can tell how soon today's successful knowledge will become obsolete, the diffusion of knowledge may be held up and the market process thus impeded. Can the market process 'digest' expectations? If it can, what is its *modus operandi*? If it cannot, is not the image of the market economy as presented to us in the Austrian writings impaired, or at least shown to be incomplete? To answer these questions we have, first of all, to ask what expectations are and how they fit into the perspective of praxeology.

The future is unknowable, though not unimaginable. Future knowledge cannot be had now, but it can cast its shadow ahead.

In each mind, however, the shadow assumes a different shape, hence the divergence of expectations. The formation of expectations is an act of our mind by means of which we try to catch a glimpse of the unknown. Each one of us catches a different glimpse. The wider the range of divergence the greater the possibility that somebody's expectation will turn out to be right.

In this way new knowledge, paradoxically, can have an economic impact before it is actually 'here'. Divergent expectations are nothing but the individual images, rather blurred, in which new knowledge is reflected, before its actual arrival, in a thousand different mirrors of various shapes. In the same way existing knowledge may become problematical even though nothing better is in existence at the moment. An expectation that it will soon be superseded by superior knowledge may suffice to stop its diffusion. In such cases, it might appear, the market process will stop for lack of digestible knowledge without anything really digestible taking its place. Must expectations, then, be fatal to the market process?

The market, of course, cannot diffuse 'superior expectations' in the sense in which it diffuses superior knowledge because *ex ante* no criterion of success can exist. It cannot make bulls and bears change their expectations but it nevertheless can co-ordinate these. To co-ordinate bullish and bearish expectations is, as Keynes showed, the economic function of the Stock Exchange and of asset markets in general. This is achieved because in such markets the price will move until the whole market is divided into equal halves of bulls and bears. In this way divergent expectations are cast into a coherent pattern and a measure of co-ordination is accomplished. This is a topic Shackle has very much made his own, which has a bearing on Austrian economics that we now have to examine.

Divergent expectations give rise to a third aspect of Shackle's model that has no counterpart in Mises's work and thus invites our attention. In studying the relevance of expectations to the market process, we come to learn that they play a different part in different markets, and these differences of their *modus operandi* will have to be explored. The relationship of the third aspect to the second is thus that of a particular instance to a general type of problem. In an ordinary product market in which an output flow is sold, most participants are either producers or consumers. Fluctuations of limited size may originate on either side. When we add stock-holding merchants, the range of possible fluctuations increases as these merchants may be buyers today and sellers tomorrow or vice versa. But in an asset market in which the whole stock always is potentially on sale and in which everybody can easily choose or change sides, we find an element of volatility that is absent from product markets. Such asset markets are inherently 'restless', and equilibrium prices established in them reflect nothing but the daily balance of expectations. In the cotton market, for example, it is likely that expectations about the probable price in July 1976 will tend to converge as this date draws nearer. But this cannot happen in the Stock Exchange, since what is being traded there are titles to (in principle) permanent income streams, which have no date that could 'move nearer'. All we get is a succession of market-day expectations tilting from one day to the next as the flow of the news turns bulls into bears and vice versa. There is here no question of a gradual approach towards long-run equilibrium. It is not surprising that this conception of a sequence of market-day equilibria in asset markets has incurred the disdain of prominent neoclassical thinkers.

> A truncated theory of temporary equilibrium in which mar-
> kets for future goods are replaced by some form of expec-
> tations, themselves functions of current prices and quantities,
> has indeed been developed, though its empirical content is
> necessarily meager if the formation of expectations is left
> unanalyzed. But the true neoclassical spirit is being denied
> in such a model.
>
> (Arrow 1974: 7)

It may be felt that the failure of the true neoclassical spirit to find adequate reflection in the list of Wall Street closing prices need cause little concern to Austrians most of whom, from Menger onwards, have been sceptical about the general equilibrium model since the days of the school of Lausanne. We may even be inclined to retort: The worse for the neoclassical spirit! But the issue, 'Restless asset markets versus long-run equilibrium', is one we cannot ignore, partly owing to the prominent part asset markets play in the market economy as a whole and partly because not all Austrians have scorned the neoclassical model. In volatile asset markets new capital gains and losses are made every day that change the distribution of resources. It is hard to see how the system can attain long-run equilibrium while these changes are taking place.

238

Professor Hayek and Mises both espouse the market process, but do not ignore equilibrium as its final stage. The former, whose early work was clearly under the influence of the general equilibrium model, at one time appeared to regard a strong tendency towards general equilibrium as a real phenomenon of the market economy. Mises, calling the Austrians 'logical' and neoclassicals 'mathematical' economists, wrote: 'Both the logical and the mathematical economists assert that human action ultimately aims at the establishment of such a state of equilibrium and would reach it if all further changes in data were to cease' (1949: 352).

It is this view of the market process as at least potentially terminating in a state of long-run general equilibrium that now appears to require revision.

CONCLUSION

In a kaleidic society the equilibrating forces, operating slowly, especially where much of the capital equipment is durable and specific, are always overtaken by unexpected change before they have done their work, and the results of their operation disrupted before they can bear fruit. Restless asset markets, redistributing wealth every day by engendering capital gains and losses, are just one instance, though in a market economy an important one, of the forces of change thwarting the equilibrating forces. Equilibrium of the economic system as a whole will thus never be reached.[7] Marshallian markets for individual goods may for a time find their respective equilibria. The economic system never does. What emerges from our reflections is an image of the market as a particular kind of process, a continuous process without beginning or end, propelled by the interaction between the forces of equilibrium and the forces of change. General equilibrium theory only knows interaction between the former.

For Shackle long-run equilibrium theory is of course an expression of the Victorian world view, a vision of a world shaped mainly by the forces of slow but orderly progress. The older Austrians, non Anglo-Saxon Victorians like Menger and Böhm-Bawerk, certainly shared this world view, though not the expression it found in the Walrasian model. Böhm-Bawerk's capital theory embodies a vision of a world of steady progress through capital accumulation without technical progress or malinvestment.

One of Menger's interests was the increasing range of variety of products in economic progress.

The kaleidic society is thus not the natural habitat of Austrian economics, but the alien soil may prove nourishing. A model in which individual plans, each consistent in itself, never have time to become consistent with each other before new change supervenes has its uses for elucidating some striking features of our world. It may even be that Austrian economics will come into its own in our society in which the apparently irreconcilable nature of economic and political forces at large finds its expression in our permanent inflation, and in which 'public policy decisions' are largely a euphemism for incoherent sequences of desperate expedients. It is quite possible that a bastion of extended subjectivism, enhanced by the inclusion of divergent expectations, will offer us an excellent vantage point from which to watch the happenings of such a society in a dispassionate perspective, a perspective superior to what we have had before.

17

G. L. S. SHACKLE'S PLACE IN THE HISTORY OF SUBJECTIVIST THOUGHT
[1990]

SHACKLE'S PHILOSOPHICAL APPROACH TO ECONOMICS

Most of us are familiar with an experience that, baffling and discouraging as it is in the narrower context of expounding subjectivist doctrine, points to the existence of a deeper problem pertaining to the way in which economists understand their own role. The experience is this: having referred a friend or student to Shackle's work, one is told after a time that, gratifying and exciting as the experience was, the reader found it hard to see what all this had to do with the daily concerns of economists.

There is of course an obvious answer to this view. Such readers would suffer from much too narrow a conception of the task of economics. Undeniably we face a problem here. Today's narrowness of professional outlook few would have tolerated fifty years ago. If this statement is correct, where is a remedy to be found? But let us first take our bearings.

For all this narrowing of outlook, the problem is not a new one. In 1926, in what in the Shackleian calendar we must reckon as the first Year of High Theory, the Oxford philosopher R. G. Collingwood wrote in a paper entitled 'Economics as a Philosophical Science':

> Philosophical thought is that which conceives its object as activity, empirical thought is that which conceives its object as substance or thing. Economics, then, is an empirical science if it is conceived as the study of a thing called wealth; philosophical if it is conceived as the study of economic action. But it is not enough, to make a science philosophical,

that it should *call* its object action; it must think of it as action.

(Collingwood 1926: 162–3)

We may learn a number of things from Collingwood. In the first place, there must be room for several approaches to economics. An approach too narrowly conceived has to be rejected. Second, there is a striking similarity between Collingwood's outlook and that which we find in Mises's *Human Action* (1949) though, to our knowledge, neither author knew of the other.[1] Finally, in the light of what Collingwood says, we have to describe George Shackle's approach to economics as a 'philosophical' one. It is not hard to find in his work passages that bear out such a description: for example, the famous 'Economics, concerned with thoughts and only secondarily with things, the objects of those thoughts, must be as protean as thought itself' (*Epistemics and Economics* 1972: 246).

But what are the roots of this philosophical approach to economics? On this question the student of Shackle's *opus* receives little instruction. Such an approach must surely have links to the past. Where are they to be found? Whom are we to regard as Shackle's philosophical masters and forebears? We are not told. Some of us, when pointing out the striking similarity between Shackle's 'solitary moment' and Bergson's *durée*, were very gently, but firmly, told we were on the wrong track, but not where we might find the right one.

It is clear nevertheless that whatever school of philosophy Shackle may be cognate to, his own approach is strongly opposed to that of Logical Positivism or Empiricism which dominated the Anglo-Saxon world for half a century, but is now in decline. It seems a legitimate surmise that at least one reason for Shackle's reticence about his intellectual lineage may have to be sought in an attempt to avoid an encounter with this school when it was at the zenith of its power in the 1950s and 1960s, the very decades in which he achieved fame. The spokesmen of this school were known to be unscrupulous in the choice of their tactics and apt to discredit their opponents. So he may have deemed it wise to address himself to economists only. Today, logical positivism is discredited as a philosophy and we can breathe more freely once again. That Shackle is neither for low-brows nor the many instrumentalists in our discipline is not new to us. That for the reason given it is at times almost as hard to persuade the studious and the philosophically minded of the true significance and value of his work, remains, to our mind, a more disconcerting experience.

RADICALIZING SUBJECTIVISM

So we have to set about our main task: namely to find a place for Shackle in the history of economic subjectivism without the benefit of instruction in the history of his philosophy. He has described himself as a subjectivist. Nobody doubts that he is. What precisely does this mean?

At this juncture it seems appropriate to remember that a few decades ago Professor Hayek described subjectivism as the chief motor of the advance of economic thought 'And it is probably no exaggeration to say that every important advance in economic theory during the last hundred years was a further step in the consistent application of subjectivism. That the objects of economic activity cannot be defined in objective terms but only with reference to a human purpose goes without saying' (Hayek 1955: 31). But what is subjectivism?

Subjectivism is a research programme of the social sciences which aims at elucidating social phenomena in terms of their *inherent meaning*, i.e. in terms of their meaning to actors.

This definition has a number of implications that need to be made explicit:

1 Elucidation of meaning is a typical research procedure of the social sciences. Phenomena and processes in the realm of nature have no meaning accessible to us. The natural sciences thus have to employ other methods.
2 Social phenomena are the result of the interaction of actors conscious of the purposes they pursue. To actors, therefore, their action had ascertainable meaning, though not the same for all participants.
3 Choice is the prototype of social action. It requires a mind capable of weighing alternatives. Meaning presupposes a mind capable of attributing it. Subjectivism without the autonomy of the human mind would make little sense.
4 The research programme of subjectivism is thus incompatible with determinism in all its forms, in particular that of the General Equilibrium model.

We explain observable events in workshop and market in terms of meaningful action causing them. That we are able to do this is due to the fact that men plan action before actually undertaking it. For us, the plan constitutes a vital link between the planning mind and the observable phenomena of action, irrespective of whether plans fail or succeed. Congruence or collision of plans of different actors does not affect their methodological meaning as keys to events – though to the economist the cases of collision may well be the more interesting of the two.

To assign to George Shackle a place in the history of subjectivist thought we have to trace a thread of historical continuity in a sequence of events. Most contemporaries may possibly have been quite unaware of the significance we, as historians, attribute to these events now. Moreover, a bewildering variety of other interpretations of past events is almost always possible. Unfortunately, there is no other way of writing history of thought, no other way to pursue the affiliation of ideas through time.

The historian faces the problem of dating his periods. For our purpose, we shall let the history of subjectivism in economic thought start with the 'subjective revolution' in the early 1870s when, in the work of Jevons, Menger and Walras, subjective theories of value won acclaim and soon superseded the classical labour theory of value. Value, which in classical doctrine was regarded as an objective, and measureable, property of goods, was now seen to consist in a relationship between an evaluating mind and an object to be valued, a result of human action. Different men would assign different values to the same object.

But the shift in the theory of value was accompanied by, and in part reflected, a more fundamental change in outlook. Classical economics, in Collingwood's phrase, undertook 'the study of a thing called wealth'. It was essentially a science of wealth, what Hicks has called *plutology* (Hicks 1976: 215), a discipline with a strongly practical orientation. It had no place for the consumer who destroyed rather than produced wealth. It had of course been recognized for a long time that the creation and accumulation of wealth depended on the efficient functioning of markets, but these were conceived as consisting of producers and merchants only. Now, however, with the subjective theory of value, the consumer could no longer be ignored. After all, it was he who bestowed value on objects. Suddenly the former outsider moved to the centre of the stage. And equally suddenly, what had been the science of wealth turned into *catallactics*, the science of markets in which the consumer occupied a prominent place.

In other words, the introduction of a subjectivist theory of value into our discipline transformed this discipline in quite unforeseen ways. Subjectivism as a research programme was seen to point beyond itself. It took a number of decades, however, before contemporaries realized what had happened. During them the potential for an expansion of subjectivism slowly built up.

In order to find George Shackle's place in the history of subjectivism we have to extend our sketch from the 1870s to the 1940s. Here we have a choice between a shorter and a longer version of our scenario.

In the shorter version the extension of subjectivism in the 1930s, from the old subjectivism of preferences to the new subjectivism of expectations, constituted the first major extension of its domain for sixty years – and Shackle took a most prominent part in it. When, in the course of the Great Depression, it became obvious that pessimistic expectations may not only prevent recovery when its other conditions are present, but actually set in motion multiplier processes of contraction, economic theory, at least trade cycle theory, could no longer avoid the subject. In Sweden, Wicksell's disciples came across it when they examined their master's heritage. Keynes used expectations as means to his end, introducing them where he needed them (marginal efficiency of capital, liquidity preference, user cost), leaving them out where he did not. What is even stranger, the Austrians, Menger's heirs, almost officially committed to the promotion of subjectivism in the spirit of the Hayek passage quoted above, failed to grasp with both hands the golden opportunity to extend it from preferences to expectations when they encountered it in the 1930s. It was left to Shackle, almost single-handed, to explore the subject of expectations. At first he received little recognition. For many years he was a lonely thinker.

So much for the shorter version of our scenario. The other one is, however, the far more rewarding. According to it, the evolution of subjectivism is less characterized by the extension of its domain from preferences to expectations (important as this remains) than by an 'inner metamorphosis', its transformation from a subjectivism of properties and 'dispositions' to one of the active human mind. This is best shown by employing a three-stage scheme.

When we come to grapple with its third stage we shall learn that we are entitled to call it 'Shackle's own'.

Subjectivism of the first stage, in the 1870s, was a subjectivism of wants. Different men had different wants and thus were inclined to attribute different values to the same object. Wants were regarded as personal attributes in much the same sense as other attributes, such as weight, body temperature, etc. There was no question of judgements of utility being utterances of the mind, hence problematical.

In Mises's work we reach the second stage. Subjectivism is now a matter of means and ends. 'In this sense we speak of the subjectivism of the general science of human action. It takes the ultimate ends chosen by acting man as data, it is entirely neutral with regard to them. The only standard which it applies is whether or not the means chosen are fit for the attainment of the ends aimed at' (Mises 1949: 21). In a world of change the mind of the actor must continuously ponder the adequacy of the means at his disposal, but not the ends themselves which are 'given' to it.

But ends lie in the future and are thus always problematical. In action our mind exercising control over the application of means to ends must ponder ends no less than means, deciding from time to time which ends are no longer worth pursuing, which ends formerly not even envisaged have now become feasible. As we learn from Shackle:

> Economic choice does not consist in comparing the items in a list, known to be complete, of given fully specified rival and certainly attainable results. It consists in first creating, by conjecture and reasoned imagination on the basis of mere suggestion offered by visible or recorded circumstance, the things on which hope can be fixed. These things, at the time when they are available for choice, are thoughts and even figments.
>
> (Shackle 1972: 96)

We have now reached the third, and thus far highest, stage, the subjectivism of the active mind, and George Shackle, the master subjectivist, has been our mentor.

WHICH WAY FORWARD?

Where do we go from here? At the start of this chapter, while deploring the narrowing of outlook of the profession of economics in our day, we emphasized that the relevance of subjectivism to the daily concerns of economists is not a matter that may be safely neglected. If subjectivism teaches that prediction of future events is impossible because the future is unknowable and will in fact itself only be created by active minds, what are economists to do? Where and how are they to exercise their talents?

It seems that they must turn from the unknowable future to the irrevocable past and draw what knowledge they can from facts that can no longer be affected by human action. Shackle recently spoke of 'two themes of the highest practical consequence', and added, 'One is the need to treat economic *history* as our chief source of instruction and understanding. The other is the need to make case studies rather than allegedly "general" theories, the vehicle of our thought' (*Economic Journal*, March 1983, p. 224). A good deal of water has flowed under the bridges since *The Years of High Theory*. I not only wish to endorse Shackle's statement, but, if I may, supplement it with one drawn from my own Inaugural Lecture of 1950. 'The chief task of the analytical social scientist is to tell the historians what factors will *not* bear a causal imputation. The general analytical schemes of theory furthermore provide the historian with alternatives of explanation' (Lachmann 1977: 178).

What about problems of the present? Does the economic adviser lose his *raison d'être* if we are no longer able to regard him as an applied scientist whose expertise enables him to predict the consequences of various courses of action open to his clients, namely those who have to make decisions on matters of economic policy? Does our inability to predict the unknowable future entail our inability to make any contribution whatsoever to the resolving of economic problems of our own day and society? Not so. The economist is able to render service to those among whom he lives by enabling them to understand how the problems, as yet to be resolved, of the present have arisen from the, by now irrevocable, heritage of the past.

Such advice, to be sure, may make no great contribution to the 'optimal solution' of these problems, but it should enable intelligent decision-makers to appreciate more fully and deeply what kind of problems they confront. And while it remains true that in a kaleidic world the lessons of history are by no means self-evident, but require careful interpretation, an activity of the mind, it is no less true that any present state of affairs (though not indeed a 'state of nature') bears the mark of the historical processes that gave rise to it. In fact, our understanding of our present depends upon our interpretation of our past. Without such interpretation we may not even be able to decide which of the problems we presently confront are more urgent and which are less. In this way the past does indeed have a bearing on all action concerning the future, but it is a subtle bearing, reflecting all the nuances of subjective interpretation. Such activity offers no room at all for relationships of a 'functional', or similarly mechanical, variety.

The question may be raised, however, in what way precisely knowledge of their historical origins would help us to overcome constraints upon our actions. Once we know them as constraints, to be sure, all we can do is take account of them. The question in this form, however, is misleading, since it ignores the nuances of the stages of action as they follow each other in 'real time'.

Historical knowledge will be of most use to us precisely at that stage of our thought when a plan, a firm product of our mind, is not as yet in existence, and when the question of what are likely to be significant constraints upon our intended action as yet awaits clarification in our own mind. At later stages of our action its utility is likely to diminish.

To overcome the artificial barriers which today separate economists from historians is an urgent task, made no easier by the circumstance that, since the darkness of the age of quasi-mechanical models fell upon us around 1930, several generations of economists have grown up who do not even know what they are separated from!

The task facing us now is no less urgent for that.

18

THE FLOW OF LEGISLATION AND THE PERMANENCE OF THE LEGAL ORDER [1979]

INTRODUCTION

Few economists will deny that the market operates within a framework of legal and other institutions, that its *modus operandi* may be helped or hindered by the varying modes of this framework, and that the outcome of market processes will not be unaffected by changes in it. That the obvious implication of these facts for the operation of the modern market economy are so rarely understood is of course to some extent due to the circumstance that in the products of the textbook industry they are commonly ignored. This neglect is largely the result of the fact that in the general equilibrium model of neoclassical economics institutions do not qualify as 'data' of the system and hence are abstracted from. This merely goes to show that, contrary to a view widely held today, abstraction is not a procedure in which arbitrary choices may be made to suit our 'analytical convenience', and that, in a significant sense, the quality of abstraction reflects the quality of the abstracting mind.

To the classical economists, as Lord Robbins has often reminded us, the economic importance of institutions was well-known. In opposing the mercantilist view that the production of wealth was not a matter to be left to chance, but required the constant attention of, and carefully designed action by, the state bureaucracy (at their time a fairly recent creation), the classical economists held that, if only the institutions of property and contract were firmly entrenched and safeguarded, the market would give rise to a continuous process in the course of which far more wealth would be produced than the wisest of bureaucracies could ever have designed. As they, however, were, in the terminology we have recently learnt from Sir John Hicks,[1] *plutologists* interested primarily in the production and distribution of wealth, and not in exchange or market processes as such in any respect other than as agencies of the growth of wealth, they had little reason to go beyond emphasizing property and contract as the basis of the institutional order of their time.

Today we face an altogether different situation. In the first place, as heirs of the catallactic revolution of the 1870s, in which the interest of economists became concentrated on market events such as prices and relative quantities of various goods, and emphasis shifted from the production and distribution of (abstract) wealth to the exchange of concrete goods and services, we have to review the classical teaching on the institutional basis of economic activity. Modern economists regard production as a form of exchange. It is evident that the catallactic perspective with its emphasis on contractual relations in a multitude of markets, while production and distribution would take place even in a subsistence or a manorial economy, calls for another look at the institutional basis of the market economy. The current revival of Austrian economics, moreover, with its emphasis on the market as a multitude of related, though not necessarily consistent, processes rather than a state of equilibrium, makes it incumbent on us to pay particular attention to the legal norms and institutions on which the complex network of market transactions rests.

Secondly, it goes without saying that our world is far more complex than was that of the classical economists and that, quite apart from the consequences of the movement of economic thought just mentioned, there is evidently a good case for having another look at the relationship between the market economy of our days and its institutional basis.

Finally we can hardly ignore the fact that a good deal of the legislation currently emanating from the *Sozialstaat* of our time, designed to gratify the various appetites of the modern mass electorate, has served to provide obstacles to market processes and to undermine the legal order on which the market must rest.

What follows is offered as a modest and preliminary contribution towards the exploration of some of the problems indicated.

Our field is cognate to the one Hayek chose for *Law, Legislation and Liberty* (1973, 1976), but it also differs from it in some important respects. We are both dealing with relations between law and legislation and concerned about the threat posed to the legal order of the modern market economy by attempts to enact a normative order inspired by the spurious ideal of *social justice*. On the other hand Hayek paints his landscape on a much broader canvas than we would dare to touch. In his work we have a whole political philosophy for our time within which relations between law and legislation play a part, even a prominent part (in chapters 4 to 6 and 8), but only one part among many all the same. 'I soon discovered that to carry out what I had undertaken would require little less than doing for the twentieth century what Montesquieu had done for the eighteenth.'[2] We have nothing comparable to offer, needless to say, and shall confine ourselves to exploring a fairly narrow strip of land in the border area between economics and the sociology of law.

We both reject the thesis of legal positivism that law is nothing but the sediment of past legislation, but we reach this position by somewhat different paths. Hayek reaches this conclusion by an argument derived from the nature of law and justice and from the historical fact that law is old and legislation a fairly recent phenomenon. We, on the other hand, at first accept the positivistic thesis at its face value, but then demonstrate that, if taken in its strictest form, it leads us to absurd conclusions, viz, the legal world in a state of chaos. In this way we hope to discover what tacit assumptions legal positivism has to make to avoid these conclusions. It will then become apparent that these tacit assumptions may be valid in some circumstances of history, but not in others, so that the thesis of positivism, so far from being a universal thesis about the identity of law and legislation, proves to be plausible only in circumstances in which legislation operates under some constraint.

We hope that, by emphasizing the part such constraints play in the legal order, our argument will serve to cast light on our contemporary dilemmas. At the same time we shall come to learn that our problem is linked to some sociological problems of even wider significance, viz. the complementarity of new and old institutions within the social order in a changing world, and, in particular, the modes of complementarity of what Menger called *organic* and *pragmatic institutions*, those that emerge as part of a spontaneous order of society and those that owe their existence to some act of the 'common will'.

LEGAL PERMANENCE AMID FLUX

A permanent legal order and a continuous flow of legislation are evidently incompatible notions. Even where the new laws, the particles of this flow, do not replace other laws that formerly existed, but are, so to speak, 'new additions' to the edifice of the legal order, they must have some effect on some part of the latter. Those who deny this incompatibility must have a conception of the legal order not unlike the way a merchant is looking at his stock, i.e. as consisting entirely of exchangeable parts, so that the stock may be maintained even when every single component has been replaced. Economists would speak of a homogeneous aggregate, but know that such homogeneity precludes all complementarity.

The coherence of the legal order, however, requires consonance, hence heterogeneity, of the norms composing it. New legal norms cannot be simply added to, or replace, old norms, they have to fit into the existing order. We could hardly speak of a legal system if we meant by it a mere aggregate of norms. The practical relevance of all this lies in the circumstances Max Weber described as follows:

> To those who had interests in the commodity market, the rationalization and systematization of the law in general and, with certain reservations to be stated later, the increasing calculability of the functioning of the legal process in particular, constituted one of the most important conditions for the existence of economic enterprise intended to function with stability and, especially, of capitalistic enterprise, which cannot do without legal security.[3]

In other words, if A lends B 10,000 DM (to choose the most stable of currencies) for twenty years, how, in a world of continuous legislation, can either creditor or debtor be sure that at the end of this period the present legal norms governing repayment of debt will still be in force in such a form that the repayment is 'calculable'? If so, what might inspire such confidence in the permanence of the present order? If not, what do we have to assume about the nature of the expectations governing long-term loans?

It is readily seen that any attempt to answer these or similar questions will have to rest on the assumption that, whatever the stream of legislation in the next twenty years may turn out to be, certain tacit conventions will be observed which impose some constraint upon the range of legislative change. It may be that legislative change is expected to be confined to what might be described as 'the outer range of the legal order'. New legislation would not affect the 'inner core', the 'lawyer's law', in other words the civil law. We find a good example in Hayek: 'Of British legislation it could be said in 1901: nine tenths of each annual volume of statutes are concerned with what may be called administrative law, and an analysis of the content of the General Acts during the last four centuries would probably show a similar proportion.'[4]

Alternatively, in our example, lender and borrower may believe in the permanence of the legal order in the sense that legislative change, even though affecting the civil law, would not affect its principles, but be confined to the revision of norms flowing from them. Such a belief would of course involve the distinction between 'inner core' and 'outer range' merely on another level. Obviously no such constraints upon the flow of legislation can ever be taken for granted. Belief in them will be more warranted in some periods of history than in others. Experience of historical change is unlikely to leave it unscathed.

Behind our conundrum there loom much wider issues. Unable as we are to do justice to them in the present context, they simply cannot be ignored. Professor Talcott Parsons has recently complained about the place of 'Law as an intellectual stepchild'.[5] So, as social scientists, we had better take heed.

Legal institutions are part of the institutional order of society. The question we have raised is merely an instance of the more general question how an institutional order can persist even though institutions change in the course of history. Behind it there lies the even more complex question of the complementarity of old and new institutions in a changing world. How can we be sure that they will actually fit into the same order? One is tempted to think of the institutional order as of an array of hinges: the institutions within each hinge can move a good deal, if within limits, but the hinges themselves cannot. The matter is of particular relevance to 'the market order of catallaxy', the subject of Hayek's chapter 10. There must be a good deal of flexibility in it of course, but some elements must persist, otherwise how could we talk of an order? We suggest that, while within the catallaxy prices and quantities of goods and services, produced and exchanged, must indeed be flexible and will actually change each market day, the order of catallaxy must derive its quality as an order from the permanence of its institutional framework, and in particular the legal norms forming part of it. Such permanence alone permits economic agents to 'take their orientation' from them in making their plans of action. Otherwise all must become precarious.[6]

AN EXAMPLE: CO-DETERMINATION

We must now turn aside to consider a noteworthy recent example of legislation disrupting the existing legal order, the German *Mitbestimmungsgesetz* of 1976 which provides that half the members of the supervisory board of German industrial joint-stock companies must be elected by the workers (where there are more than 2,000 of them) while the other half is elected by shareholders. The supervisory board (*Aufsichtsrat*) is an institution peculiar to German company law and unknown in Anglo-Saxon countries. Its main function is to appoint management (*Vorstand*) and take major policy decisions[7].

The main motive of this legislation was of course narrowly political – it is a typical piece of 'social legislation'. We shall ignore such arguments as that it is 'a major step on the way to industrial democracy'. We are interested in it solely from the point of view elucidated in this chapter: How does such legislation fit into the legal order required by a market economy? If new legislation requires some constraint imposed upon it by the need to observe certain 'tacit conventions' lest it disrupt the legal order, has any such convention been observed in this particular case? What are the principles of company law requisite in a modern industrial economy that aspires to the rank of a catallaxy, a market order?

We shall of course be told that modern joint-stock enterprise has in any case been created by a century's legislation, that the legislator in this field always had to weigh the interests of different groups, and that the new legislation is following the trend of permitting workers to participate in entrepreneurial decision-making. In order to deal with arguments such as this it is necessary to go back to the principles underlying a market order.

Company Law, as it has emerged in the Western world in the course of time, is a delicate web within which many interests, some conflicting, some complementary, have been woven into a pattern of harmony. (No doubt its very success in this task encouraged the advocates of co-determination to hope that, having achieved so much, the pattern of harmony might be expected to accommodate a few more interests without undue strain.) In this it is a true mirror image of the catallaxy as a whole.

On the other hand, there is no company law of which it could be said that it preceded legislation. As soon as the resources for organizing joint ventures with limited liability and the opportunities for their use were present, there also arose the need to give them an adequate legal form, e.g. in the form of a royal charter, or in some other way. Participants in the venture needed this minimum of 'calculability'. Modern joint-stock enterprise is of course a creation of the market (in Menger's terminology an 'organic institution'), but it could not have come into existence without a legal form expected to be permanent. It comprehends elements of *order* as well as of *organization*. The relationship between directors and shareholders, e.g., partakes of both. In the study of joint-stock enterprise, if anywhere, we learn to apply the distinction between ideal types and reality.

Company law, in short, the joint creation of market growth and the legislative embodiment of ideas pertaining to the market, is the final product of a long process of interaction of business men and lawyers who invested their experience, their ingenuity and their skills in it. In discussions of it we do well to remember Max Weber's point that law, whatever social force it may respond to, is always, in the first place, the product of lawyers (in our world academically trained). As so often in history, we have here an institution which bears the imprint of the minds of its creators long after they have vanished from the scene.

Unfortunately a deeper understanding of the nature of modern joint-stock enterprise and its environment has not been helped in recent years by the spreading notion of the 'separation of ownership and management', now widely believed to be one of its outstanding characteristics. The modern shareholder, we are told, has lost all interest in his company, rarely attends the annual meeting and is, in any case, owing to lack of information, incapable of exercising any influence on, let alone control over, management. Thus the modern 'giant enterprise' has become a law unto itself. This notion has of course been used as a weapon for the expansion of government control. It also has helped to foster an atmosphere favourable to the claims of the advocates of codetermination, at least by creating confusion about these issues in the minds of social scientists and lawyers.

This notion rests, briefly, on a failure to understand the role of the Stock Exchange in the modern market economy. Here the Stock Exchange 'monitors' the performance of managers. Brokers, investment analysts and others devote time and effort to this purpose. The daily fluctuations of market prices reflect continuously the results of this activity by specialists. The shareholder watches these prices and draws his conclusions. When he disapproves of some action by his managers he 'votes with his feet' – he sells. Far from being a passive spectator of the deeds and vicissitudes of his company, he is active in the most obvious way the modern division of functions between specialist observers and 'the public' demands. Owners and managers, so far from being 'separated' from each other, are linked together *indirectly through the market.* Managers, in public statements, often deny that stock exchange prices are of any interest to them. They know very well, however, that their creditors watch their performance and are by no means insensitive to the daily verdicts of specialist observers, and they cannot prevent shareholders from learning these verdicts.

Those who espouse the notion of the separation of ownership and management have failed to understand the function of the stock market as an intermediary of information.

We now come to the main issue. Economists distinguish between flows and stocks, between streams of goods and services and the sources of these streams. While workers sell their services, capital owners entrust the *sources* of capital services to the enterprise of their choice. In adverse circumstances they suffer not merely, as workers also might, a loss of income, but a capital loss. It seems evident that he who entrusts his capital, the source of his income stream, to others must be able to demand that these are responsible to him for their conduct, in particular where he lacks the ordinary rights of a creditor and cannot withdraw his capital. If, however, managers are responsible for their management of the (durable and often specific) capital instruments of the company, they bear such responsibility towards the owners, and not towards somebody else. Otherwise responsibility has no meaning. The worker members of the supervisory boards share in the control of management, but do not share in this responsibility.

Moreover, what exactly are the co-determinators to help determine? It is not a question of labour relations. In modern industry labour interests can hardly be said to be under-represented. The position of the firm *vis-à-vis* its customers and suppliers is given in the market. Here, as in other market relations, little can be 'determined' by a single firm, unless it held a complete monopoly, which hardly ever happens.

There is, however, one matter in respect of which each firm does enjoy some discretion. It concerns its capital. A merchant turns over his stock. A firm turns over its capital by means of depreciation. The decision, how much to set aside for depreciation out of gross revenue each year is indeed a crucial decision which, like all such, must depend on expectations. Where a wrong decision is made a capital loss will be suffered subsequently. It becomes clear, from the very nature of this case, why workers' representatives, even were they qualified for participating in such decisions, would be unable to discharge such responsibility towards those they do not represent.

It lies in the nature of productive processes that decisions concerning stocks, their rate of turnover and their composition at different points of time, are always and necessarily more crucial decisions than decisions concerning flows. The more durable and specific capital goods become, the heavier the responsibility of the decision-makers, the more crucial the nature of their decisions. It is perhaps clear (not only to economists, one hopes) why any attempt to hand decision-making power concerning capital to those who bear no responsibility to capital owners is bound to undermine not merely the legal order but the market economy. At the same time we can now see that company law, as it had developed until 'co-determination', was indeed an 'organic growth'. Political arguments cannot affect the nature of the responsibility for capital decisions.

This is most clearly seen in the case of unsuccessful firms. It is in the interest of society that capital should flow from levels of low to levels of high profitability. In a market economy competition and the motivation of capital owners will bring this about. Are we to believe that workers' representatives will quietly see capital flow out of their unsuccessful enterprise to be invested elsewhere? Yet this is precisely what should happen. Company law as it had evolved before co-determination, was shaped in such a way as to make it happen. If the power of those who have an interest in preventing it from happening is increased to the point of making them 'co-determinators', can the catallaxy remain unscathed? Changes in organization can and do affect the market order.

CONCLUSION

What do we learn from our exercise?

That politicians will readily sacrifice any principles they may hold for the sake of gaining votes, seek to erode all limits to their power, such as constitutional safeguards, and thus help to undermine the very order which confers legitimacy on their power is, alas, not a novel insight. That friends of the market economy have good reason to pay close attention to its legal and institutional framework, the more so since the style of late classical formalism that has dominated economic thought for three decades can hardly be said to provide an atmosphere congenial to such work, is also not exactly new. In fact the ORDO school has for many years taken a special interest in this framework.

That we must not expect ideal types to find full reflection in the real world is an old truth that perhaps bears repetition. Order and organization are such ideal types. It is hard to imagine any order in which, in reality, problems of organization may not arise. We saw a good example in the joint-stock company, a typical product of the modern market order, in which such organizational problems as the relationship between managers and shareholders naturally arise. Legal institutions may well come into existence in response to social needs, but nonetheless have to be given their concrete shape by lawyers whose mentality they reflect. Needless to say, it is in their concrete and permanent form alone that they can serve as points of orientation to agents. For this reason, if for no other, the legal order requires permanence.

Behind all this there remain the wider issues to which we alluded. There is the problem of the complementarity of old and new legal norms, feasible perhaps, we saw, if both are subject to, and thus, in legal logic, inferable from, the same principles, but not where these principles are in fact, if not in words, actually eroded. There is the, even wider, problem of the flexibility of the institutional order which must contain both, flexible and immutable elements and which we likened to an array of hinges; the hinges, immutable and known as such, permit other elements to 'turn' within limits. We have elsewhere suggested the distinction 'between the *external* institutions which constitute, as it were, the outer framework of society, the legal order, and the *internal* institutions which gradually evolve as a result of market processes and other forms of spontaneous individual action. It still seems to us 'that it is within a scheme such as this that the praxeological theory of institutions ... most readily finds its place.'[8]

One of the tests to be applied to a legal order is whether intertemporal transactions are possible within it without turning transactors into gamblers. It is a sobering thought that the permanent inflation of our ages has by now had precisely the same effect, and has made the same contribution to the subversion of the social order of a free society as would a stream of legislation incompatible with the principles of the market orders. This, again, is not new. Some economists have pointed out in recent years that continuous inflation must erode the basis of contract as an institution.

It is certainly important to realize that the nature of the relationship between the market and its legal and institutional framework is complex, that we must beware of undue simplification, and that, if the market may be jeopardized by clumsy legislation pandering to ignorance, it is also true that the legal order may be subverted by economic processes such as inflation, and that influences can run in both directions.

It is therefore to be hoped that, hard as is the task of conceptual clarification in such a field, all those concerned about the order of a free society will give unceasing attention, critical and constructive, to the grave problems some features of which we have attempted to adumbrate here.

SUMMARY

As the classical economists knew, the market economy is embedded in a framework of legal and other institutions. The quality of the market depends, among other factors, on the quality of this framework. This remains as true today as it was two centuries ago, as does the corollary notion that the market economy rests on the twin pillars of the institutions of property and contract.

Today this is not widely appreciated. Neoclassical formalism, whose style of thought has come to dominate academic economics since the Second World War, ignores it. Such facts are abstracted from. A broad belt of secondary reality in the form of statistical time series shields our formalists from any contact with the real world. Characteristically, today we find an awareness of the significance of our framework only in those schools of thought, (like the ORDO school, or among those whose work is inspired by

Mises or Weber) in which a vivid sense that the social sciences are concerned with meaningful human action is alive.

Hayek's *Law, Legislation and Liberty*, for all its dissent from Weber, falls into the same tradition. The market order of catallaxy comprises laws as well as market phenomena.

In the sociology of law, thus broadly conceived as an area adjacent to economics as one of the humanities, there arises the question 'Is the annual flow of legislation in the modern state compatible with the permanence of the legal order'? Without the latter intertemporal market transactions are impossible, yet the former is a fact of experience. We suggest that in modern society the gap has been bridged by means of tacit conventions which it is our task to make explicit.

Behind our question there loom much wider issues, formidable enough to make us tread warily. (It is not for nothing that Talcott Parsons recently spoke of 'Law as an intellectual stepchild'.) These are the problems of institutional change in a changing world. Some institutions must be flexible enough to adjust to change, while others, by contrast, must be sufficiently resistant to change to make the outcome of intertemporal transactions predictable. With institutional change the complementarity of old and new institutions becomes a problem.

The German Codetermination Act of 1976 (*Mitbestimmungsgesetz*) raises a number of problems of this nature. Company law, in its long process of evolution, has thus far provided the market with the institutional framework it required. Now these institutions are forced into the Procrustean bed of political expediency. Property rights are infringed.

It should be evident to all who are concerned with the market (not merely to economists) that, in the nature of the case, the law must grant stronger protection to those who entrust the stocks they own to others to be managed by them, than to those who sell time segments of a flow of service, as in the latter case the problem of confidence does not arise. Stocks and flows are different things and require different forms of protection. Also, in unsuccessful companies, co-determination may impede the flow of capital out of them that the market requires.

The true function of ideal types is to serve us as criteria of classification for real events. We must not confuse them with reality.

19

THE MONETARY SYSTEM OF A MARKET ECONOMY [1986]

INTRODUCTION

The words of our title are to denote the institutional framework of a market economy such as ours. Markets of course may exist in a centrally administered economy. 'Market socialism' has come into fashion (for good reasons) of late, but markets for capital assets, and thus for financial assets, cannot exist in a socialist economy.

By contrast, such asset markets, and in particular a Stock Exchange embedded in a network of financial asset markets, form the core of a market economy: they are in fact its central markets. The network of financial markets in the South African economy constitutes the main subject matter of the De Kock Report.[1] The Report attempts to find answers to questions of policy applicable to it.

We are thus concerned with the monetary institutions of the South African market economy, those in existence today and those to be brought into existence. In approaching our subject it will be useful to remember Menger's distinction, now a century old, between *organic* institutions, like money and the pattern of location of industry, which are the product of the interplay of market forces, as a rule over fairly long periods, and *pragmatic* institutions, like the political constitutions of modern states, which are products of the political will. Making this distinction permits us to understand better the main problem to which the Commission had to address itself: how to devise by political action those monetary institutions that would best complement the other institutions the money market has evolved in the course of the last three decades. We may say that the mode of interaction between the two kinds of monetary institutions in this country is really the underlying theme of the Report as a whole.

DANGERS OF A MODERN CREDIT SYSTEM

In the spirit of these remarks we conceive our task in this symposium as that of setting a perspective on the Commission's approach to the task it set itself, while not trespassing on the domain of the authors of the other papers, a general perspective that permits us to appreciate their economic style and to assess the quality of thought that informs the Report. In the academic jargon of our time, our task is a hermeneutical one. Our perspective is necessarily historical. For all institutions are immersed in history. Without some knowledge of their historical origins we can neither understand their present roles nor form expectations about how they might function tomorrow.

In one part of the Report the Commissioners themselves have adopted a historical method of investigation, when in chapter 14 they survey 'The Five Phases of Monetary Policy in South Africa since the Second World War', or, in the two subsequent chapters, examine the deficiencies disclosed by their survey. We, on the other hand, will have to work on a broader canvas: the monetary system of the Western world – not merely of South Africa – as it has evolved in the course of the last few centuries, will form the background for our examination of the Report.

In the general perspective from which we propose to view the Report two historical facts play a significant part. As they appear to us to have been somewhat neglected by the Commission, we wish to emphasize them from the outset. One concerns the significance of, and the dangers inherent in, the modern credit system, while the other reflects the effects of forty years of continuous inflation in the Western world.

The modern market economy, as it grew up in the West in the course of the last few centuries, at first evolved gold and silver as forms of monetary metal, but at a later stage replaced them by the modern credit system in which credit instruments are typically used as means of payment. Since credit can be created virtually without cost, while gold and silver have to be mined, the system lacks the constraints of ordinary commodity production. It is therefore an inherently unstable system.

In 1967, in one of his Critical Essays in Monetary Theory, Sir John Hicks put it forcefully:

> Metallic money is an expensive way of performing a simple function; why waste resources in digging up gold from the ground when pieces of paper (or mere book entries) which can be provided, and transported, at a fraction of the cost will do as well? That is the reason why the credit system grows: that it provides a medium of exchange at much lower cost. But on the other side there is the penalty that the credit system is an unstable system. It rests upon confidence and trust; when trust is absent it can just shrivel up. It is unstable in the other direction too; when there is too much 'confidence' or optimism it can explode in bursts of speculation. Thus in order for a credit system to work smoothly, it needs an institutional framework which shall restrain it on the one hand, and shall support it on the other. To find a framework which can be relied on to give support when it is needed, and to impose restraint just when it is needed, is very difficult. I do not think it has ever been perfectly solved. Even in this day we do not really know the answer.
>
> (Hicks 1967: 158–9)

This was the main problem the Commissioners had to address. We see no reason to doubt that the Commissioners were well aware of it on the whole, as well as of its difficulty. How often they allowed this awareness to affect their deliberations on matters of detail is another question.

Our second point of orientation concerns the effects of inflationary experience gathered over a long period. After forty years of continuous, and even accelerating, inflation this experience permeates the whole of economic life and affects decision-making at all levels. In an inflation debtors make capital gains at the expense of creditors. The firms more heavily in debt thus appear to be more profitable than firms with less debt. The urge to get into debt becomes almost irresistible.

In this atmosphere recipes for business success informed by old-fashioned prudence are tossed aside, often enough with some contempt. We have to remember that virtually nobody economically active today can remember, at least from his own experience, any period, such as the century from 1815 to 1914, in which prices were as likely to fall as they were to rise.

In such a situation the general value of lessons drawn from experience almost inevitably becomes a matter of some doubt. How the inflation originated decades ago may well become almost a matter of indifference. Whatever its origins, the inflationary process continues, and of course accelerates, under its own impact. Once all hold inflationary expectations the process is bound to continue for this very reason. If inflation is yet to be checked inflationary expectations have to be broken first.

We shall have to return to another aspect of this matter below.

DIVERSE MARKETS AND THEORIES OF MONEY

The critical assessment of a document such as the De Kock Report may be addressed to either its ends or its means, or of course to both. While to engage in an assessment of the former kind may well be more interesting, since it would have to comprehend a whole spectrum of possible ends of monetary policy, including those sought by the Commission, but also others imaginable, the fact remains that a critical assessment is likely to be the more constructive and fertile the more the critic and the authors criticized share fundamental values and desire to pursue the same ends.

Happily this is here the case. The Report proclaims as the two main aims of monetary policy in South Africa the pursuit of a 'market-related' policy, and stability of the price level as a primary objective (17. 6). We explicitly wish to endorse these aims. But a word of caution, addressed by an old partisan of market freedom to his fellows in spirit, may not be out of place.

Most contemporary discussions of 'the market' take place on a level of abstraction so high that important differences vanish from sight. But there are markets and markets. In all of them there are co-ordinating forces enabling buyers and sellers, creditors and debtors, etc. to get what they want, but there also are disco-ordinating forces. Which are the stronger depends on the circumstances of the case.

There are markets, typically those for food, in which market activity is orientated to a short flow of goods from production to consumption. There are other markets, like those for assets, in which there is no consumption and the same objects are traded over and over again. Today's sellers were buyers at some time in the past.

Expectations play their part in all markets, but, as Keynes taught us, for some purposes it is useful, and may become necessary, to distinguish between short-term and long-term expectations. The latter tend to involve some men's present expectations about other men's future expectations which will, in due time, display a similar orientation. For this and other reasons some markets are more speculative than others. Speculative markets are notoriously unstable. The balance of co-ordinating and disco-ordinating forces in them depends on circumstances, such as the extent to which 'bull' or 'bear' positions are financed by long chains of financial intermediaries. All markets for financial assets are naturally speculative markets.

It is true that a speculative market co-ordinates the plans and actions of bulls and bears, and that the price must move until a balance between them, and thus of their expectations, has been reached. But the attainment of such market-day equilibria means little, even in the short run. It is a typical feature of volatile speculative markets that strong price movements will attract outsiders to them so that either bulls or bears are continuously reinforced and a given price trend is maintained. In such circumstances market forces tending towards a balance of bullish and bearish expectations may remain weak.

It is therefore hardly helpful, and may be misleading, to discuss processes in financial asset markets as though there were no difference between the typical *modus operandi* of such and other markets. It would be unfortunate for the cause of market freedom were the impression to gain ground that its most fervent defenders neither know nor care much about what happens in the markets of the real world.

As regards monetary doctrines, an air of eclecticism pervades the Report. It finds characteristic expression in 15. 23 where we read:

> For purposes of this Report, the Commission has decided to describe and analyse the deficiencies it has identified in South African monetary policies in as 'neutral' a way as possible, in an attempt to avoid undue academic controversy and to obtain the maximum consensus among the adherents of the main schools of monetary thought in vogue today.

No doubt there is a good deal to be said for such eclecticism. Nobody who has spent any time in the universities can fail to have vivid memories of such 'undue academic controversy', while he who has spent more than a decade there will remember more than one change of 'vogue'. The Commissioners faced a hard practical task and were entitled to ignore such paraphernalia of academic life and letters. But the practising eclecticist faces some risks of which he should be aware. He must take care to see to it that the ideas he borrows from the various schools and waves of thought fit together and form a harmonious whole. Otherwise he may become entangled in a web of contradictions. It seems to us that the Commissioners have not been altogether successful in avoiding such snares. We shall examine two cases where they have succumbed to the peril.

Our problem, which we may call 'the dilemma of monetary eclecticism', first rears its head in a couple of paragraphs at the end of chapter 13 under the heading of 'Discretion versus Rules' (13.29–13.31).

Here the Commission shows that it is aware of the monetarist objection to discretion in monetary policy. (In 13.30 the Report refers to 'Some economists, including most "monetarists" ' – the air of ironic detachment expressed here by the inverted commas is not lost on the reader!) The Commission, we read, understands 'why many of those who hold this belief advocate the abandonment of discretionary monetary policy and the acceptance by the Reserve Bank of the single objective of increasing the money supply at a steady rate more or less in accordance with the long-term trend rate of increase of gross domestic product, after allowance for secular movement of the velocity of money circulation' (13.30).

In chapter 17 our problem comes fully into view when 'the Commission recommends that the Reserve Bank adopt specific intermediate objectives of monetary policy in the form of target rates of growth for one or more selected money supply aggregates' (17. 6). This of course is an idea we owe to monetarism (without inverted commas), but the Commission applies it in such a way as to obviate its roots.

> The Commission believes that monetary targeting should be applied in South Africa with a fair measure of flexibility and with a 'low profile'. More specifically, it recommends that, in setting and changing money supply targets from time to time, or in intentionally permitting them to be breached, the monetary authorities should openly exercise discretion based

on their assessment of the general economic situation and prospects at the time, including their view on the appropriate level and structure of interest and exchange rates at that stage (17. 8).

These words are hardly inspired by the spirit of monetarism, but, cut off from their roots, money supply targets can make little sense. We have to remember that monetarism is today the contemporary heir of classical monetary theory. It has inherited its distrust of any money not linked to a commodity, such as gold or silver, and its distaste for any monetary authority not bound by the closest of rules.

The monetarist, while recognizing that a return to the gold standard would be impossible in our world, endeavours to construct one which resembles the lost world of this standard as closely as possible. Under the gold standard anybody familiar with world gold output figures could calculate by how much the world gold stock was likely to increase next year. Money supply targets are to serve the same purpose today: to predict the magnitude of monetary variables. If impersonal market forces are to operate at full force, discretionary authority to interfere with them must be limited. Expressed somewhat differently, with money supply targets rigidly set down, market expectations will converge on them; with flexible targets they will diverge. For good reasons the Chicago mind abhors divergent expectations.

Needless to say, it is not our task to assess the merits and demerits of targets of money supply, flexible or inflexible. Our task here is to elucidate the dilemma of monetary eclecticism. Rigid targets would probably be unattainable, not merely in this country, but anywhere in the real world. But flexible targets of money supply are like Hamlet without the Prince, like Chicago without the Loop, like monetarism without a predictable quantity of money.

Our second example of the dilemma of eclecticism concerns the growth in this country, in recent decades, of a network of financial asset markets. The Report rightly stresses this fact at the start of chapter 1. 'For a country in its stage of general economic development, South Africa has a relatively advanced and sophisticated monetary and banking system and a set of reasonably broad, active and constantly expanding short-term financial markets' (1. 1).

Nobody who knew the South African economy in 1950 can fail to be struck by it.

What is its significance for monetary policy? 'There are two main reasons why the Commission considers well-developed and efficient financial markets desirable. The first is the significant contribution such markets can make to the growth and general soundness of the economy. And the second is the key role they can and must play in the application of effective stabilization policies in a basically free-enterprise and reasonably developed economy. These two functions are recognized as being closely inter-related' (1. 6).

As we said above, after forty years of continuous inflation, the experience of it naturally permeates the whole of economic life and affects the making of decisions at all levels. This applies to financial markets just as much, if not more, than to others. We note with obvious interest that, at times, the authors of the Report show themselves well aware of these effects of inflation on financial markets. 'The high, variable and relatively unpredictable rates of inflation of recent years have discouraged long-term and encouraged short-term lending and borrowing, and have tended to bring about distortions of relative interest rates and financing patterns. At the same time, balance sheet structures have been weakened as borrowers tended or were obliged to rely increasingly on relatively short-term sources of finance' (15. 6).

This is a clear admission that the 'relatively advanced and sophisticated monetary and banking system' of our days, mentioned earlier, has in fact evolved under the impact of inflationary forces, and that the 'constantly expanding short-term financial markets' owe their expansion to the same cause. In an inflation banks have to satisfy their customers' demand for more and more credit without having to become long-term creditors. A well-oiled money market is the answer.

Is it very likely, then, that a sophisticated system of financial markets, owing its evolution to such forces, will lend itself readily as a tool 'in the application of effective stabilization policies', or that it can 'play a key role' in checking our inflation?

We need not doubt that, after successful stabilization of the value of the currency, financial markets will adjust themselves to the new situation, perhaps even rapidly. But it is one thing to admit this, and quite another thing to expect that, before the success of the policy of stabilization has been firmly secured, these markets and their institutions will play much of a role in achieving this success.

We find here another instance of the dilemma of eclectism. But, whether this is so or not, it is very much to be hoped that questions of the kind we have broached here, viewed from our perspective, will now give rise to vigorous discussion and find a wide audience.

20

SPECULATIVE MARKETS AND ECONOMIC COMPLEXITY [1988]

Most friends of the market order are by now aware that, however successful they may be during any period of time, and especially after the volatility of the stock markets this autumn, there will always be battles to be fought and an adequate store of diverse ammunitions will have to be kept at all times. Attacks from the depth of the academic grove and from the rhetoricians at the political barricades are to be expected from time to time and have to be resisted. The importance of a long-term flexible strategy for the defence of the market is clear.

In the real world there are markets and markets, and some function more successfully than others. It is therefore curious and regrettable that many of the discussions on the market economy in recent years have been conducted at such a high degree of abstraction that these differences between markets seemed to vanish from sight. In many of the fierce controversies witnessed of late there may have lurked behind the positions occupied by the participants quite different conceptions of how markets function in reality, rather than different perspectives on the same facts. True or not, the economists and others who ignore the diversity of markets deprive themselves of a valuable weapon and, perhaps worse, prevent their friends and pupils from acquiring the skills required to handle it.

It also seems clear that in the market economy of today speculative markets play a particular role and that its student must pay due attention to them. Some critics of the market economy seem obsessed by its 'financial fragility'; others will feel that if these phenomena are studied with proper care altogether different conclusions may be derived. In any event, different markets are characterized by different constellations of market forces.

Markets differ in many ways that do not matter to the purpose of understanding the constellation, the entirety, of market forces. These differences become relevant only when they affect the character of human action in markets. But when they do, they must not be abstracted from, for in such cases talk of 'the market' is as likely to mislead as to enlighten.

I shall distinguish here between speculative and 'ordinary' markets. The contrast between these two categories can be educated by reference to a number of their characteristics, such as the constancy and transparency of the pattern of supply and demand and the 'orientation' of the participants. I shall take as my prototype of an 'ordinary' market, the vegetable market in a small town, say, that for cauliflower or carrots, while today's foreign exchange market offers itself as an obvious example of a speculative market.

The outstanding characteristic of the vegetable market is the constancy and transparency of its underlying pattern of supply and demand. It is nourished by a steady flow of supply, modified by the alternation of seasons. All participants are either buyers or sellers, except for a few merchants who are both. Some people, ordinarily buyers, may grow vegetables in their gardens, and would do so in case of an acute shortage, but this activity hardly affects the long-run pattern. Everybody is on one side of the market and stays there. Variable stocks are held, but as a matter of convenience, and their size depends on the flow. For good reasons all participants take the flow as their main point of orientation.

Here it is entirely permissible to speak of 'the market as a discovery procedure'. Producers who want to differentiate their product will soon find out whether the market likes what they have to offer, while consumers with peculiar tastes must go out to find somebody ready to cater to them.

What matters here is that everybody's attention is fixed on a more or less constant pattern of demand and supply, which provides all participants with a common object of orientation. All individual expectations converge on it.

A speculative market offers a very different picture. Nothing is easier than to change sides: a man may buy in the morning and sell in the afternoon or *vice versa*, and may repeat it on a number of days. Bulls (speculators who expect the price of securities to rise) and bears (who expect a fall in price) are not only clearly distinct groups, but may be groups formed anew every day.

The prevailing orientation is towards price change. Everybody tries to gain from differences between present and future prices. Not everybody has to be a 'speculator', in the sense of buying and selling at different prices. There are 'hedgers' who merely want to safeguard a position they had to take up for other reasons and who wish to protect themselves against price change, but this desire does not affect their orientation to it.

In such markets every transaction is a departure for the unknown, but buyers and sellers depart in different directions. The future is unknowable – though not unimaginable. Images of it take the shape of expectations. Different men hold different expectations because human minds differ. At any moment the market is thus divided not merely into bulls and bears, but also into those of mild and fierce variety. This distinction is important because the same price movement may, for instance, turn some fierce bears into mild bears but make others quit the market altogether, at least for the time being.

Divergent expectations are thus of the very essence of the speculative markets of today. Whatever certain sophists in the more deeply shaded parts of the academic grove may preach about the (ultimate?) convergence of expectations, it remains true that without divergent expectations the markets of the world in which we live could not possibly function in the way they are known to function. It is hard to see how, in a world of convergent expectations, transactions of the kind everyone is familiar with could take place.

In a speculative market, at any moment, price moves under the impact of bullish and bearish expectations, until it reaches a position in which the market is equally divided between bulls and bears. There it comes to a (temporary) rest. The market thus accomplishes, in each market day, a co-ordination of divergent expectations. This is no mean achievement. Moreover, everybody whose own expectation differs from that which finds expression in the market price is free to gain from it, if he can, by entering into a respective transaction by buying or selling.

What the future will bring, and which, if any, of the divergent expectations will eventually find 'confirmation' by future events is an entirely different matter. No one has any right to expect that markets, consisting of fallible men, will be able to know the unknowable.

Every day the stream of the news affects present plans for future action; the impact of unexpected events on these plans has to be newly assessed, and the pattern of the constellation of divergent expectations is transformed. Expectations diverge over time as well as between men.

In the light of these truths it is hardly possible to speak of 'the market as a discovery procedure' when speculative markets are under discussion. One can discover only that which *is*, not that which might – or might not – be. Future events may turn out to have been 'correctly anticipated'; they cannot be 'discovered' *now*. And for the same reason the word 'foresight' should be avoided.

What lessons can be drawn from this diagnosis of speculative markets? Friends of the market order, as I have argued, must employ flexible strategy and tactics. By the same token, an assessment of the shortcomings of any market should be conducted, in the first place, with reference to the particular circumstances obtaining on it.

The shortcomings of some speculative markets, such as the foreign exchange markets of today, are not to be denied, but it does not follow at all from this admission that a confession of 'market failure' must be made. What constitutes the failure of a market must evidently depend on a precise notion of both its primary and secondary functions. As long as a speculative market provides anyone wishing to 'hedge' existing positions with enough offers of 'cover', it fulfils at least one function. In general, the co-ordination of divergent expectations on a large scale is certainly an important and indispensable function of speculative markets.

But what about their obvious shortcomings, such as excessive and unnecessary volatility of price and volume of turnover so frequently observed, and most dramatically seen in the recent fluctuations in equities markets throughout the world? The foreign exchange markets, for example, often make it difficult to conduct business in export industries and import trades, not to mention their wider effects on employment. How many of the economists who, in the last years of the Bretton Woods system, advocated the adoption of a system of 'freely floating exchange rates under the impact of demand and supply' would have persisted in their views if they had foreseen the vicissitudes of the dollar and other currencies in the mid–1980s?

The speculative character of a market may not be inevitable. For the half-century before the First World War exchange rates were stable under the gold standard. A return to it may be out of the question today, but some international stabilization scheme, perhaps under the aegis of a rejuvenated International Monetary Fund and supported by the strongest central banks, seems possible. The most serious problem such a scheme would have to face is, of course, that capital movements have now come to overshadow the flow of funds resulting from exports and imports of goods in a way unknown in the early years of this century, and that capital movements are apt to engender further capital movements of a purely speculative kind.

An international agency attempting to stabilize exchange rates today would have to stand ready, and have the resources, to offset all these capital movements, a formidable undertaking indeed. On the other hand, the very speculative nature of today's foreign exchange markets may make the performance of the task suddenly much easier than it currently appears, for if the stabilizing agency looks strong enough to deter all speculative movements of exchange rates, these capital movements may shrink to a fraction of their present size as speculators leave these markets.

Speculation is apt to engender more speculation, volatile markets more volatility. Such a market may for a time attract many people who know very little about it and who would not dream of entering it, but for the chances of gain it seems to hold. The contrast to the ordinary market with its stable pattern of demand and supply is striking, so much so that any attempt to reduce the scope of speculative markets by restricting access to them would be futile.

The world of markets is one of complexity. Any attempt to present the simplified picture of it found in the pages of the average textbook is bound to lead the enquirer astray. The economist must neither avert his glance from the excesses and shortcomings of speculative markets, nor ascribe undue importance to them. There are many tools in his shed; each has a use of its own, although some may be awkward to handle. The market economy is a palace of many mansions; the interior decoration of some of them may not be altogether to the taste of the advocate of the market, but when it has to accommodate a large number of visitors, each of the mansions prove useful.

At a time when interest in, and understanding of, markets is growing in many parts of the world, friends of the market order face new, but by no means necessarily easier, tasks than they did thirty years ago, in the days of ignorance and neglect. As wider knowledge prompts sophistication, this increased insight may even

274

serve to improve the arguments of some of their opponents. Their own style of discourse should gain in subtlety, their arguments in depth.

Most important of all, they will have to emphasize the range and variety of markets and their modes of operation. In each market a different balance of forces can be found, co-ordinating and disco-ordinating, and each such balance will certainly tilt over time. A balanced assessment of the strengths and shortcomings of market forces calls for exactly such a perspective and entails a flexible strategy.

21

AUSTRIAN ECONOMICS
A hermeneutic approach [1991]

INTRODUCTION

In recent years, hermeneutics as a style of thought has captured
the imagination of bold minds and made its impact on a number
of disciplines for which it seems to hold a promise of exciting
departures. Economics has thus far not been among them. This is
the more remarkable since in Germany, at least before the First
World War – in the years when the *Methodenstreit* was petering
out – the merits of the method of *Verstehen*, backed by the authority of Max Weber, were widely discussed.

During the 1920s, when there was no single dominant school of
economic theory in the world, and streams of thought flowing
from diverse sources (such as Austrian, Marshallian and Paretian)
each had their own sphere of influence, 'interpretive' voices
(mostly of Weberian origin) were still audible on occasions. After
1930, however, economists all over the world followed Pareto in
embracing the method of classical mechanics as the only truly
'scientific' method. In the decades that followed this became the
dominant style of thought in almost all countries. In 1931 the
Econometric Society was founded amid much naïve enthusiasm.
An arid formalism began to pervade most areas of economics and
to sap the vigour of analytical thought. In this milieu, rational
action came to be regarded as meaning nothing but the maximization of given functions!

In subsequent decades, economists began to live as if they were
in a citadel of their own. Opening new vistas to them will not be
an easy task. To those who grew up in isolation, nourished by the
products of the textbook industry under the aegis of its scribes

and typesetters, these vistas may well become a traumatic experience. So we have reason to go about our task with some care.

As regards the scope and breadth of this chapter, let it be said at once that any attempt on my part to deal with the subject of hermeneutics as a 'style of thought' on as broad a canvas as its present significance and promise to the social sciences (let alone other disciplines) call for, would far surpass my competence and knowledge. In what follows I shall therefore have to confine myself to the significance of hermeneutics for economics – in particular, for the renewal of economic thought. I also propose to restrict this chapter's scope even further by limiting it to Austrian economics, except in the last section.

Twenty years ago, in the Festschrift for Alexander Mahr, Professor of Economics in Vienna, I attempted to show that we have to see the main contribution the Austrians made to the 'subjective revolution' of the 1870s in the 'interpretive turn' (although I did not use these words) which they managed to impart to the evolution of economic thought at that critical period (Lachmann 1977: 45–64). My present purpose is to pursue this line of thought further and explore the possible consequences if a similar 'turn' were to be given to the evolution of contemporary thought by means of ideas grounded in Austrian economics. If modern Austrians were to succeed in replacing the present neoclassical paradigm – an embodiment of desiccated formalism – by a body of thought more congenial to the spirit of hermeneutics, what exactly might they hope to accomplish? Although mainly interested in what Austrian economics might have to say on these matters, we shall find, later on in this chapter, that in this context the work of certain non-Austrian economists as a contribution to hermeneutical thought, even though they were probably unaware of it, is not to be neglected.

WHY HERMENEUTICS?

There are of course many reasons why, and respects in which, the neoclassical textbook paradigm is inadequate. Its level of abstraction is too high and, what is worse, there appears to be no way in which it could be lowered so as to enable us to approach reality gradually. Complaints about the 'scaffolding' that is never removed have been numerous. The paradigm casts no light on everyday life in an industrial world. The 'life-world' in which all our empirical knowledge of social matters is embedded does not exist for it.

But what to Austrians is most objectionable is the neoclassical style of thought, borrowed from classical mechanics, which makes us treat the human mind as a mechanism and its utterances as determined by external circumstances. Action is here confused with mere reaction. There is no choice of ends. Given a 'comprehensive preference field' for each agent, what is there to choose? The outcome of all acts of choice is here predetermined. In response to changing market prices men perform meaningless acts of mental gymnastics by sliding up and down their indifference curves. All this is far removed from meaningful action in our 'life-world'.

In reality men make plans to achieve their purposes and later on attempt to carry them out. These plans are based on, and oriented to, means available and ends freely chosen. They may collide with those of others or may turn out to be unachievable for other reasons (e.g. that in the course of action actors become aware that means counted upon are no longer available or show themselves less efficient than they were expected to be). Plans may therefore have to be revised or even abandoned. But whatever happens, observable economic phenomena – such as prices or quantities produced or exchanged – are the outcomes of the inter-action of our plans. Action guided by plans causes economic phenomena. We might say that economic phenomena are the outward manifestations of action guided by plans.

Austrian economics is perhaps regarded as lending theoretical expression to the features of everyday life in the type of market economy just described. In its essence Austrian economics may be said to provide a voluntaristic theory of action, not a mechanistic one. Austrians cannot but reject a conceptual scheme, such as the neoclassical, for which man is not a bearer of active thought but a mere bundle of 'dispositions' in the form of a 'comprehensive preference field'. Austrians are thus compelled to look for conceptual schemes informed by a style of thought that is altogether different. Perhaps hermeneutics can provide us with an answer. In this context the following points call for our attention.

Action consists of a sequence of acts to which our mind assigns *meaning*. The elements of action are thus utterances of our minds and have to be treated as such. In studying action and interaction on a social scale our task is therefore an interpretative one; we are concerned with the actors' content of consciousness.

These facts have no counterpart in nature. In our observation of natural phenomena no meaning is accessible to us. All we can do is to put our observations in a certain order, an arbitrary order. In all those cases in which our observations serve a practical purpose, the order we impose on them will depend on this latter. In the absence of a practical purpose, the order will probably conform to the direction of our research interest. Phenomena of human action, by contrast, display an *intrinsic* order we dare not ignore: that which the human actors assigned to them in the making and carrying out of their plans. As social scientists we have no right to substitute our own arbitrary designs for those which are implicit in action shaped by the human will – 'designs' here lending expression to its *intrinsic* meaning.

Plans, of course, often fail. They may fail for a large number of reasons, but one of them, already mentioned above, is of particular interest to us: the collision of one actor's plan with that of others. Such conflict of plans, so far from invalidating the importance of plans for our understanding of forms of interaction, actually shows how important a help they are for our insight into problems here arising. Who would deny that our understanding of the fact that changes in incomes and employment may be due to a failure of savings and investment plans to match, has increased our insight into macroeconomic problems?

A similar conclusion applies to the problem of tracing the unintended consequences of action. This is no doubt one of the tasks of economic theory, but how could we hope to accomplish it unless we have first mastered the theory of intended action? We have to realize that only once we are able to handle the tools of the logic of means and ends – the basis of the voluntaristic theory of action – with some adroitness, can we proceed with confidence to tackle the unintended consequences of action. No mechanistic scheme bound to confuse action with reaction is likely to be of help to us here. The fact that plans guide action and provide it with meaning enables us to find the causes of conflicts of action in the incompatibility of plans constituted by acts of diverse minds. The consequences of action, whether intended or unintended, remain the economists' concern.

Finally, we have to remember that our mind is never 'at rest'. Our thoughts are, for many purposes at least, best regarded as particles of an unending stream, the stream of consciousness. Our knowledge consists of thoughts, and can therefore hardly be regarded as a stock, except at a point of time. Time cannot elapse without the state of knowledge changing. 'Economics, concerned with thoughts and only secondarily with things, the objects of those thoughts, must be as protean as thought itself' (Shackle 1972: 246). It is the task of the social sciences to make happenings in this protean realm intelligible to us.

The answer to the question 'why hermeneutics?' is, then, to be found in our need for conceptual schemes more congenial to the freedom of our wills and the requirements of a voluntaristic theory of action than anything we have at present. Is hermeneutics likely to assist us in this endeavour?

WHAT IS HERMENEUTICS?

Hermeneutics connotes the style of thought of classical scholarship. It was at first in the scholarly exegesis of texts that those problems arose which led to the evolution of various methods of interpretation whose relative merits have to be assessed by the criteria of access to intrinsic meaning.

Whenever we read a text, we want to grasp its meaning, and an effort of interpretation is called for. Where our text is of a narrative nature, we must understand how the various parts of the story we are told are related to one another, in order to grasp its full meaning. Where it is of exhortatory character, we need to be sure we understand what we are exhorted to do or to omit. Where it contains a religious or legal prescript, we have to ascertain that we understand precisely to what kind of cases it applies. In all such cases we have to interpret the text to pervade to its meaning.

For centuries past, long before the rise of modern science, scholars have applied these methods, whether they studied the Bible or the Pandects, read Polybius or Tacitus, or translated Averroes or Avicenna from the Arabic. Theirs was a hermeneutical activity.

As we are reading a text, page by page, we do not merely grasp the meaning of sentences and passages, but while doing so we gradually form a notion in our mind of what the author wants to tell us in his work. The meaning of the text as a whole gradually emerges before our eyes from the network of meanings constituted by single passages. When we come across a passage hard to understand we must attempt to interpret it in the light of the 'major meaning' we derive from our reading of the text as a whole.

In all this we are applying a *principle of limited coherence*, the coherence of all the utterances of the same mind. From our general knowledge of life and letters, we feel we have a right to assume that an author will not want to contradict himself. A 'difficult passage' has to be interpreted so as to cohere with what we take to be 'the spirit of the whole'. In awkward cases, where this proves impossible, we may have to revise our interpretation of the 'major meaning' of the text. Or we may conclude that the author 'changed his mind' before writing the passage under examination – that our text is not the manifestation of 'one mind at one time', but that it reflects, almost as a mirror would, the change of the author's mind over time. Since a voluminous text may be the work of many years, the existence of such a possibility is not surprising.

In all these cases our interpretation is an application of critical reason. Hermeneutics is in conformity with the maxims of critical rationalism. Our interpretation of a text is in principle always 'falsifiable'.

How do we pass from letters to life, from ancient texts to modern business transactions? What texts and phenomena of action have in common is that they both are utterances of human minds, that they have to exist as thoughts before they become manifest as observable phenomena. A text needs to be thought out before it is written down, a business transaction before it is entered upon.

A great step forward was taken, and the range of application of hermeneutical method considerably enhanced, when it gradually emerged from the work of historians (already of Greek and Roman historians) that these writers did not merely provide a chronicle of events but attempted to explain these events as human action in terms of ends and means, that they thus attempted to interpret action. This was an important insight of classical scholarship.

It is but a short step from historiography to the theoretical social sciences which produce ideal types of recurrent events, and thus provide historians with the analytical tools they need. And here we reach the point at which we are able to catch a glimpse of what the role of economics as a hermeneutic discipline might be like, and of the kind of 'interpretive turn' we might hope to impart to it.

Most economic phenomena are observable, but our observations need an interpretation of their context if they are to make sense and to add to our knowledge. Only meaningful utterances of a mind lend themselves to interpretation. Furthermore, all human action takes place within a context of 'intersubjectivity'; our common everyday world (the Schützian 'life-world') in which the meanings we ascribe to our own acts and to those of others are typically not in doubt and taken for granted.

Our empirical knowledge of economic phenomena obtained by observation must in any case be interpreted as embedded within this context. Elucidation of their meaning cannot here mean that the economist as outside observer is entitled to assign to them whatever meaning suits his cognitive purpose. It must mean elucidation of the meaning assigned to them by various actors on the scene of observation within this context of intersubjective meanings.

Hermeneutic interpretation of economic phenomena therefore has to take place within a horizon of established meanings, with one such horizon for each society. Our phenomena observed have to be placed within an order constrained by this framework.

INSTITUTIONS AND THE AUSTRIAN SCHOOL

Everyone agrees that the modelling of institutions by neo-classical economics is too sparse.

(Hahn 1975: 363)

After what has been said in the preceding sections of this chapter, it is not hard to see that a more satisfactory treatment of institutions in economics, or at least one that could satisfy the demands of Austrian economists, will call for the infusion of a sizeable dose of the hermeneutic spirit. Institutions prescribe certain forms of conduct and discourage others. It is clear that those persons who conduct themselves in conformity with them must attribute some *meaning* to them. Such meaning must be elucidated to outside observers.

Or we might say that an institution is a network of constantly renewable meaningful relations between persons and groups of persons who may not all ascribe the same meaning to the same set of relations. The task of the student of institutions is to distil such meanings from his observations and to interpret them to his audience.

It is hardly possible to accuse today's orthodox economics of the neglect of institutions – in the sense that the latter are never mentioned, or at least implied, in their writings. Markets and firms, after all, are institutions. On however high a level of abstraction 'agents' may engage in exchange transactions, the enforceability of contracts and the protection of property are implied. And where would monetary economics be without financial institutions?

What strikes the student of hermeneutics when he approaches our subject is not the fact that institutions are ignored in modern orthodox economics, but the fact that, like natural phenomena, they are treated as externally given conditions of human action – whose origin may not be investigated and whose continued existence is taken for granted. *And nobody ask questions about their meaning.* In fact, few economists today possess a vocabulary that would permit them to ask such questions.

We thus confront a situation in which, while institutions are by no means ignored, most economists do not know what to do with them. They play with them like children playing with ancient coins about whose value and history they know nothing. Institutions belong to the realm of culture, not that of nature. They are immersed in history. Although we can observe their operations, our observations cannot disclose to us what meaning their objects have to those enmeshed in them, a meaning that varies from group to group and over time. It is impossible to elucidate such meaning until we realize that the mode of existence of institutions corresponds to, and varies with, the mode of orientation of those who participate in them. Such a mode of orientation is an element of culture, a web of thought – open to interpretation but not measurable. Most of our contemporaries have to ignore this fact. Plainly, owing to their lack of acquaintance with matters of culture, most of them are hermeneutically disabled. This is the real problem to which Professor Hahn's little euphemism, quoted above, gives rather inadequate expression. How are we to overcome it?

Economic institutions are situated in an area in which the realms of economics and sociology overlap. Terms of co-operation are therefore called for. Needless to say, these will be the easier to find the closer the levels of abstraction on which institutions are discussed in the two disciplines. Perhaps it will be helpful to look at some of the problems arising here from a historical perspective.

The Austrians made their contribution to this field early on, when in most of Europe sociology as an academic discipline did not yet exist. In 1883, in the *Untersuchungen*, Menger introduced the distinction between 'organic' and 'pragmatic' institutions – between those that are the products of spontaneous social processes and those that are products 'of the social will'. Money is an example of the former, legal norms are of the latter variety.

It took more than half a century before Alfred Schütz gained fame as (almost) the first sociologist of the Austrian school and a hermeneutic thinker of the first rank. Ludwig von Mises, for all his avowed apriorism, belonged to the same tradition. Professor Don Lavoie, in his contribution to the Lachmann-Festschrift ('Euclideanism versus hermeneutics: a reinterpretation of Misesian apriorism'), has convincingly argued that we should regard him as an 'interpretive' thinker. Whether von Mises, who was inclined to assign 'interpretation' to historiography only, would have liked the appellation is quite another question.

It is today almost forgotten, but we have reason to remember, that Max Weber, the great protagonist of the hermeneutic method in the social sciences, came across our problem in the early years of the century – the years when the *Methodenstreit* was gradually petering out. He concluded that in order to deal with institutions what was needed was a new discipline – 'economic sociology' – which would supplement, rather than supplant, economic theory as it then existed. In planning (as editor after 1908) what was to be a German encyclopaedia of the social sciences, the *Grundriss der Sozialökonomik*, Weber decided that he himself would write a volume, *Economy and Society*, devoted to the new discipline, while prominent economists – such as Wieser, Schumpeter and others – would write the volumes on the various parts of economics proper.

It goes without saying that the situation we encounter today in regard to economic institutions is altogether different from that which Weber faced in his time. To him, economic theory meant Austrian economics – which was then enjoying its 'golden decade', the decade before 1914. This was the economic theory to be supplemented by his own work. It seemed reasonable to hope for co-operation between economists and sociologists on an approximately common level of discourse.

Where is such a common level to be found today? As long as economic theory is conducted at a level of abstraction on which meaningful utterances are made to lose their meaning, action appears to flow from (innate?) dispositions, and cultural phenomena are made up to look as though they were phenomena of nature, there can be little hope for bringing institutions into economics. What we need is the descent to a lower level of abstraction on which hermeneutical effort is possible and worthwhile. Economic sociology as a mere supplement to neoclassical theory will not do today.

Institutions reduce uncertainty by circumscribing the range of action of different groups of actors, buyers and sellers, creditors and debtors, employers and employees. We understand how they work by grasping the meaning of the orientation of these groups towards them. For us, orientation is a fundamental hermeneutic concept. Orientation, of course, changes in time, but it cannot be regarded as a 'function' of anything else. It does not fit into a world of 'function-maximizing' agents.

Some crucial problems arise here which concern the relationship between the individual institution and the institutional order as a whole. In a world of change, it seems, each institution has to be flexible but their order must be permanent. 'Law and Order' must be maintained if the market economy is to function. How is this possible? How can the whole persist if none of its parts is permanent?

We might look upon the institutional order as a merchant looks upon his inventory – that is, as consisting entirely of exchangeable parts. In the inventory, however, every part, by virtue of its being of value, is a substitute for every other part. But are all institutions substitutes for one another? Is there no complementarity among them? To the extent to which there is, there are limits to complete flexibility.

Or do we have to conceive of such complementarity in terms of a distinction between fundamental and immutable institutions, and other mutable and flexible ones? If so, might this distinction be a matter of degree rather than category?

In facing these intriguing questions we had better understand what kind of problems they are: problems pertaining to meaning and orientation. At some time it may become desirable, as Weber originally intended, to entrust the task of dealing with these and similar problems to a task force of economic sociologists. It goes without saying, perhaps, that their effort will be more likely to flourish if they are able to count upon a wide and sympathetic audience of other social scientists – among them many, we hope, from the sister discipline of economics.

HERMENEUTICAL ALLIES OF THE AUSTRIANS

Ultimate unifying simplicity is the aim or the dream of natural science in a sense which is not permissible for the study of human affairs. For the disciplines which envisage human conduct, policy, history and institutions, or art in all its forms, are directly and essentially concerned with the manifestations themselves, the manifoldness, the richness and the detailed particular variants and individual facts of these facets of humanity, rather than with dismissing them as the contingent outcomes of some original, general and essential principle which it is the real purpose of science to identify. The science of Nature and the science of Man stand in some sense back to back, the one looking inward at the Origin and the other outward at the Manifestation.

(Shackle 1972: 29)

At this juncture it must be one of the aims of economists of the Austrian school to give their discipline an 'interpretive turn' and to bring about the infusion of a considerable dose of the spirit of hermeneutics into the, at present somewhat enfeebled, body of economic thought. No doubt it will be an arduous task. Austrians, fortunately, do not have to shoulder it entirely on their own, but are able to call on some allies for help.

Hermeneutic thought has flown in the past, and is still flowing today, from a variety of sources. Even within the narrow orbit of economic theory, as currently practised, traces of its influence can still be found today. In earlier decades of this century, as described above, it often had a noticeable influence. What matters more to our present purpose is that there have been, in this century (outside the Austrian ranks) three prominent economic thinkers whose work we may legitimately claim to have been at least strongly affected by hermeneutic influence, even though not all of them may have been aware of it: Knight, Keynes and Shackle.

Knight at least was well aware of it. He knew Weber's work well, and the influence of the latter is clearly discernible in most of his methodological writing. In his famous (1940) paper, 'What is truth in economics?' originally a review of T. W. Hutchison's first book (published in 1938), Knight had this to say:

The whole subject matter of conduct – interests and motivation – constitutes a different realm of reality from the exter-

nal world, and this fact gives to its problems a different order of subtlety and complexity than those of the sciences of (unconscious) nature.

The first fact to be recorded is that this realm of reality exists or 'is there'. This fact cannot be proved or argued or 'tested'. If anyone denies that men have interest or that 'we' have a considerable amount of valid knowledge about them, economics and all its works will simply be to such a person what the world of color is to the blind man. But there would still be one difference: a man who is physically, ocularly blind may still be rated of normal intelligence and in his right mind.

Second, as to the manner of our knowing or the source of knowledge; it is obvious that while our knowledge ('correct' observation) of physical human behavior and of correlated changes in the physical objects of non-human nature plays a necessary part in our knowledge of men's interests, the main source, far more important than in our knowledge of physical reality, is the same general process of intercommunication in social intercourse – and especially in that 'causal' intercourse, which has no important direct relation to any 'problem', either of knowledge or of action – which has been found to play a major role in our knowing of the physical world.

(Knight 1940: 27–8)

In the case of Keynes, the hermeneutic quality of his thought is not as easy to document as that of Knight. Keynes was a thinker of an altogether different style, a pragmatist who mostly took very little interest in the methodology of the social sciences. The two passages we quote to attest the hermeneutic quality of his thought are both taken from letters addressed to disciples.

In the summer of 1935, before the publication of Keynes's book, *General Theory*, Robert Bryce, a Canadian student of Keynes, addressed Professor Hayek's seminar at the London School of Economics on the fundamental ideas of the forthcoming book. He appears to have reported to Keynes that at this seminar session most of the discussion turned on the definition of income to be used in the book. Evidently exasperated at this report, Keynes said in his reply to Bryce:

It is, I think, a further illustration of the appalling Scholasticism into which the minds of so many economists have got which allow them to take leave of their intuitions altogether. Yet in writing economics one is not writing a mathematical proof or a legal document. One is trying to arouse and appeal to the reader's intuitions; and if he has worked himself into a state where he has none, one is helpless.

(Keynes 1979: 150–1)

We note that what Keynes here calls 'the reader's intuitions' is precisely what, in the language of phenomenology, would be described as our 'awareness of the life-world', and that what he means is just what Knight expressed in the excerpt quoted. The lack of a common vocabulary is one of the obstacles to the diffusion of hermeneutic thought among economists.

In July 1938, in a letter to Harrod, Keynes wrote:

I also want to emphasize strongly the point about economics being a moral science. I mentioned before that it deals with introspection and with values. I might have added that it deals with motives, expectations, psychology and uncertainties. One has to be constantly on guard against treating the material as constant and homogeneous.

It is as though the fall of the apple to the ground depended on the apple's motives, on whether it was worthwhile falling to the ground, on whether the ground wanted the apple to fall, and on mistaken calculations on the part of the apple as to how far it was from the center of the earth.

(Keynes 1973: 300)

This passage marks Keynes as a subjectivist and an exponent of the hermeneutical style of thought.

Few can doubt that, in the second half of the twentieth century, Shackle as a hermeneutical thinker has been the great torch-bearer of enlightenment in the shadowy realm of economics. The passage quoted at the beginning of this section offers an example of the calibre of his thought. Hard as it is to sum up his achievement, the following reflection provides at least a hint of what we owe to him.

The fundamental flaw of neoclassical methodology lies in the confusion of action with reaction. Man in action is seen as a bundle of dispositions and not a bearer of thought. What difference does it make if we observe rather than ignore these distinctions? In action we reflect on means and ends, trying to fit the former to the latter, make plans and carry them out. As our ends lie in the unknowable (albeit not unimaginable) future, we have to exercise our imagination in reflecting upon them, and such exercise is incompatible with mere 'response to stimulus' or even the 'decoding of signals'.

We always knew, of course, that our plans might fail and our ends prove unattainable. To Shackle we owe the more pervasive insight that any action we start now may have any one of a large number of possible sequels which, if they did occur, might affect the conditions of our own future action, our own future means, leaving thus but little room for the constancy of parameters.

To the names of these three prominent non-Austrian thinkers we must, in justice, add that of Sir John Hicks who, for the last two decades, has often reminded us that economic events take place 'in time' and that men in action do not know the future.

It is not to be denied fifty years ago the young John Richard Hicks showed himself inspired by the style of thought of classical mechanics, and with remarkable success, espoused the Paretian paradigm from which we are still suffering today. In 1936, at the Econometric Society conference in Oxford, he presided at the opening of that exhibition of Islamic art which brought him instant fame.

But all this happened a long time ago. The mature Sir John Hicks, our contemporary, has long since renounced his early beliefs and disavowed his affiliation to the Paretian paradigm. He now defends the methodological autonomy of economics. 'Economics, accordingly, if it is on the edge of the sciences (as we saw) is also on the edge of history; facing both ways, it is in a key position' (Hicks 1979: 4). He also now comes close to Mises in reminding econometricians that:

> It is just that economics is in time, in a way that the natural sciences are not. All economic data are dated, so that inductive evidence can never do more than establish a relation which appears to hold within the period to which the data refer.
>
> (Hicks 1979: 38)

What is to be done? While some conclusions to be drawn from the argument presented seem obvious, others are less readily discernible at present.

Austrians must join with non-Austrians in an effort to co-ordinate the hermeneutically relevant parts of their respective traditions, a task calling for historical perspicacity in selecting appropriate parts of these traditions as well as some dexterity in handling ideas. In short, the situation demands the typical skills of a 'broker of ideas' who has a flair for fitting together cognate ideas of various origins. Austrians and their hermeneutical allies must also attempt to establish some rapport with other social scientists and philosophers interested in exploring similar themes. The need for an 'economic sociology' in the study of institutions is an obvious example. Another is the need for reaching a new accord between economics and history in the light of what we recently learnt from Hicks (economics is 'facing both ways, it is in a key position') and of what is in any case a corollary of Shackle's teaching (see the quotation on p. 286).

Beyond the horizon constituted by these immediate tasks there loom other, more formidable, problems that will have to be tackled in the future.

The 'market process' is an item high on the agenda of the Austrian research programme. The market, needless to say, offers a particularly fascinating example of an area of intersubjectivity in which vast numbers of men interact with one another in the pursuit of their multifarious needs and interests. It calls for treatment by a method inspired by the hermeneutical style, a method which defies the spirit of orthodox formalism. As regards price formation (for example, a prominent feature of the market process), the different meanings assigned to it by different groups of participants (in particular, price setters and price takers) call for our attention.

At some time in the future the concept of 'plan' – a fundamental hermeneutic notion, as we saw – will have to be introduced into the theory of consumption. If firms make and carry out plans, why not households?

The realm of economics cannot forever remain closed to the rays of hermeneutical enlightenment.

APPENDIX

Bibliography of works by Ludwig M. Lachmann Compiled by *William Tulloh*

BOOKS AND MONOGRAPHS

1930 *Faschistischer Staat und korporative Wirtschaft,* Thesis for the degree of Doctor *rerum politicarum,* Berlin.

1950 *Economics as a Social Science: Inaugural Lecture,* Johannesburg: University of Witwatersrand.

1956 *Capital and Its Structure,* London: London School of Economics and Political Science; second edn, Kansas City: Sheed Andrews & McMeel, 1978.

1971 *The Legacy of Max Weber,* Berkeley, CA: Glendessary Press; translated by Dr L. Walentik as *Drei Essays über Max Weber's geistiger Vermächtnis,* Tübingen J. C. B. Mohr, 1973.

1973 *Macroeconomic Thinking and the Market Economy: An Essay on the Neglect of the Micro-Foundations and its Consequences,* Institute of Economic Affairs: Hobart Paper Series, no. 56 (45 pp.) (London).

1977 *Capital, Expectations and the Market Process,* Kansas City: Sheed Andrews & McMeel. Translated by Dr L. Walentik, as *Marktprozess und Erwartungen: Studien zur Theorie der Marktwirtschaft,* Munich: The International Carl Menger Library Philosphia Verlag, 1984.

1986 *The Market as an Economic Process,* Oxford: Basil Blackwell.

ARTICLES IN *CAPITAL EXPECTATIONS, AND THE MARKET PROCESS*

1940 'A Reconsideration of the Austrian Theory of Industrial Fluctuations,' *Economica* 7 (May): 179–96.

1943 'The Role of Expectations in Economics as a Social Science', *Economica* 14 (Feb): 108–19.

1947 'Complementarity and Substitution in the Theory of Capital', *Economica* 14 (May): 108–19.

1950 'Economics as a Social Science', *South African Journal of Economics* 18 (Sept): 233–41.

1951 'The Science of Human Action', *Economica* 18 (Nov): 412–27.

1954 'Some Notes on Economic Thought, 1933–1953', *South African Journal of Economics* 18 (Sept.): 233–41.

1956 'The Market Economy and the Distribution of Wealth', in M. Senholz, (ed.), *On Freedom and Free Enterprise: Essays in Honor of Ludwig von Mises*, New York: D. Von Nostrand.

1958 'Mrs Robinson on the Accumulation of Capital', *South African Journal of Economics* 26 (June): 87–100.

1959 'Professor Shackle on the Economic Significance of Time', *Metroeconomica* 11 (Sept.): 64–73.

1963 'Cultivated Growth and the Market Economy', *South African Journal of Economics* (Sept.): 165–74.

1966 'Sir John Hicks on Capital Growth', *South African Journal of Economics* 34 (June): 113–23.

1966 'Die Gestesgeschichtliche Bedeutung der sterriechischen Schule in der Volks wirtschaftslehre' *Zeitschrift für Nationalökonomie* 26 (January): 152–67. Translated as 'The Significance of the Austrian School of Economics in the History of Ideas'.

1966 'Marktwirtschaft und Modellkonstrukionen', *ORDO* 17: 261–79. Translated as 'Model Constructions and the Market Economy'.

1967 'Causes and Consequences of the Inflation of our Time', *South African Journal of Economics* 35 (December): 281–91.

1969 'Methodological Individualism and the Market Economy', in E. Streissler *et al.* (eds) *Roads to Freedom: Essays in Honour of Friedrich A. von Hayek*, London: Routledge & Kegan Paul.

1971 'Ludwig von Mises and the Market Process', in F. A. Hayek (ed.) *Toward Liberty: Essays in Honor of Ludwig von Mises*, Menlo Park, CA: Institute for Humane Studies.

1973 'Sir John Hicks as a Neo-Austrian', *South African Journal of Economics* 41 (March): 54–62.

1976 'Austrian Economics in the Present Crisis of Economic Thought', previously unpublished.

ARTICLES IN *EXPECTATIONS AND THE MEANING OF INSTITUTIONS*

1936 'Commodity Stocks and Equilibrium', *Review of Economic Statistics* 3 (June): 230–4.

1937 'Uncertainty and Liquidity Preference', *Economica* 4 (August): 295–308.

1938 'Investment and Costs of Production', *American Economic Review* (Sept.): 469–81.

1938 [with F. Snapper] 'Commodity Stocks in the Trade Cycle', *Economica* (November): 435–54.

1939 'On Crisis and Adjustment', *Review of Economics and Statistics* 62–8.

1941 'On the Measurement of Capital', *Economica* (May): 361–77.

1944 'Finance Capitalism', *Economica* (Nov.): 64–73.

1945 'A Note on the Elasticity of Expectations', *Economica* (Nov.): 248–53.

1948 'Investment Repercussions', *Quarterly Journal of Economics* (Nov.): 698–713.

1975 'Reflections on Hayekian Capital Theory', unpublished paper delivered at the Allied Social Science Association Meeting in Dallas, Texas (15 pp.).

1976 'From Mises to Shackle: An Essay on Austrian Economics and the Kaleidic Society', *Journal of Economic Literature* (March): 54–62.

1978 'Carl Menger and the Incomplete Revolution of Subjectivism', *Atlantic Economic Journal* 11: 3 (Sept.): 57–9.

1978 'Vicissitudes of Subjectivism and the Dilemma of the Theory of Choice', manuscript on file with D. Lavoie (16 pp.).

1979 'The Flow of Legislation and the Permanence of the Legal Order', *ORDO*: 69–77.

1982 'The Salvage of Ideas: Problems of the Revival of Austrian Economic Thought', *Journal of Institutional and Theoretical Economics*, pp. 629–45.

1983 'John Maynard Keynes: A View from an Austrian Window', *South African Journal of Economics* 51: 3: 368–79.

1986 'Austrian Economics Under Fire: The Hayek–Sraffa Duel in Retrospect' in Grassl and Smith (eds) *Austrian Economics: Historical and Philosophical Background*, pp. 225–42.

1986 'The Monetary System of a Market Economy', *South African Journal of Economics* 54: 1: 1–7.

1988 'Speculative Markets and Economic Complexity', *Economic Affairs* (Dec.–Jan.): 7–10.

1990 'G. L. S. Shackle's Place in the History of Subjectivist Thought' Stephen Frowen (ed.) *Unknowledge and Choice in Economics: Pro-*

ceedings of a Conference in Honor of G. L. S. Shackle, New York: St. Martins Press: 1–8.

1991 'Austrian Economics as a Hermeneutic Approach' in D. Lavoie (ed.) *Economics and Hermeneutics*, London: Routledge: 134–46.

ARTICLES NOT REPRINTED IN COLLECTIONS OF ESSAYS

1937 'Preiserwartungen und Intertemporales Gleichgewicht', *Zeitschrift für Nationalökonomie*, Feb.

1937 'Social and Political Revolutions', *Journal of Social Philosophy* 3: 1 (Oct): 24–38.

1939 'Review of Moses Abramovitz's *An Approach to a Price Theory for a Changing Economy*', *Economica* (Aug.): 369–70.

1944 'Notes on the Proposal for International Currency Stabilization', *Review of Economics and Statistics* (Nov.): 184–91.

1949 'Reply', *Quarterly Journal of Economics* (August): 432–4.

1950 'Joseph A. Schumpeter, 1883–1950', *South African Journal of Economics* (June): 215–18.

1956 'The Velocity of Circulation as a Predictor', *South African Journal of Economics* (March): 17–24.

1959 'Böhm-Bawerk und die Kapitalstruktur' *Zeitschrift für Nationalökonomie* 19: 3: 235–45.

1962 'Cost Inflation and Economic Institutions', *South African Journal of Economics*, (September): 177–89.

1963 'Wirtschaftsordnung und Wirtschaftliche Institutionen', *ORDO* 14: 63–77.

1971 'The Rationale for Economic Development Programming and the Market Economy', *South African Journal of Economics*, (December): 319–32.

1976 'On the Central Concept of Austrian Economics: Market Process', in E. G. Dolan (ed.) *The Foundations of Modern Austrian Economics*, Kansas City: Sheed & Ward, Inc., pp. 126–32.

1976 'On Austrian Capital Theory', in E. G. Dolan (ed.) *The Foundations of Modern Austrian Economics*, Kansas City: Sheed & Ward, Inc. pp. 145–51.

1976 'Toward a Critique of Macroeconomics', in E. G. Dolan (ed.) *The Foundations of Modern Austrian Economics*, Kansas City: Sheed & Ward, Inc. pp. 152–9.

1976 'Austrian Economics in the Age of the Neo-Ricardian Counterrevolution', in E. G. Dolan (ed.) *The Foundations of Modern Austrian Economics*, Kansas City: Sheed & Ward, Inc. pp. 215–23.

1976 'Review of Hollis and Nell's *Rational Economic Man*,' *South African Journal of Economics* 44 (Sept.): 336–8.

1976 'The Dilemma of Economic Policy' in M. L. Truu (ed.) *Public Policy and the South African Economy: Essays in Memory of Desmond Hobart Houghton*, Oxford: Oxford University Press, pp. 1–11.

1978 'An Austrian Stocktaking: Unsettled Questions and Tentative Answers' in Louis M. Spadaro (ed.) *New Directions in Austrian Economics*, Kansas City: Sheed Andrews & McMeel Inc., pp. 1–18.

1978 ' "Foreword" to Ludwig von Mises's *Epistemological Problems of Economics*', New York: New York University Press.

1979 'Comment: Austrian Economics Today', in M. Rizzo (ed.) *Time, Uncertainty and Disequilibrium*, Lexington, MA: Lexington Books, pp. 64–9.

1979 'On the Recent Controversy Concerning Equilibrium', *Austrian Economic Newsletter*, 2 (Fall): 2.

1980 'Review of Hayek's *Law, Legislation and Liberty, vol. III*', *Journal of Economic Literature* 18: 1079–80.

1982 'Ludwig von Mises and the Extension of Subjectivism', in I. Kirzner (ed.) *Method, Process and Austrian Economics*, Lexington, MA: Lexington Books, pp. 31–40.

1982 'Why Expectations Matter', *The Investment Analyst Journal* 20 (Nov.): 9–15.

1982 'Review of Gratoff: "The Theory of Social Action: The Correspondence of A. Schütz and Talcott Parsons" ', *Austrian Economic Newsletter*.

1983 'Preface' to reprint of Richard von Strigl [1934] *Kapital und Produktion*, Munich: Philosophia.

1985 'Review of O'Driscoll and Rizzo's, *The Economics of Time and Ignorance*', *Market Process*, 3, 2.

1988 'The Huttian Philosophy', *Managerial and Decision Economics*, Winter: 13–15.

1992 'Socialism and the Market: A Theme of Economic Sociology Viewed from a Wagnerian Perspective', *South African Journal of Economics* (March).

MISCELLANEOUS

1978 'An Interview with Ludwig Lachmann, *Austrian Economics Newsletter* 1 (Fall): 3.

OF RELATED INTEREST

Kirzner, Israel M. (ed.) (1986) *Subjectivism, Intelligibility, and Economic Understanding: Essays in Honor of Ludwig M. Lachmann on his Eightieth Birthday*, New York: New York University Press.

1992 *Lachmann Memorial Issue* of *South African Journal of Economics*, 60 (March): 1.

NOTES

INTRODUCTION: EXPECTATIONS AND THE MEANING OF INSTITUTIONS

1 From Lachmann's 1959 paper, 'Professor Shackle on the Significance of Time' ([1959] 1977:89). All the Lachmann citations are included in the Appendix at the end of this book.

2 For useful intellectual biographies of Lachmann, see Grinder (1977) and Mittermaier (1992).

3 See, for example, Addleson (1993), Boettke (1990), Ebeling (1985; 1986; 1991), Horwitz (1992), Madison (1991), Prychitko (1990) and Rector (1991).

4 Debreu's approach is a case in point. To be fair, it is apparently the case that the Austrians tried to achieve this sort of insulation of their theory from empirical challenge. At least the traditional interpretation of Mises's methodological position makes it this sort of 'Euclidean' approach. See however, Lachmann ([1966] 1977: 45–64) and Lavoie (1986) for an alternative interpretation.

5 Elsewhere (1990a) I have argued for the view that economists ought to become more like anthropologists in their empirical work.

6 For example, Donald McCloskey (1985) has been trying, so far without too much success, to awaken economists from their complacency, and consider trying to fashion post-modern re-interpretations of their ideas.

7 It might be argued that the growing influence of rational choice models in political science and sociology proves that economics is not 'isolationistic' but on the contrary is colonizing its neighbouring disciplines. But I think efforts at economic imperialism only illustrate the profundity of the problem. Neoclassical economists, who are not only to be found in economics departments, are unable to understand what is going on in sociology and political science other than what they themselves have done there. Rational choice political scientists and sociologists are as unable to truly listen to non-economistic voices in those disciplines as professional economists are.

8 Among the books that sketch the implications of hermeneutics for the social sciences in general, the two editions of Rabinow and Sullivan's (1979, 1987) *Interpretive Social Science* are among the best, though

economics is conspicuous by its absence in both editions. Two collections of essays which explicitly take post-modern themes into economics are Warren Samuels' (1990) *Economics As Discourse* and my own (1991c) *Economics and Hermeneutics*.

9 In a sense what Lachmann did with his book on Max Weber was to reconnect the Austrian school to the tradition of interpretive sociology with which it used to be closely connected. In addition to Weber's own contributions, the work of the Weberian phenomenologist Alfred Schütz – for example, Schütz and Luckmann (1973) – was brought by Lachmann back into the Austrian economic discourse. For an account of the early connections, see Prendergast (1986).

10 See Lachmann (1971: 18). We might observe that the intentionalistic language in which Lachmann puts this remark might be challenged by contemporary hermeneutical writers, who prefer to avoid talking in terms of getting at something that was in the original author's mind. This point is especially elaborated in Hans-Georg Gadamer's work on hermeneutics, for example, Gadamer ([1960] 1989; 1979).

11 Mittermaier (1992: 22). It may well be that among those who would have been shocked in the 1930s were most of the other Austrian school economists, including Mises and Hayek. Thus Lachmann may have been the first modern Austrian economist to gain a sense of the school as a perspective that is fundamentally distinct from mainstream economics.

12 See Lachmann (1977: 48–9) where he remarks that Menger 'insisted that we are dealing not only with quantitative relationships but also with the "essence" of economic phenomena,' so that 'If it is permissible to equate the "comprehension of essence" with the "interpretation of meaning", we may conclude that Menger's intention . . . was to defend the possibility of an economic theory designed to interpret meaning.' This I think makes clear what Lachmann was up to. He was *actively* reinterpreting the Austrians into a more hermeneutical position than their own words would have usually allowed. At times this may lead to an almost forced re-interpretation of the Austrians' methodological pronouncements into new positions which reflect perhaps not so much what they meant as what they *should* have meant in order to fit the methodology to the substance of their economics.

13 Indeed contemporary hermeneutics would argue that even in studying intentional action one cannot remain focused on the original intentions of the action's 'author', but must examine the unintended consequences of the author's meaning. See in this regard Lavoie (1990b).

14 On the other hand, one could question whether Lachmann did compromise when he allowed that equilibrium was appropriate in the analysis of individual action. Contemporary hermeneutics would raise a challenge to Lachmann's (and the traditional Austrian school's) conception of methodological individualism which too hastily concedes that an individual's plans can usefully be considered to be self-consistent or in equilibrium. For sketches of this sort of critique of traditional Austrian individualism, see Lavoie (1991b) and Madison (1988).

15 The implications of the phenomenology of time for economics are a

crucial concern of Lachmann's work. His focus on the issue inspired one of the most important works of the neo-Austrian revival, O'Driscoll and Rizzo's *The Economics of Time and Ignorance* (1985), which builds on Henri Bergson's work. For a radically hermeneutical analysis of time in economics, see Parsons (1991).

16 A very useful discussion of Lachmann's pivotal role in the American revival of Austrian economics is contained in Karen Vaughn (1993).

17 In the 1930s, Lachmann was criticizing Rosenstein-Rodan for using a 'functional' type of analysis (1937: 299), and in his essay 'Investment and Costs of Production' was explicitly calling for a 'causal-genetic analysis of the trade cycle' (1938: 471).

18 See Lavoie (1991a) for a discussion of the way the school judges its own progress according to how consistently it has been able to apply this principle.

19 Indeed, my personal experience with the man convinces me he had no illusions of grandeur. Here was this cultured European gentleman inviting ill-trained and ill-mannered American graduate students into his office for hours of casual conversation about economics. His manner with the brash young students was to treat us as equals, to listen to our arguments, and respond to them patiently. He was just a regular guy.

1 COMMODITY STOCKS AND EQUILIBRIUM

1 N. Kaldor, 'A Classificatory Note on the Determinateness of Equilibrium', *Review of Economic Studies*, I, 2: 133.

2 O. Morgenstern, 'Vollkommene Voraussicht und Wirtschaftliches Gleichgewicht', *Zeitschrift für Nationalökonomie*, VI, 3: 327–57.

3 Henry Schultz, *Der Sinn der Statistischen Nachfragekurven*, 1929, p. 34.

4 U. Ricci, 'Die synthetische Ökonomie des Henry Ludwell Moore', *Zeitschrift für Nationalökonomie*, III: 649.

5 O. Lange, 'Formen der Angebotsanpassung und Wirtschaftliches Gleichgewicht', *Zeitschrift für Nationalökonomie*, VI, 3: 358–65.

6 N. Kaldor, op. cit., p. 134, especially footnote 2.

7 O. Lange, op. cit., p. 363.

8 Kaldor, p. 127.

2 UNCERTAINTY AND LIQUIDITY-PREFERENCE

1 *Economica*, August 1936.

2 Op. cit., p. 272, n. 2.

3 Our italics.

4 It might be objected that the concept of liquidity-preference can be given a wider meaning by divorcing it from the demand for money and extending it to all commodities. People may thus wish to be liquid in furs and jewels as well as in money.

It seems, however, that, if thus far extended, the concept would lose all concrete meaning and liquidity-preference become indistinguishable from general preference. If every single exchange transaction can be explained by liquidity-preference on both sides, how are we to say who has become more liquid and who less?

One might even go a step further and argue that in such cases different commodities become money for different people. This would, of course, mean the end of all monetary theory.

5 As is clearly shown in ch. 17, where 'commodity-rates of interest' are treated as intertemporal exchange-rates, Mr Keynes is, at times, well aware of the necessity of introducing an intertemporal market in order to explain intertemporal exchange-relationships.

6 It is another of the cases (cf. Keynes, op. cit., p. 199) where, in the language of the financial press, 'the movement of prices is out of all proportion to the volume of dealing.'

7 Cf. Tj. Greidanus: *The Value of Money*, London, 1932, pp. 111–13.

8 We can leave out here its function of unit of account, because its utility in this respect does not depend on its actual possession.

9 It might be argued that this assertion is either tautological (if restricted to money-debts) or untrue (if extended to non-money-debts). In reality, however, it is neither the one nor the other. First, there is an important distinction between money-debts and commodity-debts: Every commodity-debt is a potential money-debt, because the debtor is able to convert his debt into a money-debt by withdrawing from the contract and paying damages. In the case of a money-debt, on the other hand, conversion into a commodity-debt is legally impossible. Secondly, it is practically impossible to conclude intertemporal loan-contracts in anything but the money-form. All attempts to do it on some other basis have so far proved entirely unsuccessful (witness the deplorable fate of the Gold Clause in the jurisdiction of all countries with depreciated currencies!).

10 D. H. Robertson: 'Some notes on Mr Keynes's General Theory of Employment', *Quarterly Journal of Economics*, November, 1936: 168–91.

11 Op. cit., pp. 176–7.

12 On the concept of Secondary Depression cf. W. Röpke, *Crises and Cycles*, London, 1936; and G. Haberler, 'Some Reflections on the present situation of Business Cycle Theory', *Review of Economic Statistics*, February, 1936: 7.

3 INVESTMENT AND COSTS OF PRODUCTION

1 G. Haberler, *Prosperity and Depression*, Geneva, 1937, pp. 81–98, 205–9.

2 J. M. Keynes, *The General Theory of Employment, Interest and Money*, London, 1936, p. 317.

3 Ibid., p. 322.

4 M. Kalecki, 'A Theory of the Business Cycle', *Rev. of Econ. Stud.*, IV, 2, Feb., 1937.

5 F. A. von Hayek, 'Investment That Raises the Demand for Capital', *Rev. of Econ. Stat.*, Nov., 1937.

6 Keynes, op. cit., p. 151, n. 1.

7 R. F. Harrod, *The Trade Cycle*, Oxford, 1936.

8 Ibid., pp. 86–7.

9 H. Neisser, 'Investment Fluctuations as Cause of the Business Cycle', *Social Research*, Nov., 1937.

10 Erik Lundberg, *Studies in the Theory of Expansion* (Stockholm Economic Series), Stockholm and London, 1937.

11 Haberler, op. cit., p. 258.

12 'Where Labour is divided into distinct groups there will be a critical level of employment, within each group, at which money wages begin to rise, and this critical point is passed in some industries when effective demand expands while unemployment in other industries is still very great.'
Joan Robinson, *Essays in the Theory of Employment*, London, 1937, p. 43.

13 Eric Lundberg, *Studies in the Theory of Economic Expansion*, p. 230.

14 Keynes, op. cit., p. 317.

15 If the increase in costs gives rise to expectations of a further rise, investment activity may continue for some time. But this effect will necessarily be of a temporary nature. Sooner or later these expectations will be disappointed.

16 Haberler, op. cit., p. 86.

17 This applies *a fortiori* if, as one would expect during a boom, costs in investment-goods industries rise more than in consumption-goods industries. For in this case the marginal efficiency of capital will *ipso facto* be reduced. Cf. Joan Robinson, op cit., pp. 44–5.

18 It goes without saying that the validity of our argument is not confined to cases of perfect competition, i.e. where price equals marginal cost. What matters is not equality of, but correspondence between, these two magnitudes. That every increase in marginal cost should be accompanied by some price rise is for our purpose a necessary and sufficient condition.

19 Keynes, op. cit., p. 263.

20 Keynes, op, cit., p. 223 ss.

4 COMMODITY STOCKS IN THE TRADE CYCLE

1 There are a few statistics of stocks of finished products, but they are not very satisfactory, e.g.
U.S.A. Survey of Current Business, Annual Supplement, 1936, p. 100.
S. Kuznets, *National Income and Capital Formation*, New York, 1937, p. 40, table 10, no. 2c 'changes in business inventories', and p. 120 (for steel sheets).
Jan Tinbergen in *De Nederlandsche Conjunctuur*, March, 1933, 11–20.

2 J. M. Keynes, *A Treatise on Money*, Vol. II, ch. 29, 'Liquid Capital'.

Also *General Theory of Unemployment, Interest and Money*, pp. 318–19.

3 Some writers have attributed these changes to sun spots. They believe that there is a sun spot cycle of about eleven years, which causes cyclical fluctuations in the size of the crops. Among the outstanding writers who have taken this view is W. Stanley Jevons and Mr S. de Wolff. The latter in his book, *Het Economisch Getij*, states that there is a longer cycle of forty-five years too. Mr D. H. Robertson (*A Study of Industrial Fluctuations*) mentions this theory without committing himself.

4 'Eenige Gegevena betreffende Grondstofffenmarkt' in *De Nederlandsche Conjunctuur*, February, 1937: 14–20.

5 J. W. F. Rowe, *Special Memorandum* no. 31, *Sugar*, London and Cambridge Economic Service.

6 *Cotton Year Book of the New York Cotton Exchange, 1937.*

7 *Treatise on Money*, Vol. II, p. 124n.

8 *Wheat Studies*, Vol. IV, p. 180, and Vol. X, p. 134.

9 Jan Tinbergen in *De Nederlandsche Conjunctuur*, March, 1933: 11–20.

10 London and Cambridge Economic Service, May *Bulletin*, 1938: 207.

11 *The Economist*, Monthly Trade Supplement, December, 1896.

12 *The Economist*, 1879, pp. 421 and 559.

13 Ibid., 1905, p. 1072.

14 Ibid., September 12th, 1908, p. 481.

15 *Stocks of Staple Commodities*, by J. W. F. Rowe and others; November, 1937, p. 24.

16 Ibid., p. 30, Table 1.

17 London and Cambridge Economic Service, *Special Memorandum*, no. 32, *Stocks of Staple Commodities*, by J. M. Keynes, J. W. F. Rowe and G. L. Schwartz, pp. 10–11.

18 Cf. L. M. Lachmann, 'Commodity Stocks and Equilibrium', *Review of Econ. Studies*, III, 3, June 1936.

19 Ralph H. Blodgett, *Cyclical Fluctuations in Commodity Stocks* (University of Pennsylvania Press), Philadelphia, 1935, Appendix C, p. 171.

20 After this paper had been completed, Mr Keynes once more took up the subject of commodity stocks in a paper read at the Cambridge meeting of the British Association in August 1938 ('The Policy of Government Storage of Foodstuffs and Raw Materials', *Economic Journal*, September 1938). While his diagnosis has remained essentially the same – 'The competitive system abhors the existence of stocks, with as strong a reflex as nature abhors a vacuum, because stocks yield a negative return in terms of themselves' op. cit., p. 449 – his therapy is new. He seems to have grown sceptical of output restrictions which 'is apt to be objectionable in general, even when it is highly desirable for the particular purpose of meeting fluctuations, because it may be part and parcel of conditions of almost uncontrolled monopoly'. What he proposes is, briefly, a government subsidy for the carrying of stocks. To this we have no objection. But it still seems to us, in the light of the statistics we have presented, that his fears about insufficient stock

carrying in a competitive world are a little exaggerated. The whole issue has, however, now become a question of degree.

21 H. Makower and J. Marschak, 'Assets, Prices and Monetary Theory', *Economica*, August, 1938: 280–1.

22 Cf above, p. 64 about the 1905 boom in 'Middlesboro' N.3'.

23 The following figures are taken from *Tin* (annually published in London by the International Tin Producers' Association). Total visible supplies as estimated by W. H. Gartsen.

24 In some markets contango and backwardation are called premium and discount.

25 J. K. Eastham, 'Rationalisation in the Tin Industry', *Review of Econ. Studies*, October, 1936: 20.

26 Blodgett, op. cit. pp. 5–8.

27 *General Theory of Employment, Interest and Money*, ch. 22: 'Notes on the Trade Cycle'.

28 *Treatise on Money*, Vol. II, ch. 29: 'Liquid Capital'.

29 Blodgett, op. cit. p. 103.

30 R. G. Hawtrey, *Capital and Employment*, London, 1937, pp. 116–17.

5 ON CRISIS AND ADJUSTMENT

1 The present paper contains results of research which the author undertook as Leon Fellow of the University of London during 1938–9.

2 By 'neoclassical' doctrine we mean the theory which before the war was generally accepted (with such exceptions as Mr Hobson and the Marxists). In its purest form, this doctrine is to be found in G. Cassel, *The Theory of Social Economy* (London, 1923), Vol. II, pp. 503–628. What practically is far more important, until very recently it was *the* business-cycle theory of the financial editors.

3 This concept has been expounded by Professor Roepke in various writings, e.g., *Crises and Cycles* (London, 1937), pp. 119–33, and 'Die sekundaere Krise und ihre Uebewindung' in *Essays in Honour of Gustaf Cassel* (London, 1933), pp. 553–67.

4 Professor Hayek in 'Der Stand und die naechsten Aufgaben der Konjunkturforschung', *Spiethoff-Festschrift* (Munich, 1933), p. 113.

5 Professor Haberler in *Spiethoff-Festschrift*, p. 97.

6 R. F. Harrod, *The Trade Cycle* (Oxford, 1936), pp. 104–5.

7 A. H. Hansen, *Full Recovery or Stagnation?* (New York, 1938), p. 279. See also Professor D. H. Robertson's review of Mr R. F. Harrod's *The Trade Cycle* in *The Canadian Journal of Economics and Political Science*, 3 (1937): 126.

8 Erik Lundberg, *Studies in the Theory of Economic Expansion* (Stockholm Economic Series, Stockholm and London, 1937), p. 230.

9 So has Professor Hansen, op. cit., p. 147.

10 L. M. Lachmann, 'Investment and Costs of Production', *American Economic Review*, XXVIII (1938): 475.

11 The latter was originally a copper crisis.

12 Melvin T. Copeland, *A Raw Commodity Revolution* (Harvard Univer-

sity, Graduate School of Business Administration, Business Research Studies, Number 19, 1938), pp. 24, 25.

13 D. H. Robertson, 'The Trade Cycle – An Academic View', *Lloyds Bank Limited Monthly Review*, New Series, 8 (September, 1937): 506.

14 F. A. von Hayek, *Prices and Production* (2nd edn, London, 1934).

15 It has, of course, often been pointed out that to distinguish between scientific doctrines according to their place of origin is a rather unsatisfactory method of classification. Nevertheless, one of the few things on which economists have found it possible to agree in recent years has been the denotation of the monetary overinvestment theory as taught by Professor Hayek as 'The Austrian Theory of the Trade Cycle'. In what follows, we shall adhere to this terminology. It should be understood, however, that in referring to the teaching of the 'Austrian School' we mean the doctrine expounded by Professors Hayek, Machlup, Mises, Robbins, and Strigl. For a brief presentation in English, see Lionel C. Robbins, 'Consumption and the Trade Cycle', *Economica*, XII (1932) 413–30.

16 Op. cit, pp. 473–4.

6 ON THE MEASUREMENT OF CAPITAL

1 Colin Clark, *The Conditions of Economic Progress* (Macmillan, 1940).

2 That actually the writing down of capital book values and not disinvestment in the ordinary sense was responsible for this apparent decline in the quantity of manufacturing capital is obvious, if not from common sense, from a glance at the Kuznets figures for capital accumulation on p. 397. In the United States total net disinvestment for the four bleak years 1931–4 was $9.6 milliards against a net investment figure of $10.1 milliards for 1929 alone.

3 Professor P. H. Douglas, the originator of this type of econometrics, was well aware of this problem. *Cf.* his cautionary remarks in his *Theory of Wages*, New York, 1934, pp. 131–2.

4 To the future student of the history of economic thought it will be a matter of some interest that the same author who on p. 281 wrote: 'Both temporal and spatial comparisons indicate that depreciation will become a question of rapidly increasing importance both in industrial management and in economic thinking', warns his readers on p. 374 that 'we must not fall into the old-fashioned error of regarding the accumulation of capital as the limiting factor in economic progress. Possibly it is not even the predominant factor' – apparently quite unaware of the inconsistency between the two statements.

5 On this point and, in connection with it, Lord Kelvin's famous dictum, everything necessary from the point of view of Social Science has now been said by Professor Knight – and with the appropriate emphasis, too! See F. H. Knight, 'What is Truth in Economics?', *Journal of Political Economy*, February, 1940: 18 n.

6 This expression is here used because after all we need a concept which covers in its totality the heterogeneous assembly of houses, mines,

shipyards, restaurant equipment, etc. (including many scrapheaps) which make up 'Capital'. The reader, we trust, will see the difference between this and 'the total quantity of capital in real terms' and not accuse us of using the same concept under a different name.

7 Solomon Fabricant, *Capital Consumption and Capital Adjustment* (National Bureau of Economic Research), New York, 1938.

8 Retirements and abandonments, important mostly in the case of railways, are, of course, only another form of asset revaluation. 'By their nature they are confined to adjustments for *unforeseen obsolescence* (my italics, L. M. L.) and inadequate depreciation, depletion and maintenance'. Fabricant p. 266. See also the two following notes.

9 'As a matter of fact, business practice ignores the distinction between ordinary depreciation and obsolescence so far as the latter is normal, that is, predictable. And replacements, renewals, and repairs incurred through ordinary (that is, minor) changes in the arts and in demand are charged to current expense. It would therefore be statistically impossible, even if logically possible or desirable, to eliminate the effects of obsolescence. But normal obsolescence at least is relevant to the economic measure of capital consumption.' (Fabricant, op cit., pp. 13–14.) It will be noticed from the first sentence that the author uses the words 'normal' and 'predictable' as synonyms.

10 This is at least implicitly admitted in Dr Fabricant's distinction between 'normal' and 'unanticipated' obsolescence, or in the sentence: 'The criterion of reasonableness must rest, as in the distinction between charges on income account and on capital account, on the kind of expectations and anticipations – usually implicit – held by those making capital commitments', p. 14.

11 Fabricant, op cit., Part IV, chapters 9, 10, 11.

12 Fabricant op cit., pp. 64–86.

13 For a tabulation of depreciation practices see Table 13, pp, 66–7.

14 Op cit., p. 194.

15 In the United States 'In 1929 the gross national product consisted of 93.6 billion dollars. To obtain a net figure, the national income, there was deducted 10.2 billion for depreciation, depletion, and losses by fire of the nation's fixed capital. In 1933 the corresponding figures (expressed in 1929 prices) were 60,5 and 9,5 billion dollars. In other words, in 1929 one-ninth, and in 1933 one-sixth of the gross product was accounted for by these items of capital consumption.' Fabricant p. 5.

16 Fabricant, pp. 195–200.

17 Fabricant, Table 33, p. 181.

18 Fabricant, Table 32, pp. 178–9.

7 FINANCE CAPITALISM?

1 Rudolf Hilferding *Das Finanzkapital*, Vienna, 1910.

2 Op. cit., p. 283.

3 V. I. Lenin 'Imperialism, the highest stage of Capitalism', *Collected Works*, Vol. XIX, p. 110.

4 Italics in original.

5 On the sociological basis and background of Company Law see Mises *Socialism*, pp. 208–10.

6 F. H. Knight *Risk, Uncertainty, and Profit*, 1933 re-issue, p. 35.

7 This distinction is mentioned on p. 316, but the point is not developed any further in its bearing on entrepreneurship.

8 Op. cit., p. 298.

9 *Report of the Committee on Finance and Industry* (Cmd. 3897), 1931.

10 The historical reasons for this lack of contact are stated with admirable precision in paras. 375–7. For the strictures see mainly paras. 385–90.

11 Lord Geddes in his address to the General Meeting of the Rio Tinto Co., May 21, 1943.

12 P. Barrett Whale (1930) *Joint Stock Banking in Germany*, Macmillan, p. 64.

13 The situation as it had then developed is well illustrated by a remark which August Thyssen is said to have made during the crisis of 1900: 'I sleep much better than my bankers in Berlin. They have lent me 50 million marks. I only owe it to them.' *Se non è vero, è ben trovato.*

14 On the development of the German chemical and electrical engineering industries see Hermann Levy (1935) *Industrial Germany*, Cambridge University Press, Chapters IV, V and VI.

15 For a brilliant pen portrait of him see Gaston Raphäel (1919) *Walther Rathenau*, Payot, pp. 15–28.

16 For particulars of his method see Whale, op. cit., pp. 57–9.

17 Whale, op. cit., p. 64.

18 'American business is eminently of a financial character, and the traffic of these financiers runs within the closed circuit of money-market strategy, with any industrial effects of this financial management coming in as incidentals. The controlling incentives are those of the market for securities, not those of the output of goods; and the final discretion rests in the investment banker, not in the engineering staff or the manager of the works. The discretionary direction of affairs has in effect passed into the hands of these financing houses, whose ostensible relation to the industrial concerns is that of underwriters only.' Thorstein Veblen *Imperial Germany and the Industrial Revolution*, New Edn, New York, 1939, Supplem. note IV, pp. 339–40.

19 Macmillan Report, para. 380.

20 T.N.E.C. *Hearings*, Part 23, p. 11847.

21 At no time later than 1905 had the 20 largest shareholders more than 11 per cent of outstanding stock. Whatever control may have been exercised over the AT & T, it certainly was not located in the majority of stock.

22 Professor R. A. Gordon, who has examined 155 of the 200 largest industrial corporations in the United States, thinks 'It is significant that there were practically no very large (10 per cent or more) holdings by banks (none by investment banks). This is not to say, of course, that banker control may not exist. Such control, in so far as it does

exist, merely does not seem to need the reinforcing power of ownership.' (R. A. Gordon (1938) 'Ownership by management and control groups in the large corporation', *Q.J.E.*, May, p. 385, n. 4.)

23 *Hearings before the Senate Committee on Banking and Currency*, Vol. 3, pp. 959–60, June 27, 1933.

24 T.N.E.C., *Hearings* Part 23, p. 11858.

25 Loc. cit., pp. 12094–5.

26 For instance, it was pointed out by Mr Whitney that the relationship between the Morgan bank and some of the railroads was very different from that with the AT & T.

27 T.N.E.C. *Hearings*, Part 24, pp. 12465–6.

28 The reader is asked to bear in mind that in what follows we are exclusively concerned with investment banking, not with deposit banking.

29 A country in the first stages of industrialization will often suffer from a lack of industrial enterprise and business experience which may well be its scarcest factor of production. In this case the task of starting new industries, one after the other, may devolve upon the bankers (and sometimes other merchants) as the specialists in engineering economic change. For a free enterprise economy adjusts itself to new problems by evolving a kind of professional problem-solver ('... that if they have a problem of a financial nature, Dr Kuhn, Loeb & Co. is a pretty good doctor to go to...'). It pays him handsomely and relieves him from all non-specialist work. And the ignorant will firmly believe in the existence of the idle rich.

30 It was when confronted with such tasks that there excelled the financial genius of Sir Ernest Cassel. A comprehensive study of his career from the point of view here indicated would perhaps throw more light on the problems of 'capital re-grouping' than many learned volumes on the applied theory of capital.

31 But, of course, it may be that the task is beyond his capacity. 'In Britain after the (last) war the intervention of bank capital was held off as long as possible, but in the 'twenties, when iron and steel prices were below the general price level and falling continuously, debentures fell more and more into the hands of the banks and they were forced to take an interest in the industry. A large part of the firms were living on frozen overdrafts and under the legal control of the banks, which did not possess the experience to exercise positive direction.' T. H. Burnham and G. O. Hoskins: *Iron and Steel in Britain 1870–1939*, London, 1943, p. 263.

32 'Scientism and the Study of Society', II, *Economica*, February, 1943; pp. 57–8. 'The Facts of the Social Sciences', *Ethics*, October, 1943, p. 9, n. 4.

8 A NOTE ON THE ELASTICITY OF EXPECTATIONS

1 On this and related aspects of the problem cf. J. A. Schumpeter, *Business Cycles*, 1939, Vol. I, pp. 55–6, 140–1.

2 J. R. Hicks, *Value and Capital*, 1939, p. 205.

3 Oscar Lange, *Price Flexibility and Employment*, Cowles Commission for Research in Economics, Monograph No. 8, Bloomington, Ind., 1944.

4 Op. cit., pp. 271–2.

5 Lange, op. cit., p. 30.

6 'He will, however, be able to select a single value which, if he could expect it with certainty, would have the same significance for him as the distribution of probabilities which he has actually in mind. We shall call such a value a certainty-equivalent.' G. L. S. Shackle: *Expectations, Investment and Income*, 1938, p. 64.

7 There is, of course, no reason why the actual market price should coincide with the median of our probability distribution. The extent to which the former deviates from the latter measures the 'bullishness' or 'bearishness' of the market. The more 'bullish' the market the lower the place on the scale at which we shall find the market price, and the more the latter will fall short of the median. And vice versa.

8 Lange, op. cit., p. 27.

9 On the significance of the interpretation of observable phenomena in the theory of expectations cf. L. M. Lachmann: 'The Role of Expectations in Economics as a Social Science', *Economica*, February, 1943, esp. pp. 15–18.

9 INVESTMENT REPERCUSSIONS

1 The sole exception is, of course, Professor Hayek's article on 'Investment that Raises the Demand for Capital', *Review of Economic Statistics*, November 1937 (now reprinted in *Profits, Interest and Investment*, 1939, pp. 73–82). The ideas there set forth by Professor Hayek have been the main inspiration of this paper.

2 'Complementarity and Substitution in the Theory of Capital', *Economica*, May, 1947.

3 *General Theory*, p. 141: 'The output from equipment produced today will have to *compete* (our italics) in the course of its life, with the output from equipment produced subsequently, perhaps at a lower labour cost, perhaps by an improved technique.' Similar statements appear on p. 143.

4 Op. cit., p. 135.

5 Paul W. Gates, *The Illinois Central Railroad and its Colonization Work* (Harvard University Press, 1934. Harvard Economic Studies, Vol. XIII). 'The Illinois Central Railroad in the first decade of its existence was primarily a land company and secondarily a railroad company. Its construction was made possible by a mortgage secured upon its lands and the interest charges were paid and the bonds retired by the proceeds from land sales' (p. 149). 'President Schuyler at first determined to withhold the lands from sale until the increase in population and the construction of the road had enhanced their value... They had been subject to sale for years at $1.25 per acre, had little

present value, and until the road was constructed would yield but a small return. *It was the construction of the road which would create their value'* (Our italics) (p. 153).

6 E. Lindahl, *Studies in the Theory of Money and Capital*, 1939, pp. 21–136.

7 E. Lundberg, *Studies in the Theory of Economic Expansion*, 1937, especially chapter IX.

8 About this function of forward markets, cf. J. R. Hicks, *Value and Capital*, pp. 135–40.

9 cf. F. A. Hayek, *Profits, Interest and Investment*, pp. 119–21.

10 E. A. G. Robinson, *Monopoly*, 1941: 'In ordinary competitive conditions when one isolated process requires a considerably larger scale of operations for its efficient conduct than is required by the other processes of manufacture, it tends to be 'disintegrated' from the remaining processes, to be handed over to larger, specialists firms who perform the required tasks for the output of a number of firms in the main industry.' (p. 64) The same view is taken by G. J. Stigler, *The Theory of Price*, p. 210.

11 'First, by vertical integration with the disintegrated firms you may attach them to yourself and deny their services to others. Second, by various types of tying clauses, or by various threats of boycott, you may give the disintegrated firm the choice between serving you and serving your competitor. If the advantage of serving you is sufficiently great, the threat will be effective.' (Robinson, op. cit., p. 64).

12 Cf. Professor Neisser's remarks on complementary investment in 'Realism and Speculation in Employment Programs', p. 94, *Planning and Paying for Full Employment*, A. P. Lerner and F. D. Graham, eds; Princeton, 1946.

13 Carl Menger, *Grundsätze der Volkswirkschaftslehre*, pp. 129–30; and F. A. Hayek, *The Pure Theory of Capital*, p. 64: 'This fact that, as investment proceeds, more and more of those natural forces which before were only potential resources are utilized and gradually drawn into the circle of scarce goods, and have in turn themselves to be counted as investments, is of great importance for the understanding of the whole process.'

14 Cf. P. T. Ellsworth, Chile: An Economy in Transition, 1943.

15 This may be an appropriate juncture to clarify the relationship in which our argument stands to Professor Schumpeter's theory of economic development.

Both are concerned with irreversible dynamic processes. In both cases the nature of the process consists in that entrepreneurs, i.e. persons with a wider expectational horizon than the 'individuals' ordinarily depicted in static theory, by their acts modify the environmental data to which such individuals 'react'. Our argument rests on the realization that all investment is a dynamic process, and relies on capital complementarity and the favourable investment repercussions it engenders as the main vehicle of change.

In Professor Schumpeter's theory, on the other hand, the relationship between entrepreneurs and the 'old firms', as well as among entrepreneurs themselves, is essentially competitive and substitutive. In spite of occasional hints at possible favourable effects of complementarity (e.g.: 'They proceed not exclusively under the stimulus of loss. For some of the "old" firms new opportunities for expansion open up: the new methods or commodities create New Economic Space.' *Business Cycles*, Vol. I, p. 134), it is clear that he regards competition as the main vehicle of dynamic change.

The two theories are thus seen to examine what are really different elements of the same process. In this respect, if not in their objects of study, they may thus be said to be 'complementary'.

10 AUSTRIAN ECONOMICS UNDER FIRE

1 At home, in Vienna, Illy and Mayer meanwhile emphasized what separated Austrian economic thought from that of the School of Lausanne, from Walras and Pareto. Their thesis that equilibrium theory, since it is unable to explain how prices are actually formed in markets, can tell us nothing about economic processes, has today a strikingly modern ring. It is to be hoped that in the Austrian revival of our days their work, today almost forgotten, will find the attention it deserves. See Illy (1948), and Mayer (1932) and also now the reprint of Schön-feld-Illy (1924).

2 In his *Reply*, Hayek wrote: 'I have been assuming that the body of existing pure economic theory demonstrates that, so long as we neglect monetary factors, there is an inherent tendency towards an equilibrium of the economic system' (1932: 238).

As Hicks says of Hayek, 'He took his model very "pure": much purer than Wicksell himself had been accustomed to take it. Prices (all prices) are perfectly flexible, adjusting instantaneously, or as nearly as matters' (Hicks 1967: 205–6).

3 We ignore here a couple of pages contributing to a symposium on 'Increasing Returns and the Representative Firm', in *Economic Journal*, 40: 89–92 (March 1930).

4 For his later view see Sraffa (1960: 38).

5 Sraffa never was a Keynesian, nor could he be. We now have Professor Joan Robinson's testimony: 'Looking back now, I see that in the tumultuous years when Keynes' *General Theory* was being written, Piero never really quite knew what it was that we were going on about' (Robinson 1979: 1).

One may regard long-run equilibrium as the centre of the economic system. Or one may hold that 'in the long run we are all dead'. One cannot hold both views simultaneously.

One of several misfortunes suffered by Austrian economics in the 1930s was that it came under fire from both sides at about the same time.

6 See also Lachmann (1956: 75–6) and Lerner (1953: 361–78).

11 THE SALVAGE OF IDEAS

1 For reasons we need not go into at length we are unable to regard Schumpeter, who followed Pareto rather than Menger and won international fame as an expositor of the former before the age of thirty, as an 'Austrian' in the sense we are using this term here.

2 Except for a brief but incursive reference to Mayer in Hutchison 1953: 327.

3 This will be so in particular where technical change has to be 'embodied' in durable and specific capital equipment. A good deal will depend here on the existence and efficiency of second-hand markets for capital equipment, including buildings, reflecting a range of versatility of such equipment. In such cases the speed of dissemination of technical knowledge is not unaffected by the state of markets. If so, our taxonomic efforts in the field of knowledge germane to economic action have their limits.

4 For an illuminating example of this confusion see Boland 1981. As economists of the present day owe some part of their education in epistemology to Professor Boland's undaunted efforts, the lapse is the more significant.

5 Böhm-Bawerk 1907: 282 ended one of his articles devoted to criticism of J. B. Clark's views on the nature of capital with the words 'With every respect for the intellectual qualities of my opponent, I must oppose his doctrine with all possible emphasis in order to defend a solid and natural theory of capital against a mythology of capital.' This is the origin of the title of Hayek's article in the same journal in 1936.

6 It is noteworthy that Keynes at once understood the classical background of Knight's views and attested that in his 'discussion which contains many interesting and profound observations on the nature of capital, and confirms the soundness of the Marshallian tradition as to the uselessness of the Böhm-Bawerkian analysis, the theory of interest is given precisely in the traditional, classical mould' (Keynes 1936: 176, n. 3).

7 We thus reach the odd conclusion that both our contestants rejected Böhm-Bawerk, but for opposite reasons: while Hayek found him too classical for his taste, for Knight he was not classical enough!

Not all Austrians agreed with Hayek's view of Böhm-Bawerk. For an able defence of the subsistence fund *see* Strigl 1934.

12 JOHN MAYNARD KEYNES

1 To most Austrians Knapp was a crank and his *State Theory of Money* seemed an outright denial of Menger's teaching. Mises must have regarded it as a gratuitous insult when his book was reviewed together, and compared, with that of a Knapp supporter.

2 Sixteen years later, in his *Treatise on Money*, we find Keynes writing, 'and if my knowledge of the German language was not so poor (in German I can only clearly understand what I know already! – so that

new ideas are apt to be veiled from me by difficulties of language.)'
(JMK, vol V, p. 178, n. 2). When writing these lines Keynes must have
forgotten his earlier review of Mises's book.

3 As the editor of his *Collected Writings* tells us, Keynes was obviously
very unhappy with the August part of the review, for his copy ... is
among the most heavily annotated of the surviving copies of his
journals, with no less than 34 pencilled marks or comments on the 26
page review. At the end of his copy of the review, Keynes summed
up his reaction by writing:

'Hayek has not read my book with the measure of "good will"
which an author is entitled to expect of a reader. Until he can do so,
he will not see what I mean or know whether I am right. He evidently
has a passion which leads him to pick on me, but I am left wondering
what this passion is.' (JMK, vol. XIII, p. 243). Keynes himself, alas,
only too often failed to live up to his admirable precept of 'good will'.

4 Professor Streissler is here using the terminology Hicks employed in
his contribution to the Lindahl-Festschrift of 1956, when he first
introduced fixprice and flexprice markets into economic theory and
called them Q- and P-markets respectively. See Hicks (1956).

5 It might be said that the type of inflation Keynes described in 1919,
with its wild fluctuations, was something altogether different from the
slow and gradual process of inflation the Western world has witnessed
during the last four decades, and that capitalism of the 1980s is sober,
restrained, and does not look 'debauched'.

But this would be a narrow and superficial view of the matter,
hardly suitable as a centenary view. For one thing, the slow process
began to accelerate in the 1970s. What is more, a slow process of
institutional erosion lasting half a century is of course apt to do far
more damage to the institutions of property and contract than the
spectacle Keynes described, which was essentially a short-run
phenomenon.

In the 1960s a few misguided economists of (then) high repute held
that inflation, when generally anticipated, would be harmless. This
view was alien to the Keynesian spirit. Few would hold it today. The
Keynesian diagnosis, by contrast, furnishes an effective antidote to it.

6 This ability to stylize the facts of a situation, and the demands it makes
on an economist's mind may have been in Keynes's mind when on 4
July 1938 he wrote to Harrod 'Good economists are scarce because the
gift for using "vigilant observation" to choose good models, although it
does not require a highly specialized intellectual technique, appears to
be a very rare one.' (JMK, vol XIV, p. 296).

7 Keynesian user cost is a good example of stylized facts seen through
the eyes of decision-makers.

13 REFLECTIONS ON HAYEKIAN CAPITAL THEORY

All references to Hayek's work are to: Friedrich A. Hayek, *The Pure
Theory of Capital*, Chicago 1941.

1 See Joan Robinson, *The Accumulation of Capital*, Macmillan, 1956: 119–20.
2 See Hayek 1941: 295 fn. 1.
3 R. Solow, *Capital Theory and the Rate of Return*, Amsterdam 1963: 15.
4 Hayek never uses this term which to us seems to epitomize the essence of the Austrian style of thought. See also E. Fossati, *The Theory of General Static Equilibrium*, New York 1957: 43–4. The term was coined by Sombart, but not to describe the Austrian method, in the form of *Kausal-genetische Betrachtungsweise* (W. Sombart, *Die drei Nationaloekonomien*, Munich 1930: 220). It was then adopted by Mayer in order to describe the Austrian method by contrast to the 'functional' method of the school of Lausanne. He, however, used the form *genetisch-kausal.* (Hans Mayer, *Der Erkenntniswert der funktionellen Prestheorien* in *Die Wirtschaftstheorie der Gegenwart*, vol. 2, Vienna 1932: 147ss.)
5 I. M. Kirzner, *Competition and Entrepreneurship*, Chicago 1973.
6 John Hicks, *Capital and Time, A Neo-Austrian Theory*, Oxford 1973: 184.

15 VICISSITUDES OF SUBJECTIVISM

1 See Robbins 1935: 16.
2 The reader will readily appreciate how much our summary of the 'subjectivist' view of action owes to Mises (1963) and Shackle (1972). See also Lachmann 1976. Behind it there lies a much older tradition going back at least to Menger which found its epitome in the work of Max Weber. For a striking defence of this tradition see Knight 1956.
3 In fairness we have to remember how eager Keynes was to achieve his aim with a minimum of theoretical innovation. 'The fact that the assumptions of the static state often underlie present-day economic theory imports into it a large element of unreality. But the introduction of the concepts of user cost and of the marginal efficiency of capital, as defined above, will have the effect, I think, of bringing it back to reality, whilst reducing to a minimum the necessary degree of adaptation. (Keynes 1936: 146).
4 Dr Kregel has rightly pointed out (in Kregel 1977) that expectations played quite a distinct part in English neoclassical economics, and in particular in trade cycle theory, before Keynes, as they indeed did in discussions of business fluctuations outside England in the 1920s. We must certainly agree with him that we owe to Keynes 'rather the recognition of the fact that any theory that took the existence of uncertainty and expectations seriously would have to formulate decision-making processes, indeed human behaviour, differently from the traditional theory' (Kregel 1977: 498).

    We also have to realize, however, that no such theory can succeed without granting full recognition to subjectivism. We cannot cope with a kaleidic world without grasping the nature of action.

16 FROM MISES TO SHACKLE

1 In 'Economics and Knowledge', reprinted in Hayek, 1948: 33–56.
2 In 'The Meaning of Competition', reprinted in Hayek 1948: 92–106.
3 Our translation. A reprint of Max Weber's 1909 essay, 'Die Grenznutzlehre und das psychophysische Grundgesetz', may be found in a collection of his writings (1929: 372).
4 Our translation. Mises quotes from the French text *Matière et mémoire* (Bergson 1911: 205).
5 For in the general equilibrium perspective Hayek adopted in the 1930s it is convergence, and the nature of the economic processes promoting or impeding it, that must be of primary interest. The divergence of expectations appears in this perspective mainly as an obstacle to equilibrium, if not as a reflection of a temporarily distorted view of the world.
6 See, however, Lachmann (1943).
7 As Shackle pointedly puts it: 'But if the rational equilibrium is an illusion, basically at odds with the human condition, the Scheme of Things, if it neglects the fact and meaning of time, that prescript of the Rational Calculus is itself an illusion' (1972: 228).

17 SHACKLE'S PLACE IN HISTORY

1 As in all such cases we have to look for a common ancestor. Our candidate for this part is Benedetto Croce, whom both authors held in high esteem. On Croce nd Mises, see I. M. Kirzner, *The Economic Point of View* (New York, van Nostrand, 1960), p. 214, n. 26 (second edition by Sheed & Ward, Kansas City, 1976); on Collingwood, ibid. p. 213, n. 8.
[Editor's note: In fact Mises knew of Collingwood, and cited him favourably in *Theory and History* (New Rochelle, Arlington 1957: 308.]

18 THE FLOW OF LEGISLATION

1 J. R. Hicks, 'Revolutions in economics,' in Sp. Latsis (ed.), *Method and Appraisal in Economics*, Cambridge 1976, ESP, pp. 212–16.
2 F. A. Hayek: *Law, Legislation and Liberty*, Vol. I, London 1973, p. 4.
3 Max Weber on *Law in Economy and Society*, ed. by Max Rheinstein, Cambridge (Mass.) 1954, p. 305. Consider also the following passage: 'It is a curious fact of history that although the older books are full of discussions of the principle that law implies general rules, there is almost no explicit recognition that the enactment of general rules becomes meaningless if government considers itself free to disregard them whenever it suits its convenience . . . Perhaps there is also operative here a confusion arising from the fact that we realize that normally a lawgiver can change any one of his laws simply by repealing it and providing a quite different law, for the governance of events thereafter

happening.' Lon L. Fuller, 'Law and Human Interaction,' *Sociological Inquiry*, Vol. 47, Nos. 3–4, 1977, p. 76.

4 F. A. Hayek, *Law, Legislation and Liberty*, loc. cit., p. 127.

5 Talcott Parsons, 'Law as an Intellectual Stepchild,' *Sociological Inquiry*, Vol. 47, 1977, p. 11.

6 It is tempting, in this context, to make use of Menger's distinction between institutions of *Organic* or of *Pragmatic* origin. The latter are those which owe their origin to an act legislative or otherwise, by a political association, or those holding power in it, while the former 'present themselves to us as the unintended result of individual efforts of members of society, i.e. of efforts in pursuit of individual interests' and are largely 'the unreflected result of social development' (*Das unreflectirte Ergebniss socialer Entwickelung*'). But while it may be tempting to say that flexible organic institutions evolve within the 'interstices' of the more durable pragmatic order, there is no warrant for such interpretation in Menger's work. In fact he took the opposite view. Carl Menger, *Untersuchungen über die Methode der Socialwissenschaften*, 1883, pp. 161–6.

7 See the following writings: Franz Böhm 'Das wirtschaftliche Mitbestimmungsrecht der Arbeiter im Betrieb', *Ordo*, Band 4, 1952. Charles Hanson 'The Bullock Report and the West Germany system of Codetermination', *Three Banks Review*, December 1977. Ernst Heuss 'Einige kritische Überlegungen zum Sachverständigengutachten über die Mitbestimmung in der Unternehmung', *Ordo*, Band 21, 1970, pp. 194–216. Hans Willgerodt, 'Der Liberale Standpunkt und die Mitbestimmungsfrage', *Ordo*, Band 21, 1970, pp. 218–42. Hans Willgerodt 'Vermögensstreuung und Mitbestimmung der Eigentümer', *Wirtschaftspolitische Chronik*, Heft 2, 1972. For the United Kingdom the 'Report of the Bullock Committee', Cmnd. 6706, January 1977 is of importance. For a succinct version of Böhm's argument against codetermination see also his famous article in the *Frankfurter Zeitung* of 22 October 1966: 'Es geht um die Menschenwürde'.

8 L. M. Lachmann, *The Legacy of Max Weber*, Heinemann, London 1970: p. 81 (German translation: *Drei Essays über Max Webers geistiges Vermächtnis*. Tübingen 1973).

19 MONETARY SYSTEM OF A MARKET ECONOMY

1 *The Monetary System and Monetary Policy in South Africa: Final Report of the Commission of Inquiry into the Monetary System and Monetary Policy in South Africa*, Pretoria, Government Printer, RP 70/1984.

REFERENCES

INTRODUCTION: EXPECTATIONS AND THE MEANING OF INSTITUTIONS

Addleson, Mark S. (1993) 'Neoclassical Theory and Subjectivism: Epistemological Perspectives on Decision-Making in Economics and Location Theory', unpublished dissertation, University of Witwatersrand, Faculty of Management, Johannesburg, South Africa.

Boettke, Peter J. (1990) 'Interpretive Reasoning and the Study of Social Life', *Methodus* 2, 2 (Dec.): 35–45.

Ebeling, Richard M. (1985) 'Hermeneutics and the Interpretive Element in the Analysis of the Market Process', *Center for the Study of Market Processes Working Paper*, 16, George Mason University.

—— (1986), 'Toward a Hermeneutical Economics: Expectations, Prices, and the Role of Interpretation in a Theory of the Market Process', in I. M. Kirzner (ed.) *Subjectivism, Intelligibility, and Economic Understanding: Essays in Honor of Ludwig M. Lachmann and his Eightieth Birthday,* New York: New York University Press.

—— (1991) 'What is a Price? Explanation and Understanding (With Apologies to Paul Ricoeur)', in Don Lavoie (ed.) *Economics and Hermeneutics,* London: Routledge, pp. 177–94.

Gadamer, Hans-Georg (1976) *Philosophical Hermeneutics,* translated and edited by David E. Linge, Berkeley: University of California Press.

—— ([1960] 1989) *Truth and Method,* revised translation by J. Weinsheimer and D. Marshall, New York: Crossroad.

Grinder, Walter E. (1977) 'In Pursuit of the Subjective Paradigm', in Ludwig M. Lachmann's *Capital, Expectations, and the Market Process: Essays on the Theory of the Market Economy,* Kansas City: Sheed Andrews and McMeel.

Hayek, Friedrich A. ([1929] 1933) *Monetary Theory and the Trade Cycle,* Clifton, NJ: Augustus Kelly.

—— (1931) *Prices and Production,* London: Routledge & Kegan Paul.

—— ([1937] (1948)) 'Economics and Knowledge', in Hayek *Individualism and Economic Order,* Chicago: University Of Chicago Press.

—— ([1940] (1948)) 'The Competitive "Solution" ', in Hayek *Individualism and Economic Order,* Chicago: University of Chicago Press.

316

—— (1941) *The Pure Theory of Capital*, Chicago: University of Chicago Press.

Horwitz, Steven (1992) 'Monetary Exchange as an Extra-Linguistic Social Communication Process', *Review of Social Economy*, forthcoming.

Knight, Frank H. (1933) *Capitalistic Production, Time, and the Rate of Return, Essays in Honour of Gustav Cassel*, London: Frank Cass.

—— (1934) 'Capital, Time, and the Interest Rate', *Economica* 1: 257–86.

—— (1935) 'Professor Hayek and the Theory of Investment', *Economic Journal*, 45: 77–94.

Lavoie, Don (1986) 'Euclideanism Versus Hermeneutics: A Re-interpretation of Misesian Apriorism', in I. M. Kirzner *Subjectivism, Intelligibility, and Economic Understanding: Essays in Honor of Ludwig M. Lachmann on his Eightieth Birthday*, New York: New York University Press.

—— (1990a) 'Hermeneutics, Subjectivity, and the Lester/Machlup Debate: Toward a More Anthropological Approach to Empirical Economics', in Warren Samuels (ed.) *Economics As Discourse*, Boston: Kluwer Academic Publishing.

—— (1990b) 'Understanding Differently: Hermeneutics and the Spontaneous Order of Communicative Processes', *History of Political Economy*, Annual Supplement to vol. 22, pp. 359–77.

—— (1991a) 'The Progress of Subjectivism', Mark Blaug and Neil de Marchi (eds) *Appraising Modern Economics: Studies in the Methodology of Scientific Research Programmes*, Gloucestershire, England: Edward Elgar, pp. 470–86.

—— (1991b) 'The Discovery and Interpretation of Profit Opportunities: Culture and the Kirznerian Entrepreneur', in Brigitte Berger (ed.) *The Culture of Entrepreneurship*, San Francisco: Institute for Contemporary Studies.

—— (ed.) (1991c), *Economics and Hermeneutics*, London: Routledge.

McCloskey, Donald N. (1985) *The Rhetoric of Economics*, Madison, Wisconsin: University of Wisconsin Press.

Madison, G. B. (1988) 'How Individualistic is Methodological Individualism?', *Groupe de Recherche en Epistemologie Comparee Working Paper* no. 8806, University of Quebec at Montreal.

—— (1991) 'Getting Beyond Objectivism: The Philosophical Hermeneutics of Gadamer and Ricoeur', in Don Lavoie (ed.), *Economics and Hermeneutics*, London: Routledge, pp. 34–58.

Mannheim, Karl ([1929] 1936) *Ideology and Utopia: An Introduction to the Sociology of Knowledge*, trans. by Louis Wirth and Edward Shils, New York: Harvest Books.

Mayer, Hans (1932) 'Der Erkenntniswert der funktionellen Preistheorien', in Hans Mayer (ed.), *Die Wirstschaftstheorie der Gegenwart*, Vienna.

Mises, Ludwig von ([1949] 1966) *Human Action*, Chicago: Henry Regnery Company.

Mittermaier, Karl H. M. (1992) 'Ludwig M. Lachmann (1906–1990): A Biographical Sketch', *South African Journal of Economics* 60, 1: 7–23.

O'Driscoll, Gerald P., Jr. and Rizzo, M. J. (1985) *The Economics of Time and Ignorance*, New York: Columbia University Press.

REFERENCES

Parsons, Stephen D. (1991) 'Time, Expectations, and Subjectivism: Prolegomena to a Dynamic Economics', *Cambridge Journal of Economics*, 15: 405–23.
Prendergast, Christopher (1986) 'Alfred Schütz and the Austrian School of Economics', *American Journal of Sociology* 92, 1 (July): 1–26.
Prychitko, David L. (1990) 'Toward an Interpretive Economics: Some Hermeneutic Issues', *Methodus* 2, 2 (Dec.): 69–71.
Rabinow, Paul and Sullivan, W. M. (eds) (1979) *Interpretive Social Science: A Reader*, Berkeley, CA: University of California Press.
—— (eds) (1987) *Interpretive Social Science: A Second Look*, Berkeley, CA: University of California Press.
Rector, Ralph A. (1991) 'The Economics of Rationality and the Rationality of Economics', in Don Lavoie (ed.) *Economics and Hermeneutics*, London: Routledge.
Samuels, Warren (ed.) (1990) *Economics As Discourse*, Boston: Kluwer Academic Publishing.
Schütz, Alfred and Luckmann, T. (1973) *The Structures of the Life-World*, Evanston: Northwestern University Press.
Shackle, G. L. S. (1972) *Epistemics and Economics: A Critique of Economic Doctrines*, Cambridge: Cambridge University Press.
Vaughn, Karen I. (1993) *Austrian Economics in America: The Migration of a Tradition*, New York: Cambridge University Press.
Weber, Max. ([1921] 1978) *Economy and Society: An Outline of Interpretive Sociology* (in two volumes), edited by Guenther Roth and Claus Wittich Berkeley: University of California Press.

10 AUSTRIAN ECONOMICS UNDER FIRE

Garegnani, P. (1976) 'On a Change in the Notion of Equilibrium in Recent Work on Value and Distribution', in Murray Brown et al. (eds), *Essays in Modern Capital Theory*, Amsterdam: North-Holland.
Hayek, F. A. von 1932) 'Money and Capital: A Reply to Mr. Sraffa', *Economic Journal*, 42: 237–49.
—— (1935) *Prices and Production*, 2nd edn, London: Routledge.
Hicks, J. (1967) *Critical Essays in Monetary Theory*, Oxford: Oxford University Press.
—— (1974) *The Crisis in Keynesian Economics*, Oxford: Blackwell.
Illy, L. (1948) *Das Gesetz des Grenznutzens*, Vienna: Springer. See also Schönfeld-Illy.
Keynes, J. M. (1930) *A Treatise on Money*, 2 vols, London: Macmillan.
—— (1935) *The General Theory of Employment, Interest and Money*, London: Macmillan.
Lachmann, L. M. (1956) *Capital and its Structure*, London: London School of Economics, 2nd edn, Kansas City: Sheed Andrews and McMeel, 1977.
Lerner, A. P. (1953) *Essays in Economic Analysis*, London: Macmillan.
Levine, D. P. (1980) 'Aspects of the Classical Theory of Markets', *Australian Economic Papers*, June.

318

REFERENCES

Mayer, H. (1932) *Der Erkenntniswert der funktionellen Preistheorien*, Vienna: Springer.

Milgate, M. (1979) 'On the Origin of the Notion of "Intertemporal Equilibrium"', *Economica*, February, 46.

Robinson, J. (1979) 'Misunderstandings in the Theory of Production', *Greek Economic Review*, August.

Schönfeld-Illy, L. (1924) *Grenznutzen und Wirtschaftsrechnung*, Vienna, repr. Munich: Philosophia, 1983.

Sraffa, P. (1926) 'The Laws of Returns under Competitive Conditions', *Economic Journal*, 36, pp. 535–50.

—— (1932a) 'Dr. Hayek on Money and Capital', *Economic Journal*, 42, pp. 42–53.

—— (1932b) 'A Rejoinder', *Economic Journal*, 42, pp. 249–51.

—— (1960) *Production of Commodities by Means of Commodities. Prelude to a Critique of Economic Theory*, Cambridge: Cambridge University Press.

11 THE SALVAGE OF IDEAS

Böhm-Bawerk, E. (1907) 'Capital and Interest Once More: I. Capital versus Capital Goods. II. A Relapse to the Productivity Theory', *Quarterly Journal of Economics*, 21: 1ff., 247ff.

Boland, L. A. (1981) 'On the Futility of Criticizing the Neoclassical Maximization Hypothesis', *American Economic Review*, 71: 1031–6.

Dolan, E. G. (ed.) (1976) *The Foundations of Modern Austrian Economics*, Kansas City.

Harcourt, G. C. (ed.) (1977) *The Microeconomic Foundations of Macroeconomics*, London.

Hayek, F. A. (1936) 'The Mythology of Capital', *Quarterly Journal of Economics*, 50: 199–228.

—— (1949) *Individualism and Economic Order*, Chicago, London.

Hicks, J. R. (1965) *Capital and Growth*, Oxford.

—— (1967) *Critical Essays in Monetary Theory*, Oxford.

—— (1977) *Economic Perspectives*, Oxford.

Hutchison, T. W. (1953) *A Review of Economic Doctrines, 1870–1929*, Oxford.

Kaldor, N. (1937) 'Annual Survey of Economic Theory: The Recent Controversy on the Theory of Capital', *Econometrica*, 5: 201–32.

—— (1960) *Essays on Value and Distribution*, London.

Keynes, J. M. (1936) *The General Theory of Employment, Interest and Money*, London.

Kirzner, I. M. (1973) *Competition and Entrepreneurship*, Chicago.

Knight, F. H. (1933) *Capitalistic Production, Time and the Rate of Return*, Essays in Honour of Gustav Cassel, London.

—— (1934) 'Capital, Time and the Interest Rate', *Economica*, N. S. 1: 257–86.

—— (1935) 'Professor Hayek and the Theory of Investment', *Economic Journal*, 45: 77–94.

REFERENCES

Mayer, H. (1932) 'Der Erkenntniswert der funktionellen Preistheorien': 147–239, in H. Mayer (ed.) *Die Wirtschaftstheorie der Gegenwart*, vol. 2, Vienna.

Pasinetti, L. L. (1974) *Growth and Income Distribution*, Cambridge.

Pigou, A. C. (1935) 'Net Income and Capital Depletion', *Economic Journal*, 45, 235–41.

Schumpeter, J. A. (1954) *History of Economic Analysis*, Oxford.

Shackle, G. L. S. (1972) *Epistemics and Economics*, Cambridge.

Strigl, R. (1934) *Kapital und Produktion*, Vienna.

12 JOHN MAYNARD KEYNES

Harrod, R. F. (1951) *The Life of John Maynard Keynes*, Oxford.

Hayek, F. A. (1931) *Prices and Production*, London: Routledge.

—— (1931–2) 'The Pure Theory of Money of Mr. J. M. Keynes', *Economica*, August 1931/February 1932.

—— (1931) 'A Rejoinder to Mr Keynes', *Economica*, November.

—— (1975) *Full Employment at any Price?* London: Institute of Economic Affairs.

Hicks, J. (1956) 'Methods of Dynamic Analysis', in *25 Economic Essays in Honour of Erik Lindahl*, Stockholm: Ekonomisk Tidskrift.

—— (1974) *The Crisis in Keynesian Economics*, Oxford: Blackwell.

Keynes, J. M. (1931) 'The Pure Theory of Money: A Reply to Dr Hayek', *Economica*, November.

—— (1936) *The General Theory of Employment, Interest and Money*, London: Macmillan.

—— (1971) *Collected Writings of John Maynard Keynes*, London: Macmillan. (Abbreviated as JMK, with relevant volume and page numbers).

Mises, L. von (1912) *Theorie des Geldes und der Umlaufsmittel*, Leipzig.

Streissler, Erich (1977) 'What Kind of Microeconomic Foundations of Macroeconomics are Necessary?', in *The Microeconomic Foundations of Macroeconomics*, (ed. by G. C. Harcourt), London: Macmillan.

14 INCOMPLETE REVOLUTION OF SUBJECTIVISM

Hicks, J. R. and Weber, W. (eds) (1973) *Carl Menger and the Austrian School of Economics*, Clarendon Press.

Jaffe W. (1976) Menger, Jevons and Walras De-Homogenized, *Economic Inquiry* (December): 511–24.

Menger, Carl, *Principles of Economics* (Dingwall and Hoselitz, trans.), Free Press.

—— *Problems of Economics and Sociology* (Trans. by F. J. Nock, with an introduction by Louis Schneider), Urbana, Illinois (1963) Originally: *Untersuchungen uber die Methode der Socialwissenschaften*, Leipzig, 1883).

REFERENCES

15 VICISSITUDES OF SUBJECTIVISM

Hicks, John R. (1976) 'Some Questions of Time in Economics', in A. M. Tang, F. M. Westfield and J. S. Worsley (eds), *Evolution, Welfare and Time in Economics: Essays in Honor of N. Georgescu-Roegen*, Lexington Books: 135–51.

Keynes, John Maynard *The General Theory of Employment, Interest and Money*, Macmillan, 1936.

Knight, Frank H. (1956). 'What is the Truth in Economics?', in *On the History and Method of Economics*, Chicago, 1956: 151–78.

Kregel, M. A. (1977) 'On the Existence of Expectations in English Neoclassical Economics', *Journal of Economic Literature* (June): 495–500.

Lachmann, Ludwig M. (1976) 'From Mises to Shackle', *Journal of Economic Literature* (March): 54–62.

Leijonhufvud, Axel (1976) 'Schools, "Revolutions" and Research Programs in Economic Theory', in Spiro Latsis (ed.) *Method and Appraisal in Economics*, Cambridge: 65–108.

Mises, Ludwig von (1963) *Human Action: A Treatise on Economics*, 2nd revised edn, Yale University Press.

Robbins, Lionel C. (1935) *An Essay on the Nature and Significance of Economic Science*, 2nd edn, Macmillan, 1935.

Robinson, Joan (1952) *The Rate of Interest and Other Essays*, Macmillan.

Shackle, G. L. S. (1972) *Epistemics and Economics*, Cambridge.

16 FROM MISES TO SHACKLE

Arrow, Kenneth J. (1974) 'Limited Knowledge and Economic Analysis', *Amer. Econ. Rev.* (March) 54 1: 1–10.

Bergson, Henri (1911) *Matière et Mémoire*, seventh edition, Paris.

Hayek, F. A. (1939) *Profits, Interest and Investment*, London: Routledge and Sons.

—— (1948) *Individualism and Economic Order*, Chicago: University of Chicago Press: London: Routledge and Kegan Paul, 1949.

Kirzner, I. M. (1973) *Competition and Entrepreneurship*, Chicago: University of Chicago Press.

Lachmann, L. M. (1943) 'The Role of Expectations in Economics as a Social Science', *Economica*, N. S. (Feb.), 10: 12–23.

Menger, Carl ([1883] (1963) *Untersuchungen über die Methode der Socialwissenschaften und der Politischen Oekonomie insbesondere*, Leipzig: Verlag von Duncker and Humblot. Translated as *Problems of Economics and Sociology*, by Frank J. Nock, edited by Louis Schneider, Urbana: University of Illinois Press, 1963.

Mises, Ludwig von (1949) *Human Action: A Treatise on Economics*, New Haven: Yale University Press.

Schumpeter, Joseph A. (1908) *Das Wesen und der Hauptinhalt der theoretischen Nationalökonomie*, Leipzig.

Shackle, G. L. S. (1972) *Epistemics and Economics: A Critique of Economic Doctrines*, Cambridge: Cambridge University Press.

321

REFERENCES

Weber, Max. ([1922] 1929) *Gesammelte Aufsätze zur Wissenschaftslehre*, Tübingen. J. C. B. Mohr.

17 SHACKLE'S PLACE IN THE HISTORY OF SUBJECTIVIST THOUGHT

Collingwood, R. G. (1926) 'Economics as a Philosophical Science', *Ethics*, January.
Hayek, F. A. (1955) *The Counter-Revolution of Science*, Glencoe: The Free Press.
Hicks, J. R. (1976) ' "Revolutions" in Economics', in Sp. Latsis (ed.), *Method and Appraisal in Economics*, Cambridge University Press.
Lachmann, L. M. (1977), *Capital, Expectations and the Market Process*, Kansas City: Sheed & Ward.
Mises, L. von (1949) *Human Action*, London: Hodges.
Shackle, G. L. S. (1972) *Epistemics and Economics*, Cambridge University Press.

21 AUSTRIAN ECONOMICS

Hahn, F. H. (1975) 'Revival of Political Economy: the Wrong Issues and the Wrong Argument', *Economic Record* (Sept.): 363.
Hicks, J. R. (1979) *Causality in Economics*, Oxford: Blackwell.
Hutchison, T. W. (1938) *The Significance and Basic Postulates of Economic Theory*, London: Macmillan.
Keynes, J. M. (1973, 1979) *Collected Writings*, vols xiv (1973) and xxix (1979).
Knight, F. H. (1940) 'What is Truth in Economics?', *Journal of Political Economy* 48 (February): 27–8.
Lachmann, L. M. (1977) *Capital, Expectations and the Market Process*, Kansas City: Sheed Andrews.
Lavoie, D. (1986) 'Euclideanism versus Hermeneutics', in I. M. Kirzner (ed.) *Subjectivism, Intelligibility and Economic Understanding*, New York: New York University Press.
Shackle, G. L. S. (1972) *Epistemics and Economics*, Cambridge: Cambridge University Press.
Weber, M. (1968) *Economy and Society: An Outline of Interpretive Sociology* (ed. by Guenther Roth and Claus Wittich), New York: Bedminster Press.

INDEX

a priorism 3, 36, 92, 232, 284
a posteriorism 3
Abramovitz, Moses 294
abstraction 15, 18, 32, 33, 118, 123, 138, 157, 173, 175, 178–9, 181, 196, 218–19, 222, 249–50, 259, 264, 270–1, 277, 283–5
abundance 131, 141, 195
academia 1, 2, 4, 167, 233, 255, 259, 262, 265–6, 270, 272, 283; *see also* scholarship
acceleration principle 43, 50, 74, 77
access to markets 65, 105, 113, 274
account, unit of 31, 300
accounting 99–103, 105, 171, 182, 305
action: *see* human action
adaptation 10, 44, 91, 313
addiction 214, 227
Addleson, Mark S. 297, 316
administration 54, 117, 253,
aggregation 12, 28, 45, 82, 84, 87, 95, 98, 101, 131, 133, 178, 180–1, 195, 206, 207, 252, 266
agriculture 25, 58, 59, 60, 65, 75
allocation 102–3, 207
ambiguity 3, 54, 67, 118, 194
Anschluss 165
anthropology 5, 297
anticipations 27, 71, 112, 126, 136–8, 273, 305, 312; *see also* expectations, bearishness, bullishness
arbitrage 35, 161

Aristotle 216, 217
art 108, 157, 286
assets 30, 35, 36, 38, 39, 40, 44, 94–5, 100–5, 115, 134–5, 143, 155, 189, 194, 207–8, 226–7, 237–9, 261, 264–5, 267
Austrian School 1, 149, 154, 161, 163, 164–8, 185, 186, 217, 282, 284; business cycle theory of 55, 67, 73, 83–7, 148, 153, 304; capital theory of (*see* capital theory); decline of 1; heyday of 1, 167; methodology of 4–8, 10, 14, 17, 162, 168–76, 229–40, 276–90, 298
autonomy of the human mind 205, 243

banking 30, 38, 40–1, 43, 87, 107–23, 152–62, 188–9, 266–7, 274, 306–7
barter 152, 161
bearishness 35, 207, 226, 308
Bergson, Henri 123, 131, 234, 242, 299
Böhm, Franz 315
Böhm-Bawerk, Eugen von 176–81, 202, 239, 311
Boland, L. A. 311
bonds 34–5, 51–2, 115–17, 308
booms 40–4, 57, 64, 70–4, 133, 149, 302
bottlenecks 67, 69, 208
Bretton Woods 273

Bryce, Robert 287
bullishness 64, 70–1, 163, 207, 226, 237, 265, 272, 308
Bullock Report 315
bulls and bears 10, 163, 173, 207, 221, 237–8, 265, 271–2
bureaucracy 171, 249
bygones 12, 28, 137

Cambridge controversies 200, 203
capital theory 8, 153, 176–83, 153, 203, 239, 311; capital gains and losses 86, 120, 134, 140–1, 155–6, 190, 207–8, 238–9, 256–7, 263, 304–5; capital goods 6, 74, 188–9, 311; complementarity of capital 13, 82, 132–8, 141, 157, 201, 208–9, 222, 309, 310; demand for capital in the trade cycle 40–5, 52, 65, 68, 73, 78, 85; expectations and, 50, 226, 245; financial decision-making 13, 65, 108–23, 256–60, 261, 274, 307; fixed capital 53, 68, 73–4, 94, 202, 257; heterogeneity of capital 7, 12, 46, 48, 65–7, 85, 120, 131, 157, 183, 193–6, 199–202, 304–5; intellectual capital 164–8, 175; Knight's critique of Austrian 14, 168, 176–184, 201; liquid capital 67, 74; maintenance 47, 82, 84, 177–8, 182, 194–5, 252; measurement of capital 92–106, 183, 199–200, 204–6; regrouping of capital 13, 133–8, 307; relationship to equilibrium theory 16, 48, 91, 132–3, 190, 199–201, 208–9, 239, 313; relationship to interest rates 49, 52–3, 79–81, 155, 160; substitutability 13, 37–9, 47–8, 132–3, 136, 144, 201, 285, 310; time structure of capital 7, 12, 55, 73, 81, 162, 190, 201–2; working capital 47, 52, 67, 74
capitalism 13, 107–22, 157, 189–90, 312
cash-balances 29–40

Cassel, Ernest 307
Cassel, Gustaf 168, 170, 303
catallactics: see microeconomics
causal-genetic explanation 15–16, 31–2, 45, 169–72, 203, 299, 313
Chamberlin, Edward H. 147
Chicago School 201, 267
choice 3, 17–18, 216, 218–25, 231–4, 243, 246, 278, 297; see also human action
Clark, Colin 92–7, 304
Clark, J.B. 111, 177, 311
Clark, J.M. 74,
codetermination 254–8
Collingwood, R.G. 242, 244, 314
complexity 2, 191–2, 201, 215, 270, 274, 287
complementarity: see capital
context 227, 281–2
Cournot 168
Croce, Benedetto 314
culture 283
cumulative process 40–1, 42–3, 45–9, 57, 68, 74, 77–80, 137, 264
credit 39–40, 48, 51, 54–5, 65–6, 154, 155, 262–3, 268

Davidson, Paul 171
Debreu, Gerard 297
debt 34–8, 85, 116, 152, 252, 263
decentralization 174
deduction: see a priorism
deficit 191
deflation 41, 81, 87, 93, 190
depression 41, 42–3, 47, 51, 53, 57–8, 64, 66, 67, 71–2, 76, 78, 80–5, 144, 149; secondary 10, 12, 40–1, 56, 77–8, 87; see also Great Depression
determinism 169–70, 216, 229, 234, 243
development 107, 110, 140–3, 268, 309–10, 315
diffusion of knowledge 174–5, 237, 288
disco-ordination 265
discovery 231, 271–3
disequilibrium 16, 28, 86, 151, 162, 171, 204, 231

disinvestment 52, 58, 68, 181, 304
dislocation 78, 81–3, 190
disruption of the legal order 254
dissemination of knowledge 173–4, 206, 231, 236, 311
Douglas, P.H. 97, 304
dynamics 10, 12–13, 23–8, 43, 54, 78, 82, 91–2, 98–100, 107, 110, 112, 124, 133, 137–8, 199–200, 309; *see also* time

Ebeling, Richard M. 297
eclecticism 144, 264–9
econometrics 91–2, 97, 276, 289, 304
economizing 214–16
efficiency 311
egalitarianism 208
elasticity: expectations 124–130; of monetary system 43, 46, 51, 53; of substitution 47; of supply and demand 11, 24–5, 43, 45–6, 48, 60, 79–80
employment and unemployment 12, 33, 42–3, 46–56, 58, 60, 76–9, 82, 85–7, 124, 131, 140, 143, 147, 185, 194, 226, 273, 279
entrepreneurship 13, 27, 38–9, 44, 46–7, 51, 65, 78, 82, 84–6, 110–13, 121–2, 125, 136–8, 141, 154–5, 160, 166, 171, 200, 204–5, 236, 254, 306, 309–10
epistemics 19, 166, 172–5, 206, 229, 242
epistemology 7, 175, 311
equilibrium 10, 12, 15–16, 23–8, 50, 56, 82, 83–8, 133, 139–40, 149–51, 155, 157–63, 164–83, 189–91, 195, 198–209, 225–6, 230–1, 236, 238–9, 243, 249–50, 265, 298, 310, 313, 314; *see also* Walrasian economics
error 78, 121, 192–3, 215–17, 288
expectations 9, 39, 124–30, 236, 264–5, 308; as an aspect of all human action 111, 139, 227–8, 313; balance of 10, 207, 237–8, 265, 272–3; capital theory and 157, 179, 182, 195, 199–200, 206,

305, 313; divergence of 9, 137–9, 155, 163, 173, 182, 195, 199, 204–8, 221, 226–7, 236–40, 267, 271–3, 313–14; equilibrium theorizing and 10, 86, 91, 139, 152, 157–8, 161–3, 204–7, 238, 309, 313–14; errors and 86, 94, 129, 204, 278; futures markets and 35, 158, 163, 227; history and 262; holding of stocks and 11, 25, 194; imagination and 18; interest rates and 34–5, 40, 86, 158, 163, 187; investment and 44, 49, 69, 80, 94, 136–8, 187–8, 257; legislation and 252–3, 255; macroeconomics and 225–8, 267; price level and 52, 70, 264; subjectivity of 9, 17, 128–30, 152, 162, 192, 199–200, 213, 219–21, 227, 234–7, 240, 245, 272, 288, 308; *see also* anticipations, bearishness, bullishness
exploitation 140–2

Fabricant, Solomon 100–5, 304–5
falsifiability 3, 216, 281
feedback 204
financial institutions 2, 9, 13, 30, 38, 40, 52, 70, 86–7, 107–23, 137–8, 155, 188–9, 194, 226, 261, 265, 267–8, 270, 283, 303, 306–7
fixprice and flexprice markets 171, 188–9, 196, 312
flows vs. stocks 11, 177–8, 207, 227, 237–8, 256–7, 260, 264, 271; *see also* time
forecasting 25, 44, 78, 138
formalism 4, 10, 15, 16, 18, 118, 170, 173, 227, 258–9, 276–7, 290; *see also* Walrasian economics
Fossati, E. 313
Fuller, Lon L. 314–15
functionalism 15, 168–72
fundism 179, 181–2; *see also* capital theory

Gadamer, Hans-Georg 18, 298
Garegnani, P. 150

genetic-causal explanation: *see* causal-genetic explanation
Great Depression 8, 10, 14, 64, 94, 245
Greidanus, Tjardus 300
Grinder, Walter E. 297

Haberler, G. 300, 301, 303
Hahn, Frank H. 282, 283
Hansen, A.H. 79, 303
Hanson, Charles 315
Harcourt, G.C. 171
Harrod, R.F. 45, 74, 147, 187, 192, 288, 301, 303, 312
Hawtrey, R.G. 74–5, 303
Hayek, Friedrich A.: on capital theory 12, 14, 16, 44, 91–2, 141, 153, 156, 176–83, 198–209, 301, 308, 309, 311, 312; on complexity 191–2, 201; on economic methods 123, 191, 213, 233, 236, 243, 245, 287, 298, 313; on equilibrium 16, 86, 149–51, 160–2, 172, 190–1, 200, 203–4, 207, 216, 236, 239, 310, 313–14; on expectations 236; on inflation 190; on knowledge 15, 166, 168, 172–5, 191, 205–6, 231, 236, 313; on political philosophy 10, 166, 187–8, 250–1, 253, 260, 314; on trade cycle theory 7, 10, 12, 14, 83–7, 147–63, 165, 185–8, 190, 303–4, 308, 311
Heidegger, Martin 18
Henderson, Leon 116–17
hermeneutics 3–6, 16, 18, 262, 276–90, 297, 298, 299
Heuss, Ernst 315
Hicks, Sir John 9, 124, 147–8, 154, 165, 166, 171, 179, 182, 188, 193, 207, 214, 223, 224, 226, 244, 250, 263, 289–90, 308, 309, 310, 312, 313, 314
Hilferding, Rudolph 13, 108, 110, 114, 305
Hobson, John A. 303
Horwitz, Steven 297
Hoskins, G.O. 307

human action 9, 19, 110, 119, 123, 130, 166, 169, 194, 205, 219–21, 225, 227–8, 231–3, 235, 239, 242, 244, 246, 247, 260, 271, 279, 281–3
Hutchison, Terence W. 164, 286, 311

ignorance 179, 215–17, 230; *see also* uncertainty, unknowability
Illy L. 310
imagination 18, 30, 86, 246, 289
immobility of factors 42, 47–8, 55, 131
imperialism 141, 297, 306
indeterminacy of equilibrium in oligopoly 132, 139
indifference curves 23, 150, 223–4, 278
industrial democracy 254
inflation 48, 54, 84, 101–3, 115, 122, 155, 189–91, 240, 259, 262–4, 268, 312
information 129, 173–4, 213, 255–6; *see also* knowledge
innovation 119–20
institutionalism 8, 36
institutions 6, 9, 17–18, 30, 37–8, 53, 105, 113, 143, 161, 190–1, 249–55, 258–60, 261–3, 268, 282–6, 290, 312, 315; *see also* language, law, money
intelligibility 13, 30, 33, 36, 98, 123, 233, 280; *see also* meaning
intentions 9, 110, 172, 266, 298; *see also* plan
interaction 176, 225, 239, 243, 255, 261–2, 278–9, 290
interest rates 33–5, 40, 43–6, 49, 51–5, 79–81, 83–4, 95, 119, 132, 134–5, 154–63, 187–9, 194, 203, 267–8, 300
interpretation 1, 3, 6–11, 14, 16–19, 36, 58, 68, 97, 107, 115, 118, 127–30, 144, 174, 187, 194, 196, 205, 213, 216, 220, 224, 233, 235, 244, 248, 276–90, 297, 298, 308, 314; *see also* orientative process analysis, subjectivism, *verstehen*

intersubjectivity 282, 290
intertemporal exchange 34–8, 52–3, 70–1, 81, 199–202, 259–60, 300
introspection 192, 288
investment: *see* capital theory

Jaffe, W. 217
Jevons, W.S. 149, 179, 217, 244, 302
judgement 19, 112, 117, 128–9, 184, 190, 214, 216, 246

Kahn, Otto H. 116
Kaldor, N. 23–4, 169, 177, 299
Kalecki, M. 44–5, 300
kaleidic society 18, 229–40, 248, 313
Kant, E. 232–3
Kelvin, Lord 304
Keynes, J.M.: interpreting 16, 167, 184–5, 196–7; on Austrian economics 16, 185–9; on the commodity rates of interest 52–3; on disequilibrium 171, 310; on the downturn of the trade cycle 44–5, 74, 148; on expectations 17, 50, 217, 226–7, 237, 245, 264–5, 313; on fixprice and flexprice markets 188–9, 195–7; on fluctuations in commodity stocks 57–8, 62–3, 67–9, 74, 302; on investment 131, 143–4, 155, 193–5, 311; on inflation 189–91, 312; on liquidity preference 12, 33–5, 40; on macroeconomic policy 189–91, 194; on the multiplier 12, 155; on (neo)classical economics 8, 149, 170–1; on own rates of interest 157, 300; on the short term 200–2, 265; on subjectivism 17, 191–3, 221, 226–7, 286, 287–8; on the transactions motive for the demand for money 38; on the upturn of the trade cycle 67; *see also* Keynesian economics and post-Keynesian economics
Keynesian economics 16, 147–8, 154, 163, 165–6, 184–5, 191;

Austrian economics 16, 189; full employment policy in Nazi Germany 147; Hayek's trade cycle theory 12, 16, 148; investment 12–13, 193, 195, 206; savings and investment divergence 154
Kirzner, Israel 11, 166, 179, 182, 203–4, 236, 313, 314
Knapp, G.F. 185, 311
Knight, Frank: on subjectivism 14, 286–8, 304; on capital theory 14, 16, 111–12, 168, 176–83, 201, 306, 311, 313
knowledge: causal explanation 3, 171, 191; equilibrium and 163, 171, 204, 230; historical 247–8, 262; importance of in economy 15, 141, 166, 168, 170–6, 220, 230; intentions and 112, 172, 223; investment in, 133; objectivity 3, 218; perspectives and 184, 196, 205–6, 220, 230–2, 236–7, 280–3, 287; practical know-how 15, 175–6, 220–2, 230–1, 278; progress of 118, 206, 274; specialized 121, 175–6, 220–2, 225, 230–1, 311; substitutes 199; theory as an aid to 109; *see also* dissemination of knowledge, information

labour 42–3, 47–8, 55, 79, 84–6, 96–7, 111, 136, 140–1, 177–8, 193, 256, 300, 308
labour theory of value 244
Lachmann, Ludwig M. 1–20, 247, 277, 284
Lachmann's Law 16, 196–7, 280–1, 312
land 84, 94, 111, 133, 177, 251, 308
Lange, Oskar 11, 24–5, 124–8, 299, 308
language 3, 4, 218
Latsis, Spiro 314
Lausanne School: *see* Walrasian economics
Lavoie, Don 284, 297, 298, 299

law 9, 18, 110–11, 116, 138, 249–60, 284–5, 288, 306, 314–15
learning by doing 174
legal interpretation 280
legal tender laws 36–8,
Leijonhufvud, Axel 218
Lenin, V.I. 109–10, 114, 189–90, 306
Lerner, Abba 10, 309, 310
Levine, D.P. 150
Levy, Hermann 306
Lindahl, Erik 136, 309, 312
liquidity 12, 29–41, 193, 226–7, 245, 299–300
Luckmann, T. 298
Lundberg, Eric 12, 46, 49–51, 79, 136, 301, 303, 309

Mach, Ernst 216, 232
Machlup, Fritz 10, 207, 304
macroeconomics 1, 182, 221, 279; aggregates 180, 183, 195, 200, 206; growth theory (plutology) 9, 15, 174, 180, 244, 250; 'the Islamic art' (IS/LM analysis) 289; macrodynamics 57, 120, 131, 133; short-run 193, 200; subjectivism in 17, 221, 225–8
Madison, G.B. 297, 298
Mahr, Alexander 277
Makower, H. 303
maladjustment 78, 82–4
malinvestment 92–5, 120–1, 154, 155, 159, 190, 239
Mannheim, Karl 8, 18
marginal efficiency of capital 41, 44–5, 50–1, 131–5, 143, 187, 195, 226, 245, 301, 313
Marschak, J. 303
Marshall, Alfred 7, 150, 171, 190, 194, 227, 239, 276, 311
Marxism 13, 303
mathematical economics 3–5, 77, 191, 216, 234, 239, 288
maximization 122, 134, 171, 215, 276, 285
Mayer, Hans 15, 168–72, 310, 312
McCloskey, Donald N. 297
meaning 6, 9–10, 11, 98, 109–10,

128–30, 162, 167, 179–80, 182–3, 189–91, 200, 206–7, 213–15, 224–5, 227, 233, 243–4, 260, 278–85, 290, 298, 314; see also intelligibility
measurement 12–13, 85, 91–106, 120, 124–6, 135, 179, 182–3, 195, 199–200, 204–6, 230, 234, 244, 283, 305
mechanism 16–17, 128, 130, 203–6, 222–4, 234, 248, 276–9, 289
Menger, Carl 7–8, 17–18, 141, 149–50, 163, 201, 213–17, 232, 238–40, 244–5, 251, 255, 261, 284, 298, 309, 311, 313, 315
mercantilism 249
methodenstreit 148, 276, 284
methodological individualism 123, 298
methodology 1, 3, 5–9, 14–18, 61, 92–7, 100–5, 111, 122–3, 127, 135, 150–1, 164, 169, 176, 180, 188–9, 191, 196, 203, 205, 218, 221, 232–5, 243–4, 262, 276, 280–90, 297, 298, 313, 314
microeconomics (catallactics) 1, 9, 15, 17, 131–3, 180, 183, 219, 221–8, 245, 250, 253–7, 260
Milgate, M. 150
mind 6, 18, 110, 123, 128, 162, 176, 182–3, 192, 196–7, 198, 205, 215, 217, 220, 224–7, 231, 237, 243–8, 249, 255, 267, 272, 276–82, 298
Mises, Ludwig von 10–11, 19, 165–6, 229–40, 298; on apriorism 232, 284, 297; on equilibrium 239; on econometrics 289; on expectations 236–7; on interest rates 154, 187; on law 306; on monetary theory 7, 185–6, 311–12; on political philosophy 188; on probability 234–5; on socialism 7; on subjectivism 7–8, 17–18, 215, 230, 232–6, 242, 246, 259–60, 284, 297, 313, 314; on time 231–2, 234, 236, 289, 313; on trade cycle theory 7, 165, 304
mistakes: see error
Mittermaier, Karl 8, 297, 298

mobile resources 200–1, 222
monetarism 266–7
monetary equilibrium 155, 160
monetary policy 42–3, 46, 51–6, 83–7, 127, 185, 261–9, 273–4
monetary theory 7–8, 14, 29–41, 73, 83–7, 148, 151–3, 157–60, 186, 189, 190–1, 227, 265–6, 283, 304, 310
money 9, 18, 29–41, 43, 52–3, 79, 83, 117, 120, 126, 157–8, 161, 171, 185, 190–1, 226, 261–9, 284, 299–300
monopoly 45, 55, 64, 69, 72, 108–9, 114–15, 119, 131, 139, 257, 302, 308
monopsony 141
Montesquieu, Charles Louis 251
Morgan, J.P. 66, 115–16, 306
Morganstern, Oskar 299
multipier 12, 39, 77, 131, 155, 193, 226, 245
Myrdal, Gunnar 154, 187

narrative 123, 280
National Socialism 147
nationalism 140
Neisser, Hans 45, 301, 309
neoclassical economics 1–7, 17, 77–87, 107, 151, 166, 170–1, 174, 202, 222, 225, 229–30, 236–9, 249, 259, 277–8, 282, 285, 288, 297, 303, 313; see also Walrasian economics
nihilism 2, 151
norms 250, 252–4, 258, 284
numeraire 161, 227

O'Driscoll, Gerald P., Jr. 299
obsolescence 100–1, 174, 205, 220, 232, 236, 304, 305
oligopoly 131–2, 139
order 2, 18, 230, 249–60, 270, 273–4, 279, 282, 285, 315
organic institutions 191, 251, 255, 257, 261, 284, 315; see also spontaneous order
organized markets 9, 34–6
orientative process analysis 16–18,

138, 168, 203–6, 254, 258, 264–5, 271–2, 278, 283–5; see also interpretation, subjectivism, verstehen
ownership 255–6, 306–7

paradigms 8, 218, 229, 277, 289
Pareto, V 33, 149–50, 168, 221, 223, 276, 289, 310, 311
Parsons, Stephen D. 299
Parsons, Talcott 253, 260, 315
Pasinetti, L.L. 170
perspective 8, 14–16, 150, 168, 170, 174, 180–1, 189–91, 196–7, 215, 218–23, 229, 236, 240, 250, 262, 269, 270, 275, 283, 298, 313
phenomenology 288, 298–9
philosophy 2–6, 9, 10, 15, 147, 166, 182, 187–8, 203, 216, 233–4, 241–3, 251, 290
Pigou, A.C. 179, 182
plan 102–3, 110–13, 118, 135–43, 172, 182, 187–8, 202, 204, 208, 219–23, 234, 244, 248, 279, 290; see also intentions
plutology: see macroeconomics
Poincare, Jules Henri 216, 232
Popper, Karl 19
positivism 19, 216–17, 232, 234, 242, 251
praxeology 232–6, 259
Prendergast, Christopher 298
prices: adjustment of 23–6, 44–5, 58–75; equilibrium 15, 26, 151, 159, 162–3, 168–72, 222, 231, 238, 301; expectations of future 11, 25–7, 31–5, 49, 52, 134, 158, 161–3, 207, 224–5, 236–8, 256, 265, 271–2, 307–8; flexibility of 124–30, 137, 152, 182, 188–90, 199, 206, 250, 253, 256, 271, 273, 300, 310; formation of 15, 168–72, 222–6, 233, 290, 310; interpretation of 6, 91–106, 272, 278; in the trade cycle 42, 52–5, 60, 78–87; knowledge of 173, 215, 230–2; level of 34, 51, 71, 78–87, 153, 190, 263–4
probability 125, 234–5, 308

profits 34, 38–9, 45–56, 70, 77, 80–7, 98, 111–14, 134–41, 161, 175, 198–9, 203, 207–9, 232, 236, 257, 263
Prychitko, David L. 297

quantifiability 3–4, 94, 97–8, 135, 191–2, 206, 215, 234, 298

Rabinow, Paul 297
Raphael, Gaston 306
Rathenau, Emil 114
Rathenau, Walther 111, 115, 306
rationalism 3, 281
Rector, Ralph 297
redistribution 208, 239
regrouping: see capital theory
reputation 116
Ricardianism 9, 15, 149–57, 162, 170, 176, 180, 199, 202, 232
Ricci, U. 24, 33
Rizzo, Mario J. 299
Robbins, Lionel 10, 219, 249, 304, 313
Robertson, D.H. 38, 300, 302, 303
Robinson, E.A.G. 139, 309
Robinson, Joan 147, 221, 301
Roepke, W. 300, 303
Rosenstein-Rodan, Paul 12, 30–3, 299

Samuels, Warren 298
Sauerbeck's index numbers
savings 55, 83–6, 119–20, 140, 143, 152–6, 159, 203, 206, 279
Say, J.B. 111
scarcity 42, 47–8, 54–5, 67, 71–2, 84, 131, 193, 199, 201, 216, 307, 309, 312
scholarship 4–5, 148, 167, 196, 280–1; see also academia
Schönfeld-Illy, L.: see Illy
Schultz, Henry 24, 299
Schumpeter, Joseph 108, 111, 144, 165–6, 176, 229, 232, 235, 284, 307, 309–10
Schütz, Alfred 18, 282, 284, 298
science (natural and social) 3, 9,

188–92, 206, 215–16, 229, 234, 243, 286–9
search theory 172
Shackle, G.L.S. 19, 147, 229–48; compared with Mises 17, 229–40; on diffusion of knowledge 236–7; on divergent expectations 237–9, 245–6, 289, 308; on history 247–8; on kaleidic society 230, 232, 239–40; on Keynes 17; on mainstream economics 2, 166, 229–32, 242, 314; on philosophy 241–3; on practical knowledge 15, 175; on quantifiability 206; on subjectivism 17–18, 166, 217, 233–6, 241–8, 280, 286, 288–90, 313
Snapper, F. 12, 57–75
socialism 7, 207, 261; see also Marxism
sociology 251, 260, 283–5, 290, 297, 298, 306
Solow, Robert 202, 312
Sombart, Werner 7–8, 313
spontaneous order 9, 205, 235, 251, 258, 284; see also organic institutions
Sraffa, Piero 14–15, 147–63, 176, 310
Stigler, George J. 309
stock market 2, 86, 103, 138, 207, 237–8, 256, 261
stocks: see flows vs stocks
Streissler, Erich 189, 312
Strigl, R. 304, 311
subjectivism: applied to perspectives in social thought 16, 196–7, 218; in the measurement of capital 105, 199–200; learning and 174–5; of preferences (value) 7–9, 17–18, 105, 149–51, 162, 170, 175, 213–15, 219, 221–5, 232–3, 244–6, 277; of ends (action) 9, 17–18, 162, 193, 196, 215–16, 219–27, 233, 243, 245–6, 288, 313; of expectations 9, 17–18, 32, 128, 152–3, 162–3, 199–200, 213, 219–21, 226–8,

235–40, 245–7; of interpretations 196–7, 220, 243, 248, 277; psychological explanations of trade cycle phenomena 30; radical 1–2, 8–11, 15–17, 166, 196, 213, 226–8, 240, 243–8, 276–90; *see also* interpretation, orientative process analysis
substitutability: *see* capital
Sullivan, W.M. 297

technological change 43, 47–8, 102, 106, 113, 133, 174–6, 201, 222, 230–1, 239, 308, 311
time: adjustment to change 23–6, 44, 48, 65, 67, 71, 73, 80, 93–4, 158, 163, 240; concept of 3, 123, 234–5, 248, 298–9, 314; continuity of markets over 105; dynamic economics and 10, 107, 111, 122–3, 133, 137, 173, 200, 203, 209, 219–21, 225–6, 239, 289; holding of stocks and 27, 99, 105, 178, 257, 260; knowledge and 174, 184, 199, 205, 220, 231, 273, 280–1; labor skills, erosion of 47; liquidity and 193; perspectives limited by time horizon 107, 219–20, 231, 283, 285; policy timing 76, 78, 85; statistical time series 93, 96–7, 259; temporal structure of capital 7, 12, 49, 55, 80–1, 99, 153, 179, 201; *see also* dynamics
Thyssen, August 306

Tinbergen, Jan 63, 192, 301, 302
trust 263

uncertainty 12, 30–40, 112, 125–9, 136, 139–40, 163, 169, 179, 192, 217, 220–1, 226, 234–7, 246, 273, 285, 288–9, 313; *see also* ignorance, unknowability
unemployment: *see* employment and unemployment
unknowability of the future 199, 220, 230, 236–7, 247, 272, 289

value, theory of 7, 9, 14, 17, 149, 157, 170, 183, 233, 244–5
Vaughn, Karen I. 299
Veblen, Thorstein 115, 306
verstehen 8–9, 14–18, 169, 196, 214, 276; *see also* interpretation, orientative process analysis, subjectivism

Walrasian auctioneer 171, 231
Walrasian economics 7, 10, 15, 32, 149–50, 168, 170, 172, 191, 217, 229–30, 238–9, 244, 310, 313; *see also* Neoclassical economics, equilibrium, formalism
Weber, Max 6, 10, 18, 19, 167, 214, 233, 252, 255, 260, 276, 284–6, 298, 313, 314, 315
Weber, W. 214
Wicksell, Knut 7, 12, 157, 165, 187, 245, 310
Wieser, Friedrich 284
Wolff, S. de 302

ᵗed in the United States
ᵉr & Taylor Publisher Services